CANARY
ISLANDS

CANARY
ISLANDS

CONTENTS

DISCOVER 6

EXPERIENCE 48

NEED TO KNOW 204

Left: Cactus plants on the island of Lanzarote
Previous page: Kiteboarding in Fuerteventura
Front cover: The Tenerife village of Masca

DISCOVER

Buildings of Las Palmas de Gran Canaria

WELCOME TO THE CANARY ISLANDS

Rugged landscapes, scenic towns, warm weather year-round: the Canary Islands have it all. Whatever your dream trip to these islands includes, this DK travel guide is the perfect companion.

1 A hiking trail through the ancient forests of El Hierro.

2 Traditional *paella*, served alongside a drink.

3 The Old Town of Tenerife's Puerto de la Cruz.

4 The looming Punta Teno lighthouse in Tenerife.

There really are few places in Europe like the Canary Islands. This sunny Spanish archipelago – clustered in the Atlantic Ocean just 100 km (60 miles) west of Morocco – was formed millions of years ago by volcanic eruptions from the Atlantic seabed, and the islands that make up this region today bear the marks of this explosive start. Dark volcanic sands, rugged landscapes and swathes of foggy forests are just some of the stunning terrains that can be explored on one of many trails here. And, with 500 beaches to choose from, there is plenty of coastline for both sunseekers and thrill-chasing adventurers to enjoy.

While islands like La Palma and La Gomera are famous for their jaw-dropping natural beauty, head to Gran Canaria and Tenerife for a dose of culture and heritage. These are the archipelago's two busiest islands, full of insightful museums, restaurants serving up local cuisine and buzzing bars that make up the famously vibrant nightlife scene. Across the Canary Islands, towns big and small are home to a variety of historic architectural styles, from whitewashed buildings to intricate churches.

With such variety, it can be tricky to know where to start. We've broken down the islands into easily navigable chapters, with detailed itineraries, expert local knowledge and colourful, comprehensive maps to help you plan the perfect trip. However long you plan to stay, this DK travel guide will ensure that you see the best of these spectacular islands. Enjoy the book, and enjoy the Canary Islands.

REASONS TO LOVE
THE CANARY
ISLANDS

Volcanic landscapes, stunning coastlines, vibrant cities and a creative local cuisine, not to mention year-round sunshine. There are so many reasons to love the Canary Islands, but here are a few of our favourites.

1 IMPRESSIVE HIKING

With trails through the laurel forests of Parque Nacional de Garajonay *(p164)* and crater-turned-oases like the Caldera de Taburiente *(p196)*, the islands are ideal for an active break.

SANDY SHORES 2

The beaches of the Canary Islands are legendary, with endless coastline to enjoy. Don't miss the epic sand dunes of Maspalomas *(p71)* and Parque Natural de Corralejo *(p84)*.

3 ISLAND HISTORY

You'll find a story around every corner here, from cave houses and grain stores left behind by the islands' Indigenous inhabitants, to 15th-century colonial towns.

SPECTACULAR STARGAZING *4*

Home to the largest single-aperture optical telescope on the planet, the Canary Islands are renowned for being one of the best places in the world to see and study the stars.

SPLENDID ART AND ARCHITECTURE *5*

From colonial churches to modern sites, architecture here is as varied as it is breathtaking. No artist left a greater mark than César Manrique, whose nature-inspired works abound.

FLORA AND FAUNA *6*

Prehistoric laurel forests, the world's oldest dragon tree, the yellow canary: there are plenty of stunning plants, animals and birds thriving across the Canary Islands.

DRAMATIC LANDSCAPES 7

It's easy to find show-stopping scenery in the Canaries, from the lofty heights of El Teide *(p147)*, Spain's tallest peak, to otherworldly natural crags like the looming Roque Nublo *(p29)*.

COLOURFUL CARNIVALS 8

One of the world's biggest carnival celebrations takes place each year in Santa Cruz de Tenerife *(p130)*. Join in the fun at bright parades, street parties and carnival queen galas.

9 UNDERWATER PARADISE

The islands are home to Europe's first Whale Heritage area, but it's not just cetaceans in these waters. Divers can also see Europe's first underwater museum, the Museo Atlántico *(p28)*.

10 WONDERFUL WATERSPORTS

Surfers, paddle-boarders, sailors and other watersports enthusiasts make their way to the Canary Islands to hone their craft and enjoy near-perfect conditions.

BUZZING NIGHTLIFE 11

Whether it's the impressive Maspalomas Winter Pride or simply the endless great bars, clubs and restaurants open year-round, the islands have no shortage of places to party.

CANARIAN CUISINE 12

The best food on the islands features traditional techniques and fresh, local ingredients. Try milled *gofio*, goat meat, cheese and seafood to experience the full Canarian flavour palette.

EXPLORE
THE CANARY
ISLANDS

This guide divides the Canary Islands into seven colour-coded sightseeing areas: Gran Canaria, Fuerteventura, Lanzarote, Tenerife, La Gomera, El Hierro and La Palma, as shown on this map. Find out more about each area on the following pages.

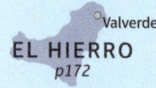

LA PALMA
p186
Santa Cruz
de La Palma

Puerto de la Cruz
Santa Cruz
de Tenerife
La Orotava

LA GOMERA
p158
San Sebastián
de La Gomera

TENERIFE
p124

Valverde

EL HIERRO
p172

Atlantic Ocean

Scale

0 kilometres 40
0 miles 40

N

Atlantic Ocean

Alegranza

Montaña Clara

La Graciosa

LANZAROTE
p100

Arrecife

Isla de los
Lobos

Puerto del
Rosario

FUERTEVENTURA
p78

Gáldar

Las Palmas
de Gran Canaria

Arucas

GRAN
CANARIA
p50

Maspalomas

LOCATOR MAP

Azores

PORTUGAL

*Atlantic
Ocean*

SPAIN

Madeira

MOROCCO

Canary
Islands

ALGERIA

WESTERN
SAHARA

MAURITANIA

GETTING TO KNOW
THE CANARY
ISLANDS

Situated in the Atlantic Ocean around 100 km (60 miles) from the African continent, the Spanish archipelago of the Canary Islands is famous for its steady climate. It's made up of many islands, the biggest of which are Gran Canaria, Fuerteventura, Lanzarote, Tenerife, La Gomera, El Hierro and La Palma.

GRAN CANARIA

PAGE 50

Gran Canaria is the third largest of the Canary Islands and it's also one of the most popular, drawing around 3.5 million visitors each year. Its natural landscapes are so diverse that it's become known as "the miniature Continent", and nearly half of the island is part of a Biosphere Reserve. Within the reserve is the island's highest point, Pico de las Nieves, while beyond it you'll find stunning beaches and the epic rolling dunes of Maspalomas. The island's capital, Las Palmas de Gran Canaria, is surprisingly cosmopolitan, with many historic sights and a lively nightlife scene among its charms.

Best for
Varied beaches, culture, nightlife

Home to
Las Palmas de Gran Canaria

Experience
The incredible dunes of Maspalomas on foot or by bike

PAGE 78

FUERTEVENTURA

The island of Fuerteventura is all about sun, sea and surf. The longest of the seven main islands in the Canary Islands, it has 150 km (93 miles) of white-sand beaches, which draw watersports enthusiasts and sun-seekers alike. The sweeping, windy shores of the Península de Jandía offer ideal conditions for surfing and windsurfing, while the vibrant marine life that surrounds the island make it a great destination for divers of all levels. Beyond the coast lies the island's breathtaking volcanic landscape, full of stunning nature reserves and hiking routes to discover.

Best for
Beaches, watersports, dramatic scenery

Home to
Parque Natural de Corralejo, Isla de los Lobos, Morro Jable

Experience
Trekking on Isla de Lobos, Fuerteventura's smaller, wilder island.

PAGE 100

LANZAROTE

From lively tourist resorts to tranquil, white-washed villages, the towns of Lanzarote are as varied as the rich landscape that make up the island. Swathes of sandy beaches beside beautifully clear waters have added to Lanzarote's popularity with tourists. Its volcanic topography, meanwhile, makes up much of the island and plays a key role in local life, from volcano-powered restaurants to a thriving wine-making industry. Local artists have also made their mark on the landscape, like the stunning structures designed by the Lanzarote-born artist César Manrique.

Best for
Volcanoes, beaches, picturesque towns

Home to
Parque Nacional de Timanfaya, Jameos del Agua, Cueva de los Verdes, Mirador del Río

Experience
The unique underwater display at the Museo Atlántico off Lanzarote's southern coast.

→

PAGE 124

TENERIFE

Named after the Guanche word for "white mountain", Tenerife is home to Spain's tallest peak, the great Pico del Teide. Rising over 3,700 m (12,100 ft) above sea level, this volcano dominates the landscape and is the centrepiece of a popular national park. Beyond its natural wonders, Tenerife has plenty of resorts and well-maintained beaches, plus a vibrant nightlife scene, all of which draw visitors year-round. The island's towns also feature museums, historic buildings and abundant opportunities to explore the island's rich cultural and natural heritage.

Best for
Hiking, beaches, nightlife

Home to
Santa Cruz de Tenerife, Parque Nacional de Anaga, La Orotava, Puerto de la Cruz, Parque Nacional del Teide

Experience
The vibrant annual Carnival celebrations.

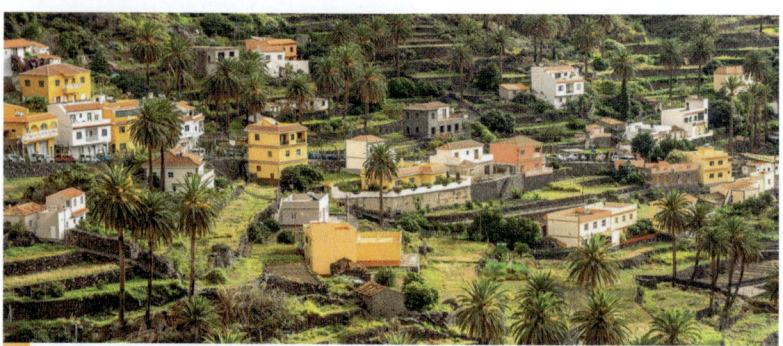

PAGE 158

LA GOMERA

Known as "the round island", La Gomera is one of the smallest and greenest islands of the archipelago. Despite its small size, it's rich in natural attractions and unspoiled landscapes (picture plunging ravines, rocky summits and mist-shrouded laurel forests), which make it an excellent place for outdoor pursuits. The highlight of these is the Parque Nacional de Garajonay, with its stunning ancient forest filled with around 450 species of plant and tree. The island's tranquil capital city, San Sebastián de La Gomera, is steeped in history, and traditions here are carefully maintained.

Best for
Peaceful escapes, unspoiled nature, walking trails

Home to
Parque Nacional de Garajonay

Experience
A whale-watching cruise to see the many species that frequent the surrounding waters.

EL HIERRO

PAGE 172

The westernmost point of the archipelago, El Hierro is also the smallest of the seven main islands. Despite its diminutive size, nature is in abundance across this island: highlights range from the lush greenery of the native pines, juniper trees and laurel groves, to striking volcanic landscapes and natural lava pools. The marine reserve, La Restinga, is an underwater paradise with a range of flora and fauna within it. The island's capital Valverde is home to half of El Hierro's 11,000 inhabitants and is also a great place to browse local handicrafts and village markets.

Best for
Natural sea pools, picturesque towns, peaceful escapes

Home to
Las Puntas, La Restinga

Experience
Diving into the waters of Mar de las Calmas, part of La Restinga.

LA PALMA

PAGE 186

The stunning nature across La Palma is unparalleled, so much so that it is often referred to as *isla bonita*, or the "beautiful island". It's home to rugged volcanic landscapes – dotted with verdant forests – which slope down to the coast to form black sandy beaches. Beneath the water, stunning volcanic seascapes are protected by a marine reserve; up above are breathtaking views of the night sky. Established as a world-renowned astrophysical research destination, La Palma is a certified Starlight Reserve, and one of the best places in Europe to stargaze.

Best for
Natural pools, black sand beaches, stargazing

Home to
Santa Cruz de La Palma, Parque Nacional de la Caldera de Taburiente

Experience
An evening stargazing from the Llano del Jable viewpoint.

Golden Sands

There are golden beaches all over the Canary Islands, if you know where to look. Las Teresitas near Santa Cruz de Tenerife is a stunning spot, where you can lounge on white sand that was imported from the Sahara Desert in the 1970s. For epic vistas, take to the sandy hills of the Parque Natural de Corralejo *(p84)*, or explore the undulating dunes of Maspalomas *(p71)*.

← Palm trees along the golden shores of Tenerife's Las Teresitas

THE CANARY ISLANDS FOR
BEACHGOERS

With more than 1,500 km (930 miles) of coastline and just about 500 beaches, it's little wonder that the Canary Islands draw sun and sea worshippers. There are shores to suit every beachgoer, from huge stretches of powder-soft sands to small coves with super-clear waters.

TOP 3 ECO-FRIENDLY TRAVEL TIPS

Protect local species
Refrain from taking rocks, sand or any other natural formations home.

Leave no trace
Avoid polluting the local environment by disposing of your rubbish properly.

Respect the wildlife
Always observe any local wildlife from a distance and don't feed the animals you may encounter.

Sheltered Seawater Pools

Often naturally formed, stunning seawater pools that provide shelter from mighty ocean waves can be found on most of the islands. The pretty Charco Azul in La Palma is one of the best for a scenic dip. To get even closer to nature, cool off at one of the natural pools at Lanzarote's Punta Mujeres, or try the Mesa del Mar pool in Tenerife, surrounded by natural rock formations.

→ Taking a sheltered dip in La Palma's scenic natural pool, Charco Azul

Secluded Coves

Some of the most stunning Canarian beaches lie off the beaten track, where you can seek out your own hidden gem away from the busy resorts and tourist crowds. Some of these quiet coves might be a little tricky to reach, but beaches like Playa de Guïguï in the west of Gran Canaria, El Verodal in El Hierro and Las Conchas in La Graciosa are well worth the trek. At each cove, it's easy to unwind among the unspoiled stretches of sand, the lapping sea your only companion.

→

The quiet shores of Gran Canaria's Playa de Guïguï

Pebbled Expanses

They may not be the best place to lay your towel, but the rare pebble beaches here are worth visiting for the clear waters that surround them. At Las Nieves beach, one of the most famous and popular pebble shores, enjoy a dip in the with a view of the majestic cliffs that back it. The rocky El Cabezo beach in Tenerife, meanwhile, is home to many small rock pools as well as perfect conditions for windsurfers.

←

Relaxing along the rocky shores of Gran Canaria's Las Nieves beach

Volcanic Shores

One of the most common types of beach found throughout the Canary Islands is the black-sand beach, a product of the islands' volcanic make-up. Some of the best include the coastline around La Orotava *(p136)*, Playa de Santa Catalina in La Gomera and Los Cancajos in La Palma.

→

The volcanic sands of La Orotava's Playa del Bollullo

Mighty Volcanoes

The Canary Islands are famous for their epic volcanoes, as impressive as they are imposing. Explore the lush, green Caldera de Taburiente crater of La Palma *(p196)* on a scenic hike, or hit the trails of one of the largest volcanoes in the world and Spain's highest peak, El Teide in Tenerife *(p146)*. Experience the power of all this tectonic activity at Restaurante El Diablo in the Montaña del Fuego of the Parque Nacional de Timanfaya *(p106)*. Here, delicious dishes are carefully prepared using natural geothermal heat.

↑ Tenerife's mighty volcanic peak El Teide against a clear blue sky

THE CANARY ISLANDS FOR
NATURAL WONDERS

There's more to the Canary Islands than its stunning coastline. Home to everything from huge volcanic landscapes to rolling sand dunes – much of which is protected – here you'll find epic landscapes at every turn.

↑ Vibrant marine life thriving in the waters surrounding the Canary Islands

A Watery World

For centuries, the waters surrounding the Canary Islands have been plied by a whole host of marine species, including cetaceans big and small. Indeed, spotting a whale here is a very real possibility: to increase your chances, head to one of the scenic viewpoints overlooking the strait between La Gomera and Tenerife, which became Europe's first Whale Heritage site in 2021 *(p168)*. Below the surface, vibrant fish and lush marine vegetation awaits: see it for yourself by diving underwater to volcanic reefs at Las Galletas in Tenerife or Mar de las Calmas in El Hierro *(p181)*.

Stunning Stargazing

Protected dark skies and very little light pollution make the Canary Islands one of the best places in the world to stargaze. After nightfall, hike to the top of El Teide in Tenerife (p146) or to one of the peaks of La Palma – two of three Starlight Reserves on the islands – to witness whole galaxies come to life.

→

Seeing the starry Milky Way above the Canary Islands

Flourishing Flora and Fauna

With over 4,000 endemic animal species and 500 plant species, the archipelago is a nature haven. Drago trees and fire-resistant Canarian pines can seen on all islands, while the prehistoric laurel forests of Parque Nacional de Anaga (p134) and Parque Nacional de Garajonay (p164) are botanical treasure troves worth seeking out. Bird spotters, meanwhile, can scour the mountains of Gran Canaria for the elusive blue chaffinch.

←

A rare blue chaffinch perched in a pine tree in the mountains of Gran Canaria

Driving through sand dunes, Parque Natural de Corralejo

POPCORN BEACH

Known as Popcorn Beach, Fuerteventura's Playa del Bajo de la Burra is famous for its shores of white rhodoliths shaped like popcorn. While these rhodoliths look like coral, they're actually made of calcareous algae and white sand. They not only create a unique landscape, but are also said to help manage carbon dioxide levels in the sea and provide a breeding site for marine species.

Rolling Sand Dunes

Swathes of rolling, sandy hills characterize the otherworldly landscapes of Gran Canaria and Fuerteventura. For a scenic view, watch the sun set below the dunes of Parque Natural de Corralejo (p84). Dedicated routes around Maspalomas (p71), meanwhile, showcase and protect the beauty of the dunes.

FLORA OF THE CANARY ISLANDS

From bananas to date palms, cacti to dragon trees, there are a whole host of plant species that thrive on these islands. In fact, more than half of the islands' 1,800 species are native to this archipelago, making it home to some of the most unique and varied plants in the world.

The vegetation of the Canary Islands is distinct, in part thanks to its geography. Located 100 km (60 miles) from the nearest continent, the islands have a distinct ecosystem in which exceptional plants have thrived for centuries. Many of the plant types are historic relics of the old Mediterranean flora, which became extinct throughout the region as the climate began to change. Their historical relevance, coupled with the unique character of the plants, has long drawn the interest of botanists to the region.

Of the many plants found in the Canaries, one of the most emblematic is the dragon tree *(Dracaena draco)*. With its swollen branches, tufts of spiky leaves and bright red sap, it makes for a striking sight. It was once used in pigments, paints and varnishes, as well as in medicinal powders. One of the oldest examples is the Drago Milenario in Icod de los Vinos *(p150)*, said to be 1,000 years old.

Canary Island juniper

Canary Island date palm (Phoenix canariensis) is endemic here.

Canary samphire (Astydamia latifolia) is found on volcanic slopes.

← The heavy branches and long, pointed laves of the Canarian dragon tree

PLANT ZONES

The local flora, along with a variety of colourful, exotic imported plants, have flourished here thanks to the fairly stable and relatively humid climate of the Canary Islands. The mountains of the region provide a home for a diverse array of flora, with different plants growing at each level. As the ground rises, the salt-tolerant and semi-desert vegetation gives way to humid rainforests, pine forests and, in the highest regions, to hard-leaf shrubs and rock plants.

Coastal areas are home to plants that can tolerate salt and temperature variance.

Semi-desert regions have flora that store water within their leaves and stalks.

Balsamic spurge grows in semi-desert areas.

Erysimum scoparium, a shrub, grows in the islands' highest regions.

Canary Island pine, a native species, grows at altitudes of over 1,000 m (3,300 ft).

Viper's bugloss (Echium vulgare)

Canary samphire (Astydamia latifolia) is found on the coastal basalt rocks of the Canary Islands.

Canary Island spurge (Euphorbia canariensis)

Limonium papillatum

This type of spurge olive has silvery leaves.

Canary Island strawflower (Helichrysum gossypium)

↑ Illustration showing some of the flora typical of the Canary Islands

Higher ground and areas with little rainfall see low shrubs flourish.

Northern slopes, where humidity is high, are home to Laurel forests.

Slopes up to 2,000 m (6,560 ft) high see pine trees and shrubs thrive.

Mountain areas above 2,000 m (6,560 ft) feature cushionlike shrubs.

Colonial Monuments

With Spanish colonization from the 15th century came countless building projects that transformed the islands into European outposts. The striking Catedral de Santa Ana in Las Palmas de Gran Canaria *(p60)* and Tenerife's Basílica de Nuestra Señora de Candelaria *(p156)*, are just two examples of religious monuments from this time. Meanwhile, large fortifications like Castillo de la Luz *(p57)* were also built, a sign of the islands' strategic and geographic importance to their former sea-faring rulers.

→

Tenerife's imposing Basílica de Nuestra Señora de Candelaria

Did You Know?

In 1797, Horatio Nelson unsuccessfully attempted to claim Tenerife for Britain.

THE CANARY ISLANDS FOR
HISTORY BUFFS

Everywhere you turn there are reminders of the far-reaching history of the Canary Islands: prehistoric artifacts, Guanche heritage and remnants of colonial takeover. Head to one of many museums to learn more or simply stumble across signs of the past as you explore the region.

Pirates and Smugglers

Due to the islands' strategic location between Europe and the Americas, they often drew pirates and privateers seeking precious loot. French, British, Dutch and Portuguese navigators all sailed here at different times, frequently attempting to pillage the islands. Time your visit for mid-October, when the annual re-enactment of the Battles of Tamasite and El Cuchillete takes place in Fuerteventura, celebrating the historic victories over British privateers in 1704.

←

Re-enacting the historic Battles of Tamasite and El Cuchillete in Fuerteventura

TENERIFE'S BOTANICAL GARDENS

Botanical study was of interest to colonial navigators, who collected plant specimens as they travelled. However, the plants brought back from South America often didn't thrive in mainland Spain's climate. As a result, the Jardín Botanico was opened in Puerto de la Cruz *(p145)* in 1788 to acclimatize plant specimens, with an offshoot in La Orotava following 150 years later *(p136)*.

Historic Towns

Colonial trade from the 16th century onwards brought wealth, which led to more towns being built. Betancuria *(p94)* and La Laguna *(p148)* both have some of the best examples of colonial-era buildings; La Laguna's grid layout later influenced colonial towns in South America. The Casa de Colón *(p62)* is a typical colonial mansion; visit to learn about its history.

→

Strolling down a colonial-era street in pretty La Laguna

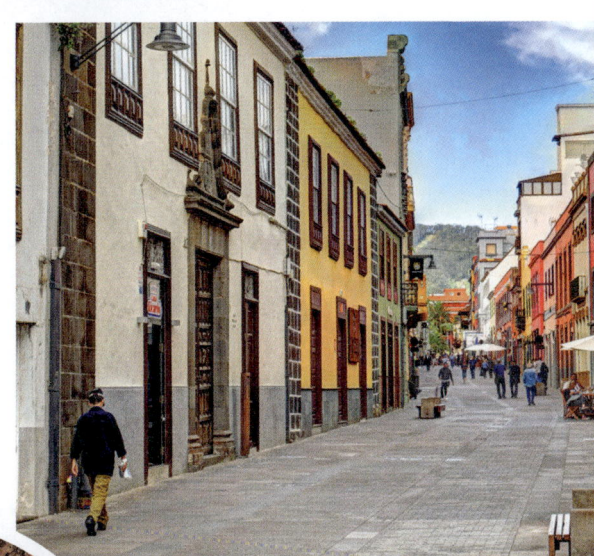

Guanche Heritage

The Guanche people only lived in Tenerife, but the term is used to refer to Indigenous peoples of all the islands. Deep-dive into centuries of Guanche culture and history through artifacts displayed at the Museo Canario *(p61)* or at one of the people's former dwellings, like the Cueva Pintada *(p69)* or the 300 caves that make up the Cenobio de Valerón *(p69)*.

←

Exploring the historic dwellings at Gran Canaria's Cenobio de Valerón

Take to the Canyons

With their many gorgeous canyons and ravines, the Canary Islands are ideal for scenic canyoning. Hike, rock climb or rappel among the many volcanic *barrancos* (deep ravines), like Gran Canaria's Barranco de las Vacas or Barranco de Los Cernícalos. The latter is uniquely lovely, with forests, streams and waterfalls to traverse.

↑ Climbing a rockface while canyoning through the Canaries

THE CANARY ISLANDS FOR
ADVENTURERS

With its year-round steady temperatures, diverse landscapes and powerful ocean swells, the Canary Islands are made for outdoor adventures. Test your mettle with a scenic hike past volcanic ridges and mighty ravines, or harness the wind and set sail across the mighty waves.

↑ Exploring the striking underwater sculptures of the Museo Atlántico

Underwater Finds

The waters here are a dream for divers: several sunken vessels, volcanic underwater seascapes and vibrant sea life can be found beneath the Atlantic waves. Enjoy a dive off the shores of Las Palmas de Gran Canaria *(p56)* to see La Catedral, a striking 30-m (100-ft), cathedral-like natural rock formation that makes for epic underwater snaps. Near the coast of Lanzarote is the eerie Museo Atlántico – comprising over 300 underwater human casts by British sculptor Jason deCaires Taylor – while the sunken wreckage of the Douglas DC-3 plane can be seen in the waters near Gran Canaria's Playa de Vargas.

Brave the Waves

With plenty of breeze and swells, the archipelago is ideal for hitting the waves. A great place to try out all kinds of surfing is Fuerteventura, with surf schools in Corralejo *(p90)* and the René Egli Windsurfing school in Sotavento. To try stand-up paddleboarding or kayaking, head to the popular Club La Santa in Lanzarote. If you're not up to braving the waves, catch one of the major windsurfing and surfing competitions that take place here each summer instead.

↑ Windsurfers getting ready to hit the waves in Fuerteventura

Get a Bird's-Eye View

Thanks to prevailing trade winds, paragliding is a great way to witness the Canary Islands from above. Nearly all of the islands have gasp-worthy views, but one of the best and most scenic glides can be found at the tiny town of Sabinosa in El Hierro *(p180)*. For pure thrill, there's no better spot than Izaña in Tenerife: gliders set off from 2,200 m (7,200 ft) above sea level before gently soaring all the way back down.

← Paragliders soaring through the sky across the stunning landscapes of the Canary Islands

---

TOP 4 HEAVENLY HIKES

Camino de Jinama
A challenging 8-km (5-mile) route in the green heart of El Hierro.

Roque Nublo
This easy 1.5-km (1-mile) hike leads to the 80-m- (260-ft-) high basalt monolith in Gran Canaria.

Ruta Espigón del Roque
This moderate trail leads to views of La Palma's Taburiente crater.

La Laguna Grande
One of Parque Nacional de Garajonay's 18 routes, this 10-km (6-mile) trail is among the prettiest.

↑ Walking past rock formations on route to Tenerife's El Tiede

Hit the Hiking Trail

This archipelago is a paradise for hikers. On Tenerife, the *cañadas* (ancient shepherds' paths) are the best way to trek El Teide *(p146)*. The smaller islands of El Hierro, La Gomera and La Palma, meanwhile, all have trails of varying difficulty levels with truly impressive views.

▷ **Spectacular Saltworks**

The Canarian coastlines are dotted with salt flats. The resulting mineral-rich salts are used in local dishes and make for a great souvenir. See its extraction at Salinas de Janubio in Lanzarote, or head to the Museo Salinas de Carmen (*Barrio las Salinas, 2*) to learn more about the process.

INSIDER TIP
Salt Ecosystems

While visiting one of the saltworks, keep an eye out for some of the biodiversity that thrives in these saline ecosystems, including migratory birds.

THE CANARY ISLANDS FOR
FOOD AND DRINK

Sweet and savoury toasted *gofio*; salty *flor de Guía* cheese; thirst-quenching Malvasia wines: the Canary Islands offer a whole host of tasty local specialities. Get ready to discover a distinct blend of Spanish, North African, Indigenous influences and more with every sip and bite.

◁ **Craft Beer Spots**

Local beer brands may dominate bars, but craft breweries have made a name for themselves too. The Cervecera Malpeis microbrewery in Lanzarote serves three beers inspired by local beaches, while Cervecería Isla Verde in La Palma offers tours and tastings of their brews.

▷ Wonderful Vineyards

It's said that playwright William Shakespeare demanded a barrel of Canarian wine as part of his salary, so prolific was the grape juice of the islands in the 16th century. Today, many bars across the islands serve the good stuff, but for a wine education, head to Bodegas Ferrera in Tenerife *(www.bodegasferrera.com)*, or join a local wine tour in Lanzarote for insider access.

◁ Say Cheese

A lack of dairy cattle doesn't stop the islands making incredible cheese. Mostly made with goat's milk, the cheeses of the Canaries range from soft, creamy varieties such as Gran Canaria's *flor de Guía*, to potent hard cheeses. The most famous, however, is *queso majorero* from Fuerteventura – so loved that it has Protected Designation of Origin status.

▷ Get to Know Gofio

Gofio is a toasted flour made mainly of corn, wheat or barley, and is the quintessential Canarian ingredient. It's said to have first been cultivated by the Indigenous populations, and its popularity endures today: it features in sweet and savoury dishes, like *gofio escaldado* dip. Try it in most restaurants across the island or, to learn more about what it is, head to the Molino de Gofio El Amparo *(Camino el Aserradero, 24)* and witness the *gofio* milling process.

◁ Speciality Coffee

Believe it or not, coffee plants are harvested on the islands, though they're something of a rarity. Follow the journey from bean to cup at the verdant Agaete Valley in Gran Canaria, on a tour of the Bodega Los Berrazales *(Calle de los Romeros)* coffee plantation. Looking for something even more potent? Try a *barraquito* at a café in Tenerife. This local specialty is a mix of condensed milk, the Spanish liqueur Licor 43, coffee, milk, foam and a twist of lemon, topped with a dusting of cinnamon.

Fantastic Carnivals

Head and shoulders above all religious festivals is this annual party before Lent begins. Though celebrated across the islands, the best carnivals are jointly held in Santa Cruz de Tenerife and Las Palmas de Gran Canaria, which are said to be the biggest outside of Rio de Janeiro. Head out to either and take in joyful costumes, parades and parties.

Parading down the streets of Santa Cruz de Tenerife for carnival

THE CANARY ISLANDS FOR
FESTIVITIES

The Canarian calendar is packed with fun-filled annual festivities that bring towns and cities to life throughout the year. Expect raucous carnivals, lively arts events and elaborate religious festivals, which together celebrate the rich culture of the islands.

TOP 4 TRADITIONAL FESTIVALS

San Juan (23 June)
Bonfires line the shores of Gran Canaria to ward off evil spirits and purify.

Bajada de la Virgen de los Reyes (5 July)
Follow the saint from her shrine to El Hierro's capital city *(p178)*.

Fiesta del Fuego (31 July)
This festival celebrates the divine intervention that stopped lava flows in Lanzarote in 1824.

La Traída del Agua (August, dates vary)
Splashing water marks a wish for rain in this Telde tradition.

Religious Festivals

With a strong Catholic presence across the islands, there's no shortage of exuberant religious festivals throughout the year. Corpus Christi in July is marked in La Orotava *(p136)*, where swathes of intricate sand art takes over the square. Nearby, San Bartolomé festivities take place in Tejina every August, where wooden crosses with two large heart shapes covered in flowers take centre stage.

Colourful art being added to La Orotava's main square for Corpus Christi

Pride Bonanzas

The Canary Islands are one of the most popular spots for LGBTQ+ travellers. While most islands have Pride events, it's Gran Canaria that goes all out: it has the ten-day Maspalomas Pride in May and the week-long Winter Pride in November. For quieter celebrations, head to La Palma for the Isla Bonita Love Festival in July.

INSIDER TIP
Pride Events

For Pride events beyond the main parade, go to the world's only LGBTQ+ shopping centre, the Yumbo Centrum in Maspalomas. Expect global artists, parties, costumes and more.

↑ Revellers enjoying the Pride parade celebrations in Maspalomas

Indigenous Celebrations

The islands' rich Indigenous heritage is celebrated in countless festivals. Gran Canaria's annual Fiesta de la Rama in August, which is thought to be of Indigenous origins, sees locals march through the town with palm branches to summon rain. Of more obscure origins are holidays like the Los Finaos celebrations, when loved ones who have passed away are remembered.

← Palm branches being collected as part of the annual Fiesta de la Rama in Gran Canaria

Cultural Festivities

Buzzing music, art and film events can be found across all of the islands. The world-famous WOMAD Festival – bringing together music, arts and dance – draws huge crowds to Gran Canaria in the summer. Street art fan? Don't miss the colourful works of the International Street Art Festival (Mueca) in Tenerife's Puerto de la Cruz in May.

→ Crowds cheering on the acts at Gran Canaria's yearly WOMAD Festival

Traditional Pottery

Pottery-making on the islands goes back to the time of the ancient Indigenous Guanche people, whose distinct wares were made using dark clays and natural textures. In Las Palmas de Gran Canaria, the Museo Canario *(p61)* holds the most beautiful collection of storage vessels and beads, while over in La Orotava's Museo de Cerámica *(p140)* you'll find over 1,000 ceramic items and pottery-making workshops.

→

Stunning handmade Canarian ceramic plates for sale

THE CANARY ISLANDS FOR
ARTS AND CRAFTS

From the Guanche-style pots of Tenerife to the woven rugs of La Gomera, the Canary Islands are home to rich arts and crafts traditions. Whether you're looking to pick up a delicate lace souvenir or learn from the masters, the craft scene of the Canaries offers something for everyone.

Intricate Embroidery

Canarian embroidery is prized for its distinct patterns, which add a flourish to tablecloths, sheets and napkins. Go on the hunt for the best of these on Santa Cruz de Tenerife's Calle Castillo *(p131)*, where there are many handicraft centres selling unique embroidery. The islands' national costumes are also often embroidered; check out some beautiful examples on display in La Orotava's Casa de los Balcones *(p138)*.

 ←

Dressing in traditional Canarian costume, with many embroidered details

Wonderful Weaving

Carefully produced using simple hand-looms and woven in an array of bright colours and geometric patterns, narrow carpets are the pride and joy of many Canarian homes. One of the best places to buy one for yourself is over at the handicraft centre Los Telares in Hermigua *(p169)*, a town famous for its intricately designed handmade rugs and other woven products. Or, if you fancy trying out some weaving yourself, get hands-on at the Casa-Museo Monumento al Campesino in San Bartolomé *(p120)*, which offers artisanal workshops; the textile dyeing demonstration is a particular highlight.

← Weaving delicate silk on a hand-loom in a traditional workshop setting

Creative Carvings

Nearly every city and town brims with stunning woodcraft, with wooden gates, doors, shutters and wooden balconies all carved with centuries'-old motifs. For some examples in Las Palmas de Gran Canaria, look up at the wooden balconies of Casa de Colón *(p62)*. A stroll around Teror's Plaza de Nuestra Señora del Pino *(p66)*, meanwhile, reveals the carved features of the mansions around the square.

→ An intricately carved wooden balcony in a typical Canarian style

Did You Know?

The five-stringed, wooden *timple* is a traditional Canarian instrument still carved on the islands.

Fun-Filled Amusement Parks

There are many parks here to keep the whole family busy. The popular Siam Park *(p154)* has water slides aplenty, while Lanzarote's Aqualava Waterpark features a lazy river and wave pool. Looking to stay dry? Head on over to Sioux City in Gran Canaria and be transported into the Wild West.

→

Exploring the slides and climbing frames at the ever-popular Siam Park

THE CANARY ISLANDS FOR
FAMILIES

The Canary Islands are the perfect place for a family holiday, no matter your budget or interests. With (almost) guaranteed good weather and plenty of outdoor spots to explore, not to mention family-friendly beaches, resorts and activities, the islands are sure to keep the whole family entertained.

The Great Outdoors

For a fun-filled learning experience, there's nothing better than exploring the great and varied nature of the Canary Islands. Take the family out to see the views on one of the easier hikes to Roque Nublo *(p29)* and Roque Bentayga *(p76)*. For a first-hand lesson in local geography, head out onto the trail towards Calderón Hondo Volcano in Fuerteventura to peek into the giant crater, or explore the pine trees of Tenerife's Forestal Park.

Did You Know?

All school children on La Gomera learn the island's unique whistling language, Silbo Gomero.

Taking in the views on a hike to Gran Canaria's Roque Nublo ↑

Hit the Water

It's hard to beat the memorable experience of seeing whales, dolphins and other marine life in their natural habitat. Home to the first Whale Heritage area in Europe, the Canary Islands offer many cetacean-spotting opportunities. Head out on one of the boat tours from the major resorts in Tenerife and Gran Canaria to catch a glimpse of these wonderful sea creatures. Looking for smooth sailing? The hourly boat taxi from Puerto Rico *(p72)* to Puerto de Mogán *(p70)* in Gran Canaria is ideal for little ones; the boat has a glass bottom, making it easy to spot fish and other marine life below.

→

Spotting whales emerging from the water on a boat trip near Tenerife

Wildlife Adventures

To meet Canarian wildlife in nature, let the experts lead the way and head out on a guided bird watching or hiking tour with local tour companies like Gran Canaria Sightseeing. Youngsters will also delight in the botanical gardens of Maroparque in La Palma *(Calle la Cuesta, 28–30)*, home to many local and non-native animals, like meerkats, pythons and cranes.

←

Long-beaked dunlin strolling the shallows looking for food on Gran Canaria's sweeping shores

Marvellous Museums

One of the best museums for children in the Canary Islands is the Museo Elder *(p58)*. At this hands-on science and technology museum, visitors can learn through exhibitions, 3D screenings and more. For engaging displays, visit Santa Cruz de Tenerife's Museum of Nature and Archaeology *(C/Fuente Morales s/n)*.

→

Historic planes on display at the exciting Museo Elder

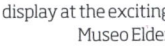

A YEAR IN
THE CANARY
ISLANDS

JANUARY

△ **Noche de los Reyes** *(5 Jan)*. Colourful parades are held to celebrate Epiphany.

Festividad de San Sebastián *(20 Jan)*. Farmers drive their animals into the sea for a symbolic purification in the town of Adeje in Tenerife.

FEBRUARY

△ **Fiestas del Almendro en Flor** *(early Feb)*. An annual celebration of the blossoming of almond trees across Gran Canaria.

Carnival *(Feb–Mar)*. Parties and parades build up to the main event on Shrove Tuesday.

MAY

Pride *(mid-May)*. Pride celebrations take over Maspalomas in Gran Canaria.

△ **Día de Canarias** *(30 May)*. Also known as the Day of the Canary Islands, this holiday sees locals gather to celebrate Canarian culture.

JUNE

Corpus Christi *(Jun)*. Bright religious processions are held across the islands.

△ **Día de San Juan** *(24 Jun)*. Held in Las Palmas de Gran Canaria to commemorate the city's foundation.

SEPTEMBER

Fiesta de la Virgen del Pino *(6–8 Sep)*. A yearly procession where offerings of produce are made to the patron saint of Teror.

△ **Fiesta del Charco** *(7–11 Sep)*. Held in La Aldea de San Nicolás, this celebration sees participants jump into a pool of salt water to catch fish.

OCTOBER

Festival Internacional de Cine de Las Palmas *(Oct–Nov)*. A film festival held annually in Gran Canaria, drawing many international stars.

△ **"El Río" Crossing** *(early Oct)*. The highlight of this popular festival is the long-distance swimming event between Lanzarote and La Graciosa.

APRIL

Fiesta de Ansite *(29 Apr)*. Festivities in Gran Canaria mark the final Guanche uprising and Spain's colonization over the island.

Fiesta de Los Pastores *(late Apr)*. This traditional festival celebrates the shepherding history on El Hierro, dating back to the 16th century.

△ **Mes del Vino** *(Apr)*. The month of April sees an annual fair of Canarian wine take over Tenerife's village of Tegueste.

MARCH

△ **Entierro de la Sardina** *(Mar)*. A symbolic Spanish festivity which officially marks the end of the Carnival period.

Semana Santa *(Mar–Apr)*. Holy Week is celebrated across the Canary Islands, usually with a Good Friday procession.

Good Friday *(Mar–Apr)*. This Christian holiday is observed across the Canary Islands, in the lead up to Easter Sunday.

AUGUST

Bajada de la Rama *(4 Aug)*. Colourful parades are held in Agaete, Gran Canaria, based on a Guanche tradition to summon rain.

Assumption of Mary *(Aug)*. This Christian holiday is celebrated across the islands each year.

Los Corazones de Tejina *(Aug)*. This annual ancient festival in Tenerife sees revellers enjoying heart-shaped displays of treats like cakes, fruit and other produce.

△ **PHE Festival Tenerife** *(late Aug)*. An annual music festival held in Puerto de la Cruz, Tenerife.

JULY

△ **Fiesta del Carmen** *(16 Jul)*. This yearly celebration is held in Gáldar on the island of Gran Canaria to honour the patron saint of fishermen and sailors.

Festival Internacional Canarias Jazz *(mid-Jul)*. Buzzing jazz concerts are held across all of the Canary Islands in July, when a range of international musicians are hosted at this annual jazz festival.

NOVEMBER

△ **Fiestas de San Andrés** *(late Nov)*. Wine makers in Tenerife open bottles of the latest vintages.

Festival del Cacharro y de las Castañas *(30 Nov)*. In Santa Cruz de Tenerife, locals bang on pots to scare away evil spirits and eat roasted chestnuts.

DECEMBER

Día de Santa Lucia *(13 Dec)*. Villages in Gran Canaria are illuminated for this saint day.

Santos Inocentes *(28 Dec)*. Across the islands, tricks are played for the Spanish equivalent of April Fools' Day.

1

A BRIEF
HISTORY

Forged by fire and chiselled by waves and wind, the volcanic Canary Islands archipelago has been in constant geological change since it sprang up from the Atlantic Ocean floor more than 20 million years ago.

The First Canary Islanders

It's estimated that the Canary Islands have been inhabited for over 3,000 years. Research suggests that early island dwellers may share DNA with historic north African tribes, but how they would have crossed the 100-km (60-mile) stretch of Atlantic water to reach the archipelago remains a mystery. The term "Guanche" is often used to describe all Indigenous populations of the Canary Islands, but in reality this term only

1 A map of the Canary Islands from the 18th century.

2 A 19th-century Italian illustration of a Guanche cave.

3 Colonizing forces and Indigenous tribes battling in 1494.

4 Ships approaching the islands in the 17th century.

Timeline of events

20–11 million years ago
Islands are formed by volcanic eruptions.

1st century BCE
Guanches establish settlements on the islands.

1st Century CE
Pliny the Elder describes them as "the Fortunate Isles".

c 40 BCE
King Juba II of Mauritania makes an expedition to the islands.

BATALLA DE ACENTEJO

pertains to those of the island of Tenerife. Although recent discoveries have also shown evidence of Roman presence, it appears that the Indigenous Canary Islanders enjoyed relative solitude for millennia, subsisting off the land and sea and living in caves.

Arrival of the Europeans

The Genoese navigator Lancelotto Malocello landed on Tyterogaka in 1312 and renamed it Lanzarote after himself. More than 100 years passed before the islands were fully colonized, this time led by Jean de Béthencourt, who arrived in 1402 at the behest of the Castilian crown. The following years saw a wave of conquests across the seven main islands: Gran Canaria fell in 1483, followed by La Gomera in 1488 and, in 1496, La Palma. Tenerife, which had put up the fiercest resistance, fell to the Spanish in 1495. The Indigenous tribes, deprived of their land and forced into slavery, soon saw decreased numbers.

THE GUANCHE TRIBES ON THE CANARY ISLANDS

The Indigenous inhabitants of the Canary Islands were known as the Guanches. The term comes from the words *guan* (meaning "man") and *che* (meaning "white mountain"). The latter is thought to be in reference to the snow-capped El Teide volcano on Tenerife, where the Guanche tribes lived.

999 CE
Arabic traders land on Gran Canaria.

1312
Lancelotto Malocello lands on Tyterogaka and renames it Lanzarote.

1402–96
Spanish colonize the archipelago, starting with Lanzarote.

1400s
First grape vines planted on the archipelago.

1   St. Maria   Nina   Pinta

Crossing the Ocean

In the 15th century, the Canary Islands were the last stop for the navigator Christopher Columbus before he sailed to the Americas, and the ports of the islands – particularly Las Palmas de Gran Canaria – have been crucial stopping, refuelling and trading points ever since. It's from these ports that many islanders and others sailed to the New World looking for a better life. Many returned with increased wealth, bringing prosperity to what were then relatively poor islands.

Arrival of Industry

From the 16th century, sugar, cochineal, bananas and tomatoes were major exports for the archipelago. This boom in industry coincided with a rapid growth in the number of European settlers, particularly in Gran Canaria and Tenerife. Sugar cane, imported from Madeira, was used to produce sugar, which quickly became the main export from each island. Large sugar cane plantations sprang up, relying on the labour of enslaved people and European workers, despite Spain's ban on the slave trade in 1537. This industry resulted in the transformation of

1 Caravels in port of Luz in Las Palmas.

2 Admiral Horatio Nelson during the attack on Santa Cruz de Tenerife.

3 Traditional wine making on Gran Canaria.

4 A 16th-century illustration of a pirate attack on Las Palmas de Gran Canaria.

Timeline of events

1492
Christopher Columbus stops to refuel and restock before his voyage of discovery.

1537
The Spanish introduce a ban on the slave trade.

1500s
Exports from the island take off.

1570
The islands' first cathedral, Santa Ana, opens in Las Palmas de Gran Canaria.

the local ecosystem. Stripped of their trees, forests gave way to sugar cane fields, and bare slopes became prone to erosion. Soon, the growth of the sugar industry was halted by the colonization of America and the Caribbean, where sugar was produced more cheaply.

Wine from the islands, produced mainly in Tenerife and Gran Canaria, saw a growing export demand at this time and was especially popular in Britain. By the turn of the 18th century, however, income from wine production fell drastically.

Islands Under Attack

Spanish rule of the Canary Islands was threatened almost from the start. Pirates and slave traders, mostly from Europe and the northwest coast of Africa, set their sights on the islands. Several castles were built between the 16th and 17th centuries to defend port entries from French, Dutch and British fleets, and provide shelter for the locals. The last attempt at conquering the Canary Islands was made in 1797 by British admiral Horatio Nelson, who launched an attack on Santa Cruz de Tenerife. He not only failed to take the town, but lost his arm in the battle.

Did You Know?

———

Grape vine varieties were first brought to the Canary Islands in the 15th century.

1665
Establishment of the Canary Islands' Company, in London.

1706
Garachico destroyed by the eruption of Volcán Negra.

1730–36
Timanfaya volcano erupts, covering a third of Lanzarote in lava.

1797
Admiral Nelson loses his right arm trying to claim Tenerife for the British.

New Rule and Later Trade

In 1821, the Canary Islands became a province of Spain, with Santa Cruz de Tenerife made its capital. This intensified the rivalry between the two most populated islands – Tenerife and Gran Canaria – and led to the division of the archipelago into two provinces in 1927. During this period, the archipelago's economy refocused on the banana trade, which became the main export product. Production peaked in 1913, when more than 3 million bunches of bananas were exported from Tenerife, Gran Canaria and La Palma.

Changing Politics

The proclamation of the Second Spanish Republic in Madrid, in 1931, led to increased tension. In 1936, fearing a coup d'état, the Republican government "exiled" General Francisco Franco to the Canaries. In July 1936, Franco seized control of the islands, marking the beginning of the Spanish Civil War, which lasted until 1939. Around this time, economic development in the Canary Islands slowed and resulted in many local inhabitants emigrating.

[1] Packing bananas for export in Gran Canaria.

[2] Santa Cruz de Tenerife's Civil War memorial.

[3] Beach-goers enjoying this popular tourist spot.

[4] Crescent shore of Las Teresitas in Tenerife.

Did You Know?

London's Canary Wharf was named after the Canary Fruit Lines company.

Timeline of events

1843
Spanish novelist Benito Pérez Galdós is born in Gran Canaria.

1880s
Bananas become a main export of the islands.

1852
Queen Isabella II makes the archipelago a free trade zone.

1883
Work begins to construct La Luz Port in Las Palmas de Gran Canaria.

Rise of Tourism

The local economy began to shift its focus onto tourism from the 1960s onwards. Drawn to the year-round temperate climate, a wave of sun-seeking, package holiday visitors started to arrive. Major resorts sprung up around the sandiest spots, including Maspalomas in Gran Canaria and Los Cristianos in Tenerife. The first hotel in Fuerteventura opened in 1969 in Corralejo – then a small fishing village – to coincide with the opening of the island's airport. This industry has, in turn, accounted for the majority of the islands' revenue ever since.

The Canary Islands Today

Today, the islands maintain both their tourist appeal and their distinct cultural heritage. Protection of the natural environment is another key area of focus. Several programmes have been initiated to protect the vast geological wealth of the islands, with many national parks and sites gaining UNESCO World Heritage status since the 1980s. Faced with questions around sustainable tourism and finite resources, the Canary Islands continue to maintain their wild and vibrant nature.

↑ General Francisco Franco, who was later Head of Spanish State

1919
Lanzarote architect César Manrique is born.

1982
The Canary Islands become an autonomous region of Spain.

2021
The Cumbre Vieja volcano in La Palma erupts for 85 days, destroying 1,000 homes.

1954
El Teide National Park is established.

2024
Thousands of locals protest against mass tourism.

THE FORMATION OF THE CANARY ISLANDS

Like other Atlantic islands, such as Madeira, the Azores and the Cape Verde Islands, the Canaries are volcanic. The oldest of the islands, Lanzarote and Fuerteventura, are believed to have emerged from the sea between 16 and 20 million years ago; Gran Canaria, Tenerife and La Gomera followed around 8–13 million years ago; and the remaining islands much later. Today, most of the islands have a central volcanic cone and areas of solidified lava, around which communities have been built.

VOLCANIC VINEYARDS

The stunning vineyards of La Geria (p122) on Lanzarote are truly unique: these crops flourish in the fertile, dark volcanic soil of the island. Semicircles of stones protect vines from the prevailing winds, and the resulting grapes are used to produce the famous, amber-coloured Malvasía wine.

An illustration of the topography around the Canary Islands ↓

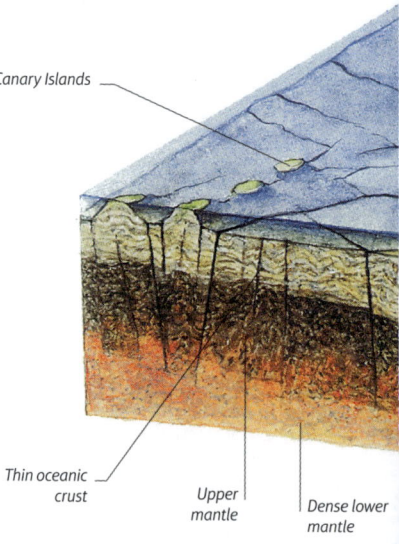

Canary Islands

Thin oceanic crust

Upper mantle

Dense lower mantle

EVOLUTION OF VOLCANIC ISLANDS

The Canary Islands are in fact the tips of volcanoes, which have been pushed up from the floor of the Atlantic Ocean by the movement of the Earth's crust over time. As a result, the islands are home to dormant calderas, volcanic black-sand landscapes and epic mountain peaks. Most of the islands in this archipelago are still in their geological evolution. Tenerife, El Hierro, Lanzarote and La Palma are still volcanically active; La Palma experienced its last eruption in 2021.

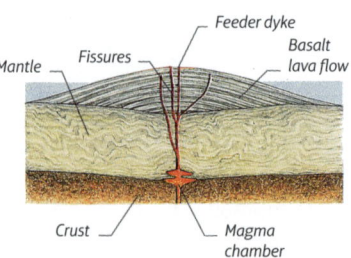

Mantle   Fissures   Feeder dyke   Basalt lava flow

Crust   Magma chamber

△ The islands of La Gomera, El Hierro and La Palma are really the tops of volcanoes that rise from the ocean's bed. They consist of basalt rock produced by solidified lava. Below, the Earth's crust bends under the weight of the islands.

The dramatic volcanic landscapes of Tenerife seen from above

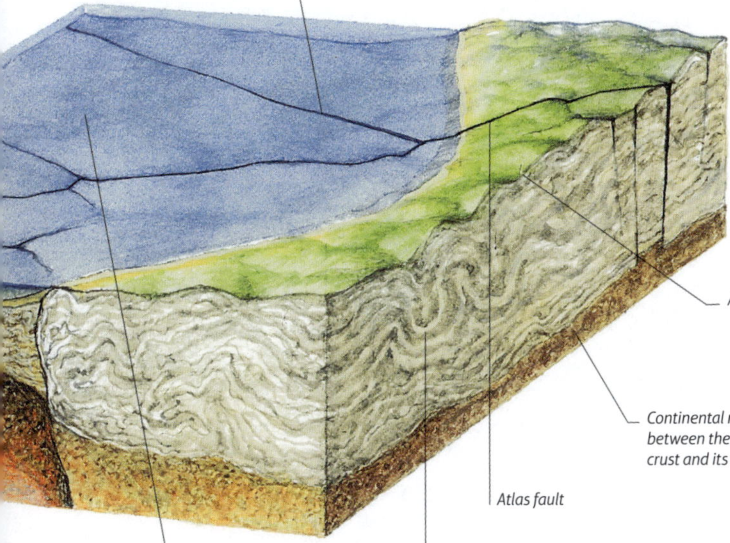

Transform fault

Africa

Continental mantle between the Earth's crust and its core

Atlas fault

Atlantic Ocean

Thick continental crust

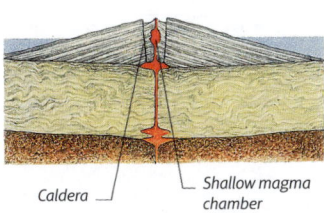

Caldera   *Shallow magma chamber*

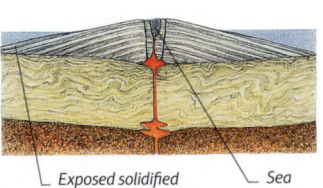

Exposed solidified magma chamber   *Sea level*

△ When the magma chamber empties during an eruption, the top of the cone collapses. This creates a crater, known as a caldera, like the Caldera de Taburiente on La Palma *(p196)*. This stage of volcanic evolution is marked by great flows of lava.

△ When the eruption has ended, the volcano begins to erode. The mountains of Gran Canaria are in the early stages of erosion. Fuerteventura's volcanic chambers, with their solidified lava, are in a more advanced stage of evolution.

EXPERIENCE

Laurel forests near Los Tilos, La Palma

GRAN CANARIA

It's thought that Gran Canaria was first inhabited in the 5th century BCE, with its earliest dwellers being the Guanche people of the Canary Islands. One of the most significant remnants of Guanche life can be found at the Cueva Pintada in Gáldar, where geometric cave paintings indicate the artistic traditions of the Indigenous people.

Between 1478 and 1483, the island was conquered by the Spanish, and by the 1520s it officially became a part of Spain. The Guanche people of the island faced significant oppression during this time, with many losing their lives; those who survived were compelled to adopt Spanish customs and traditions.

Gran Canaria's capital city, Las Palmas de Gran Canaria, was founded soon after colonization in 1478 as Real de las Palmas. A significant chapter in the city's history is linked to the navigator Christopher Columbus, who spent some time here in 1492 on his way to the Americas.

Trade through and from the islands increased in subsequent centuries, and with it slowly came tourism. Visitor numbers really took off in the mid-19th century, with tourists drawn to the island's good climate and stunning natural beauty, which was something later recognized by UNESCO.

GRAN CANARIA

Must See

1 Las Palmas de Gran Canaria

Experience More

2 Tafira Alta
3 Caldera de Bandama
4 Santa Brígida
5 Vega de San Mateo
6 Teror
7 Arucas
8 Firgas
9 Moya
10 Guía
11 Gáldar
12 Puerto de Mogán
13 Maspalomas
14 San Bartolomé de Tirajana
15 Puerto Rico
16 Agaete
17 La Aldea de San Nicolás
18 Agüimes
19 Ingenio
20 Barranco de Guayadeque
21 Santa Lucía
22 Telde

Punta de Ortiz

El Sobradillo

Punta de Sardina

Barranquillo del Vino

Sardina

GÁLDAR **11**

San Isidro

GC2

Los Quintanas y Piso Firme

Hoya de Pineda

Playa Sotavento

Puerto de las Nieves

16 **AGAETE**

El Saucillo

Playa de Guayedra

San Pedro

Berrazales

Fagajesto

Playa del Risco

Tamadaba
1,443 m (4,734 ft)

El Risco

Juncalillo

Punta de la Arenas

GC200

Coruña

Artenara

Casas de Lentisco

Parque Natural de Tamadaba

Acusa

Caserones

LA ALDEA DE SAN NICOLÁS

17

GC210

El Carrizal

Montaña de Pino Gordo
647 m (2,123 ft)

Lomo del Mulato

El Toscón de Arriba

Punta de la Soga

Artejevez

El Hoyo

Montaña de Sándara
1,570 m (5,15 ft)

El Juncal

Reserva Natural Especial de Güigüí

GC200

Cueva las Niñas

Playa de Güigüí

Tasartico

Tasarte

Las Tetas

La Huerta Nueva

Soria

Embalse de Soria

El Pie de la Cuesta

Loma de la Palma

Atlantic Ocean

La Cardonera

Lomo Central

Mogán

La Solana

Playa de Tasarte

Molino de Viento

GC200

Los Navarros

Lomo de Gamona

Cercados de Espinos

El Llano

Playa de Veneguera

Las Burritas

Los Peñones

PUERTO DE MOGÁN

12

Taurito

PUERTO RICO **15**

La Playa del Cura

El Motor Grande

GC500

GC1

Las Crucitas

Playa de Patalavaca

El Pujar

GRAN CANARIA

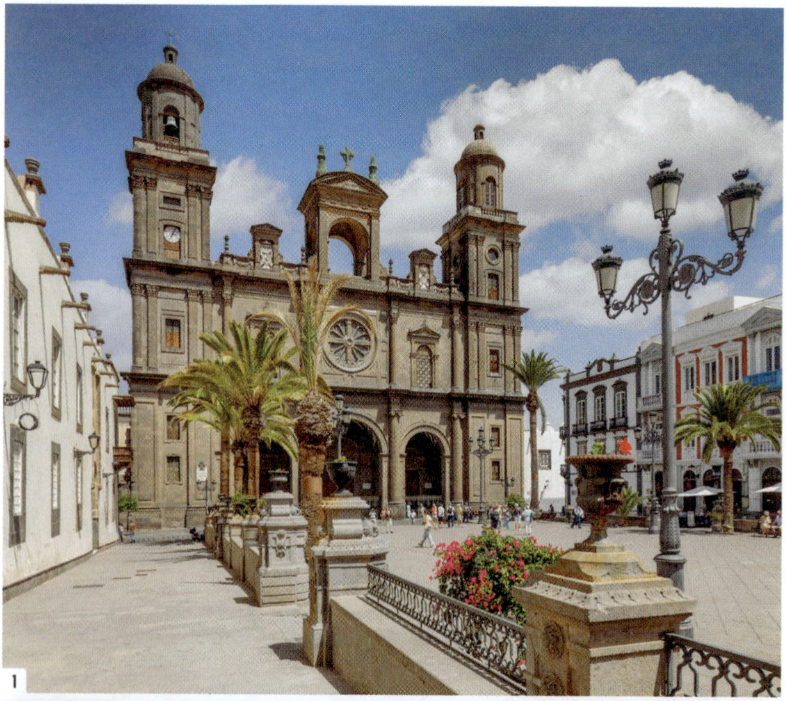

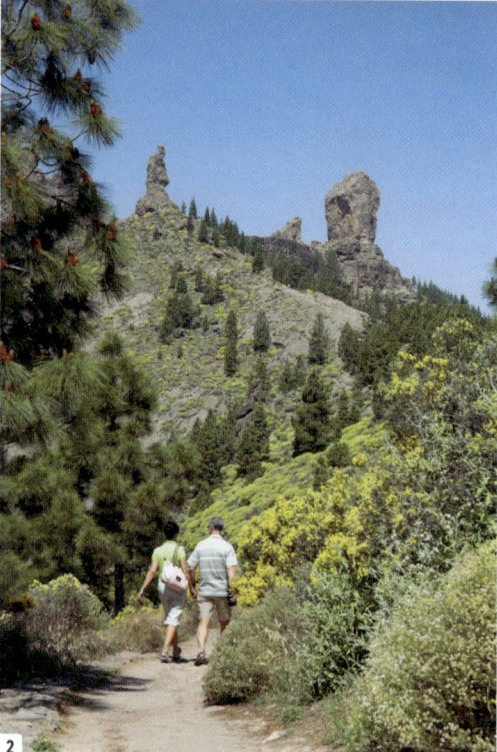

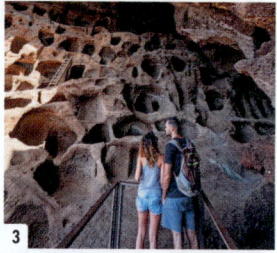

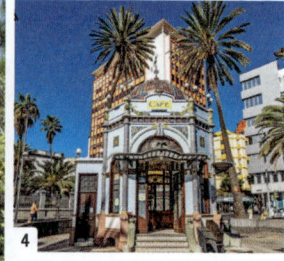

1

2

3

4

←

1 Santa Ana Cathedral in Las Palmas de Gran Canaria.

2 The stunning Roque Nublo.

3 Inside on of the caves of Cenobio de Valerón.

4 A café in Parque San Telmo.

5 DAYS
in Gran Canaria

Day 1

Beginning in Las Palmas de Gran Canaria *(p56)*, grab a bite from one of the brunch spots at the Mercado de Vegueta *(Calle Mendizábal, 1)*. Make your way over to Casa Colón *(p62)* and learn about pre-Hispanic culture on the islands, before strolling over to Plaza de Santa Ana to admire the cathedral *(p60)*. Continue south, stopping at the Art Nouveau café in Parque San Telmo *(p59)* for a bite. Walk to the west side of the park to rent a bike from a Sítycleta dock and cycle to Castillo de la Luz *(p57)*, returning your bike at the nearby dock. Explore this culture space before strolling to Playa de Las Canteras *(p56)* as night falls for a seafood dinner at one of the many beach-side restaurants.

Day 2

Rent a car and drive along the north coast, stretching your legs with a walk to the natural sea pools of Playa Charco de Las Palomas *(Calle Océano Atlántico, Arucas)* along the way. Continue west to Santa María de Guía *(p69)* and see the 300 caves of Cenobio de Valerón. Drive to Gáldar *(p69)* and stop at Plaza de Santiago for lunch. Belly full, walk over to the striking Cueva Pintada Museum and Archaeological Park *(Calle Audiencia 2)*, where you can get up close to the pre-Hispanic paintings here. Spend the evening strolling the town, pausing for a drink and, later, dinner at the historic Hotel Agaldar *(Plaza de Santiago 14)*.

Day 3

Fuel your day with a hearty breakfast on the Plaza de Santiago. Make your way to the Mercado *(Calle Capitán Quesada 29)* to stock up for a picnic before heading south on the windy GC-70 road towards the GC-150. Take in the sweeping views from the lookouts along the way, until you reach Degollada de La Goleta walking route. From here, it's an easy 1.5-km (1-mile) walk to the Roque Nublo. Take a break to enjoy your picnic among the stunning rock formations, then drive north to the mountain village Cruz de Tejeda in the centre of the island. See out the day with a drink at the Parador *(Cruz de Tejeda s/n)* before resting for the night.

Day 4

It's back in the car, this time to the town of Santa Brígida *(p65)*. After a stroll, stop off for an early lunch at one of the town's charming restaurants. Fuelled up, make your way to the Caldera de Bandama walking route – it may be just under 3 km (2 miles), but be prepared to take on the rather steep gradient. After the walk, drive over to the town of Tafira Alta *(p64)* and stop here for the night, enjoying dinner and a restful sleep.

Day 5

It's your last day on the island, so spend it relaxing on the beach. Start the day with a drive of just under one hour to Playa del Inglés and enjoy a morning swim and rest by the water. Have a snack from a beach bar before setting off to explore the nearby Maspalomas Dunes on an e-bike tour from the beach, taking in the rolling sand dunes along the way *(p171)*. After a day on the beach, drive up to Puerto de Mogán *(p70)* to toast the end of the trip with a sundowner from Restaurante Mogán Mar *(Avenida Varadero 32-3)*.

❶

LAS PALMAS DE GRAN CANARIA

  Parque de San Telmo; www.laspalmasgc.es;
www.grancanaria.com

The largest city of the archipelago, Las Palmas was founded on 24 June 1478 by Spanish conquistadors. It soon became an important port for ships heading for the Americas and has remained an essential stop for visitors of all kinds ever since. Today, its historic architecture (a legacy of its colonial rulers), vibrant nightlife scene and annual carnival celebrations provide a hit of culture for holidaymakers and locals.

①

El Puerto de Las Palmas

The driving force behind the development of Las Palmas, the city's port has seen all manner of seafaring traffic, from Spanish conquistadors to modern cruise ships. Though it's not as busy today as it once was (especially when the Canary Islands enjoyed duty-free status), some 1,000 ships dock here each month.

The port area includes a marina, which is the starting point for the annual winter boat race from the Canary Islands to Saint Lucia.

②

Playa de Las Canteras

This gorgeous stretch of sand is one of the best beaches in Las Palmas. At 2.8 km (1.7 miles) long and

 INSIDER TIP
Stand-up Paddle Boarding (SUP)

Thanks to the sandbar protecting it from big waves, Playa de Las Canteras is great for SUP; try it out with MojoSurf School (*www.mojosurf.es*).

in places up to 100 m (330 ft) wide, it's ideal for days spent sunbathing and sandy walks. La Barra, a natural rock barrier protecting the beach here against strong surf, makes bathing possible, even in rough conditions.

The seaside promenade Paseo de Las Canteras has plenty to entertain between swimming and sunbathing, lined with many cafés, bars, restaurants and shops, as well as hotels. At the southern end of the beach is the Auditorio Alfredo Kraus, the home of the Philharmonic Orchestra of Las Palmas. The building, named after the Canarian

←

El Puerto de Las
Palmas illuminated
in the evening

tenor Alfredo Kraus (1927–99),
has ten concert halls that are
also used as meeting venues.
The area around the beach
is also home to one of the
city's biggest shopping
centres, Las Arenas.

③
Playa de Alcaravaneras

Located south of the ferry
terminal at Muelle de Santa
Catalina in the district of
Alcaravaneras, the golden
sands of the Playa de
Alcaravaneras make up this
city beach. Stretching along
the coast for 1 km (0.6 miles),
this is the second-longest
of the Las Palmas beaches
after Las Canteras.

The beach is a popular spot
for sports by the sea; take a
dip, join in a game of beach
volleyball or head out for a
walk along the promenade
close to the shore. South
of the beach, the modern
yacht marina of the Real
Club Náutico, a beautiful spot,
is often packed with several
glamorous boats.

④
Santa Catalina

At the heart of the scenic
Santa Catalina district is
the Parque Santa Catalina,
which is not a park as the
name suggests but instead
one of the city's major
squares. Thanks to its
proximity to the port, it's
one of the first places visited
by those who arrive by
boat; as a result, there
are many great bars and
restaurants here. There is
also a tourist information
office located here.

Leading off from the
square are narrow streets

lined with shops which
specialize in all manner
of goods, including clothes,
jewellery, alcohol and
electronics.

⑤
Castillo de la Luz

📍 C/Juan Rejón, s/n
📞 928 463 162 🕐 11am-
7pm Mon-Sat, 10am-2pm
Sun (by appt)

On the delightful south
shore of La Isleta, near the
harbour, stands Castillo de
la Luz – the Castle of Light.
This well-preserved fortress
dates back to the 16th
century, when it was built
to guard the town of Las
Palmas against pirates. It
was restored to its former
glory in 1990, and is now
home to the Martín Chirino
Foundation and its many
art exhibitions.

ISLAND DEFENCES

Facing the threat of
pirates and privateers,
who came in search of
treasure brought from
the Americas, the city
constructed several
fortifications. Castillo
de la Luz, Castillo de la
Mata, Castillo de San
Cristóbal and Castillo de
San Francisco all helped
protect Las Palmas from
the likes of Peter Van
der Does and even Sir
Francis Drake *(below)*.

EAT

Poemas by Hermanos Padrón

Situated in the historic Hotel Santa Catalina, this Michelin-starred restaurant serves up dishes rooted in Gran Canarian tradition with innovative twists.

 C/Leon y Castillo 227
🌐 restaurante poemas.com

€€€

Restaurante Terraza Elder

Next to the Museo Elder, this family-friendly gourmet restaurant serves up Canarian and international cuisine. Tuck in while enjoying the views over the Muelle Santa Catalina.

 C/Eduardo Benot 2
🌐 terrazaelder.com

€€€

The Hook

Dining is a relaxed affair at this reasonably priced spot near the Muelle Santa Catalina. The menu offers a mix of different cuisines, so there's something for everyone.

 C/José Franchy Roca 9
🌐 thehooklpa.com

€€€

Restaurante Terraza Pantalán

Sample Mediterranean cuisine and sip a cocktail as you admire spectacular views over the marina.

 C/Blanco Torrent s/n
🌐 restaurante pantalan.com

€€€

↑ Lovely statue atop a fountain in the Parque Doramas

⑥ Muelle de Santa Catalina

 Santa Catalina Pier s/n
🕙 10am–10pm daily
🌐 ccelmuelle.es

This towering shopping and leisure centre is located at the foot of the ferry terminal. It houses a range of local and international fashion and homeware brands, as well as several restaurants. Located on the south side of Avenida Marítima del Norte, the ferry terminal offers cruises and hydrofoil services to Tenerife and the other islands.

---

⑦ Museo Elder

🏛 Parque Santa Catalina s/n 🕙 10am–8pm Tue–Sun 🌐 museoelder.org

The wonders of technology and science are explored in this interactive museum. Exhibits explain everything from gravity and supersonic speeds to intelligent robots.

Did You Know?

Visitors to Hotel Santa Catalina in its heyday included Winston Churchill and Agatha Christie.

⑧ Parque Doramas

One of the main highlights of the verdant residential district of Ciudad Jardín, aptly dubbed the "Garden City", is this beautifully landscaped park. An oasis of peace in the otherwise bustling city of Las Palmas, the park features pretty water cascades and a municipal swimming pool.

The park is named after the Guanche chieftain Doramas who, in the late 15th century, put up a fierce resistance against the Spanish invaders. His struggles are symbolized by the monument depicting Guanches tumbling over a precipice to escape capture.

NÉSTOR MARTÍN FERNÁNDEZ DA LA TORRE

Néstor Martín Fernández de la Torre (1887–1938), known simply as "Néstor", was one of the most original artists to come from the Canary Islands. Born in Las Palmas, he studied in Paris and went on to produce paintings, stage designs, theatre and opera costumes, and interior designs, but was known principally for his murals. In 1934, he settled in Gran Canaria and devoted the last years of his life to developing and publicizing Canarian art forms.

 ⑨

Hotel Santa Catalina

🏠 C/Leon y Castillo 227
🌐 hotelsantacatalina.com

Set among the subtropical greenery of the Parque Doramas is the imposing Hotel Santa Catalina. Originally built in 1890 for the British employees of the Canary Island's Company, the building was redesigned between 1947 and 1952 to blueprints left by the late Canary artist Néstor Martin Fernandez de la Torre. Views of the park can be enjoyed by non-resident visitors from the bar.

 ⑩

Parque San Telmo

🏠 Avda Rafael Cabrera 30

This small city park is a popular spot for a stroll in the city centre. At the edge of the Parque San Telmo stands the 17th-century San Telmo Chapel, devoted to this patron saint of fishers. On the edge of the park is the Gobierno Militar building, where, on 18 July 1936, General Franco declared his opposition to the Republican government, signalling the start of the Spanish Civil War.

Nearby is Calle Bravo Murillo, along which runs the old city wall. This street leads up to an old castle, Castillo de Mata. Take a stroll down Calle Mayor de Triana and admire the Modernist houses that line this historic street.

Nestled into a corner of the park is the La Modernista café. Built in 1923, today this stunning Art Nouveau kiosk serves up refreshments in the leafy park setting.

 ⑪

Museo Néstor

🏠 Pueblo Canario
🕐 Temporarily, check website 🌐 laspalmasgc.es/mnestor

Opened in 1958, this museum exhibits works by Néstor, including sketches and symbolic paintings. One of the museum's highlights is the dome of the rotunda, which is decorated with eight murals illustrating Torre's "Poema del Mar" ("Poem of the Sea").

↓ The Art Nouveau kiosk in the leafy Parque San Telmo

Centro Atlántico de Arte Moderno (CAAM)

🏠 Los Balcones 11 🕐 10am-9pm Tue-Sat, 10am-2pm Sun 🌐 caam.net

CAAM is located in the heart of Vegueta, the oldest district in Las Palmas. Housed in a former hotel that retains its 18th-century façade, the space has a history of its own. The interior, by contrast, is modern and airy, with plenty of natural light and white spaces.

CAAM organizes a host of exhibitions, mainly of avant-garde art, as well as its own collection of works by artists influential in shaping 20th-century Canarian art. The space is also a venue for academic symposia on the subject of modern art; you'll find exhibits on Spanish artists such as José María Sicilia, Cristina Iglesias, Alberto García Alix and Luis Gordillo.

After ambling around the centre, it's worth exploring Vegueta's labyrinth of narrow streets, lined with historic houses and beautiful patios. Equally charming are the old town squares, including Plaza de Santo Domingo.

Catedral de Santa Ana

🏠 Pl Santa Ana

It took 400 years to complete this cathedral, the building of which started in 1497. The lengthy gestation resulted in a mix of architectural styles and interior furnishings. The Neo-Classical façade hides Gothic vaults resting on slender columns, altar retables, Baroque pulpits and sculptures by José Luján Pérez. The crypt contains the tomb of José de Viera y Clavijo, Canarian traveller and the author of *History of the Canary Islands*. Another chapel is the resting place of diplomat Fernando de León y Castillo (*p75*). A lift in the south tower whisks visitors to the viewing terrace, which offers outstanding views.

Casa-Museo Pérez Galdós

🏠 C/Cano 2 & 6 🕐 10am-6pm Tue-Sun (last adm: 5pm) 🌐 casamuse-operez galdos.com

The Museum of Benito Pérez Galdós celebrates the most distinguished writer from the Canary Islands. Occupying the house in which Galdós was

The Neo-Classical façade of Catedral de Santa Ana hides Gothic vaults resting on slender columns, altar retables, Baroque pulpits and sculptures by José Luján Pérez.

← Vaulted nave of Catedral de Santa Ana, and *(inset)* its Neo-Classical façade

SHOP

Mercado de Vegueta

Located right at the edge of the busy Vegueta district, this indoor market sells a huge variety of goods, including fruit, fish, meat and cheeses, as well as local handicrafts.

📍 C/Mendizábal 1
📞 928 33 41 29 🕐 Sun

Palmas and one of the most famous in the Canary Islands. It hosts plays, operas, musicals, concerts and dance performances all year round.

Museo Canario

📍 C/Dr Verneau 2 🕐 10am–8pm Mon–Fri, 10am–2pm Sat & Sun 🌐 elmuseocanario.com

The renowned Canary Island Museum opened in 1879 and was refurbished in the mid-1980s. The collection features archaeological finds from all seven islands, including statuettes of gods, pottery, jewellery and tools of the Guanches, as well as skulls, skeletons and mummies. Among the star attractions are copies of the paintings discovered in Gáldar's Cueva Pintada, as well as several *pintaderas* – terracotta stamps used for printing geometric patterns on clothes.

born and where he lived until 1862, this five-storey building still has the original interior decor. The museum, which opened in 1964, contains objects associated with the writer's life, as well as photographs of many actors who appeared in his plays. There's also a small patio adorned with a statue of the writer outside.

---

⑮ Teatro Pérez Galdós

📍 Pl Stagno 1 🌐 teatroperezgaldos.es

In the south of Triana, almost opposite Mercado Municipal de Vegueta, stands a theatre named after the writer Benito Pérez Galdós (1843–1920). Built in 1919, this structure is the work of architect Miguel Martín Fernández de la Torre. The opulent interior and the auditorium for 1,400 spectators were designed by his brother, Néstor Martín Fernández de la Torre. Today this is the best theatre in Las

↑ Historic Canarian pottery on display at the Museo Canario

⑰

CASA DE COLÓN

⌂ Colón 1 🕙 10am–6pm Mon–Sat, 10am–3pm Sun 🚫 1 & 6 Jan, 1 May, 24, 25 & 31 Dec 🆆 casadecolon.com

In the oldest district of Las Palmas stands the palace of the first governors of the island. This charming building may have been rebuilt in 1777, but it retains its charm with its beautiful wooden balconies.

↑ Admiring the cartography displays at the museum

Stories say that the infamous navigator Christopher Columbus stayed in this palace in 1492 during a break in his voyage while one of his ships was repaired, hence the name Casa de Colón, or Columbus House. Since 1952, it has housed a museum that includes models and artifacts relating to voyages made by Columbus. Temporary exhibitions are also held regularly.

The permanent displays are arranged on three levels, in 12 rooms surrounding two inner courtyards and in underground chambers, which contain treasures of

Did You Know?

Casa de Colón hosts a colloquium on Canarian-American History every two years.

Since 1952, Casa de Colón has housed a museum that includes models and artifacts relating to voyages made by Columbus.

pre-Columbian art. The ground floor is given to Columbus's expeditions, the growth of cartography and the history of the Canary Islands as the gateway to the Americas and life on the islands before that. The first-floor rooms present an overview of Las Palmas history, from the 15th until the 19th century. There are also separate rooms displaying items on loan from Madrid's Museo del Prado.

Building Highlights

External Portal

▷ Casa de Colón features a magnificent portal crowned by a Tudor arch. This exquisite ornament combines plant and animal motifs, with two lions supporting the town's crests.

St Lucia

Guamart de Amberes' painting is part of the museum's vast collection of works by 16th-century Dutch and Italian painters. Some of these collections belong to the Museo del Prado. They include paintings by Guido Reni, the Carracci brothers and Guercino.

Pre-Columbian Art

An extensive collection of pre-Columbian artifacts of gold and other metals includes original items and replicas associated with the Spanish conquests in Central and South America.

Santa María

Models of the three ships from Columbus's fleet (Santa María, La Niña, La Pinta) and navigation instruments illustrate the equipment available to mariners in the early 16th century.

Astrolabe

One of the early navigational instruments, the astrolabe was developed in the 2nd century BCE. It was used to measure the height of heavenly bodies above the horizon. The collection here includes a bronze astrolabe from the first half of the 16th century.

Ship's Interior

▷ A reconstructed, full-size fragment of the interior of La Niña, one of the ships that sailed with Columbus's expedition, demonstrates the conditions that the sailors endured.

Courtyard

At the centre of the inner courtyard stands an old well. Centuries-old galleries and arcades, in typical Canary style, keep the rooms cool and shady.

← The Casa de Colón's striking portal and *(inset)* a pretty courtyard inside

EXPERIENCE MORE

❷ Tafira Alta

🛈 Jardín Canario; 928 219 580

Set among the hills is the small town of Tafira Alta, famous for its many beautiful residences surrounded by gardens. These colourful villas feature a variety of eye-catching architectural forms and details, with many houses showing the influence of Moorish or Bauhaus style. Little wonder, then, that Tarifa Alta is a favourite spot among Las Palmas' well-heeled visitors and locals.

At the beginning of the 20th century, the British built several elegant hotels here, including Los Frailes. This hotel was used as a meeting place by General Franco's supporters as they plotted to overthrow Spain's Republican government in 1936.

Situated on the outskirts of Tafira Alta is the **Jardín Botánico Viera y Clavijo**, named after José de Viera y Clavijo (1731–1813), the author of the *Canary Islands Dictionary of Plants*. The beautiful gardens were originally created in 1952 by the Swedish botanist Eric Sventenius (1910–73), who remained their director until his death. Set on terraces and growing in their natural subtropical environment are plants sourced from all the islands in the archipelago. These include species of the native Canary palm, Canary pine and heathers. Also featured are plants from other regions including the Azores, Madeira and the Cape Verde Islands. One of the highlights of the Jardín Botánico are the 2,000 succulents, which were brought here from all around the world.

PICTURE PERFECT
Mirador Bandama

The Mirador Bandama offers stunning views across the northeastern part of the island and of the lush crater below. Take a snap at sunset of the shadow stretching over the caldera.

Jardín Botánico Viera y Clavijo

📍 Ctra del Centro, km 7 (GC-110), 35017 Las Palmas de Gran Canaria 🕐 Hours vary, check website
🌐 jardincanario.org

❸ Caldera de Bandama

It is worth travelling the 5-km (3-mile) distance from Tafira, half of which is over a narrow mountain road, to reach the peak of the volcano Pico de Bandama where the Caldera de Bandama lies. This low

→ Massive Candelabra cacti at the Jardín Botánico Viera y Clavijo, and *(inset)* a Golden Barrel cactus in bloom

mountain (570 m/1,870 ft high) provides one of the best viewpoints on Gran Canaria from the Mirador de Bandama. From here, visitors get a great view over the whole of Las Palmas and the mountainous centre of the island. Below is the volcanic caldera of Bandama, 1,000 m (3,300 ft) in diameter and 200 m (650 ft) deep. It is named after a Flemish merchant, Daniel von Damme, who grew vines inside the crater in the 16th century, together with his Gran Canarian wife Juana Vera. Today the area is overgrown with orange and fig trees and palms. Eucalyptus and agaves grow on the slopes, among shrubs and bushes.

A golf course, located on the mountain just south of Pico de Bandama, was set up by English residents of the island in 1891. It is the oldest golf course in Spain.

↑ Exploring the weekend market in Vega de San Mateo

---

④

Santa Brígida

📞 928 648 181

The prosperous old town of Santa Brígida lies on the slopes of a gully covered with cypress and tall palms. Its narrow streets are lined with eucalyptus trees and flower-filled balconies. This pretty town is a popular destination for a day out for locals from Las Palmas, its narrow streets perfect for walks.

The town's Santa Brígida parish church is fronted by a terrace that provides a good view over the surrounding palm groves. This impressive triple-nave, Neo-Gothic basilica was built in 1904 on the site of a chapel constructed in 1520 by Isabel Guerra, the granddaughter of Pedro Guerra – one of the conquerors of Gran Canaria. The chapel was replaced by a church built in 1580. This, in turn, was almost destroyed by fire in the late 19th century. The only part that escaped destruction was the tower, built in 1756. Vineyards nearby produce Vino del Monte, one of the best Canarian red wines.

> **Santa Brígida is a popular destination for a day out for locals from Las Palmas, its narrow streets perfect for walks.**

26 km (16 miles) from Las Palmas. It is known for its large agricultural market, which is held every weekend. As well as fruits, vegetables and numerous types of cheese, the local farmers also bring goats, pigs and cows for sale. San Mateo is equally known for its wickerwork baskets and for producing Canary Island knives, leather goods and woodwork. These and other local arts and crafts are often on sale at the bustling weekend market.

On Calle Principal stands the church of San Mateo, a fine example of neo-Canary architecture. Above this two-nave building hangs a bell sent from Cuba by local emigrants. The church also houses a 17th-century statue of St Matthew, the town's patron saint.

WINEGROWING IN GRAN CANARIA

Gran Canaria's rich, volcanic soil and mild, subtropical climate support nearly 40 grape varieties across 110 sq km (42 sq miles). Popular varieties include Listán Negro, Listán Blanco, Tintilla, Malvasia Volcánica and Muscat of Alexandria. The fertile lands near Santa Brígida and Tafira Alta contribute significantly to the island's wine industry, producing wines with complex flavours, pronounced mineral notes and an intense, lingering finish.

---

⑤

Vega de San Mateo

📞 928 661 350

This small town is situated in a fertile, green valley

↑ The 18th-century basilica of Nuestra Señora del Pino, Teror

Large historic houses line the town's main square, Plaza de Nuestra Señora del Pino. Some of these mansions date from the 16th century and have lavishly carved wooden, stone and wrought-iron balconies, which speak to the wealth of the mansions' former occupants.

The basilica of Nuestra Señora del Pino, completed in 1767, was the third church to be built on this site. Only the tower remains from the earlier church; it dates from 1708. The octagonal shape and striking mix of Moorish and Baroque elements make

6

Teror

✉ ℹ C/Padre Cueto 2; www.teror.es

Teror is famously the religious capital and spiritual heart of the island. The town owes its spiritual status to the saint Nuestra Señora del Pino

(Our Lady of the Pines), who is said to have first appeared here atop a pine tree in 1481. Later, in 1914, Pope Pius XII proclaimed her the patron saint of the island.

Since then, the town has been visited every year in early September by many pilgrims, who travel here from all over Gran Canaria.

Did You Know?

The town of Teror is also famous across the island for its delicious sweet pastries.

HOW RUM IS MADE

Rum, a by-product of sugar production, is a drink normally associated with the Caribbean, but thanks to the Canary Islands' sugar plantations, it's made in abundance here too. The local rum is generally valued for its outstanding flavour and its warming and even medicinal properties. Its alcohol content can vary from 40 to 80 per cent. One of the Canary Islands' specialities is *ron miel,* a honey rum.

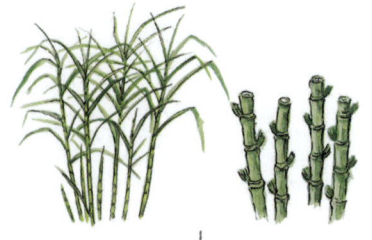

Production

Processing

▲ Rum is made from sugar cane, which is processed in order to obtain sugar syrup and molasses - both are used in the later stages of production.

Distillation

▲ Inside these large vessels, sugar juices or molasses undergo a fermentation process. The alcohol obtained by fermentation subsequently undergoes a distillation process.

the tower a distinctive landmark. The main feature of the large, triple-nave interior is the vast, Baroque altar with its 15th-century carved figure of the Virgin, who is the patron saint of the island and the reason for one of the biggest fiestas in the Canary Islands (p38). Some of the other attractions here include the fascinating Treasure Room, which contains an eclectic mix of precious gifts, donated at past festivals, to celebrate the saint.

Not far from the church is Plaza Doña María Teresa de Bolívar, named after María Teresa, the wife of Simón Bolívar – a figure of South America's fight for independence. Her family came from Teror, and the family crest adorns the square.

Around 2 km (1 mile) from the centre of Teror is the Molino Bridge. Built between 1824 and 1828, it is the oldest bridge on Gran Canaria.

❼ Arucas

🚌 🛈 C/León y Castillo 10; 928 623 136

On approaching Arucas, the first sights you'll encounter are the impressive towers of the Neo-Gothic parish church of San Juan. The church, often mistakenly referred to as a cathedral, was designed by Spanish architect Manuel Vega March and built in 1909. As well as the fine stained-glass windows and retable, the interior features a wonderful sculpture of *Cristo Yacente* (the Recumbent Christ), which is the work of a local sculptor and artist, Manuel Ramos.

The old town hall in Plaza de la Constitución, designed by José A López de Echegarret, was built in 1875 and then rebuilt in 1932. On the opposite side of the square is the leafy town park, which is home to many species of rare tropical tree, including the evergreen soapbark tree (*Quillaja saponaria*).

Encircling the park, Calle de la Heredad features one of the town's most beautiful buildings, Heredad de Aguas de Arucas y Firgas, which was built in 1908 and now houses the Water Board. In the second half of the 19th century, and the early years of the 20th century, the Board initiated the construction of an irrigation system and the town itself acquired its present shape.

The Canary Islands' largest rum factory was built in Arucas in 1884. The factory has a good museum devoted to the history and distillation method of the spirit. Near the factory entrance stands an early 18th-century chapel – La Ermita de San Pedro.

About 2 km (1 mile) north of Arucas is the Montaña de Arucas. At the highest point of the town is a restaurant that offers panoramic views of the town and the entire island.

⒈ Molasses combine with the foam (collected from the boiling juices) and the brew in large vats to produce strong rums.

⒉ Traditional oak barrels are used to age the resulting rum to ensure a refined flavour.

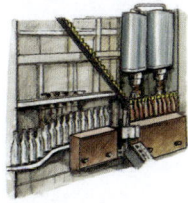

Aging
⚠ The rum is left to mature in oak barrels, a process that can last between three and ten years.

Bottling
⚠ Bottling and labelling are the final stages of rum production. This is a fully automatic process.

Final product
⚠ One of the island's most popular rums is from La Palma; the best brand is said to be Ron de la Aldea.

8

Firgas

📠 ℹ️ 928 616 747

Firgas is famous for its production of sparkling mineral water. The water is drawn from a spring some 6 km (4 miles) away, in Barranco de la Virgen, and 200,000 bottles a day are produced. Firgas water is very popular throughout the islands, where there is a shortage of fresh water.

A feature of the town, which celebrated its 500th anniversary in 1988, is the Paseo de Gran Canaria, where cascades of water flow along passages that were laid out in 1995. On either side of the passage, by the walls of surrounding houses, are benches with backrests decorated with landscapes or historic symbols of Gran Canaria. The white walls of the houses feature colourful town crests. Above Plaza de San Roque, the passage is filled with giant slabs with ceramic maps and views of the individual islands. These provide an unusual lesson in the geography of the Canary Islands. Still further along the passage there is a fine display of the flags of all the Canary Islands fluttering in the breeze.

The historic 15th-century Molino de Gofio and the 19th-century fountain were restored in 1988. The whole town is decorated with modern sculptures, including an amusing statue of a peasant with a pink cow.

TOMÁS MORALES (1884-1921)

Born in Moya, Tomás Morales is hailed as one of the Canary Islands' best poets. Although he completed medical studies at the university in 1909, his true passion was poetry. He started writing poems at the age of 15 and had his first works published in 1902. In 1908, his first book, *Poems of Glory, Love and Sea* appeared, and two years later Las Palmas Theatre Group staged his dramatic prose poem *Dinner at Simon's House*. His strong identification with his homeland is reflected in his work.

9

Moya

📠 ℹ️ C/Juan Delgado, (Parque Pico Lomito) 6; 928 612 348

Tucked away from the main tourist attractions, the road to this small town meanders through volcanic valleys, with countless turns and bends. The town is worth visiting for its vast Neo-Romanesque church, dating from the first half of the 20th century. The church is imposing with two towers and a position at the edge of the Barranco de Moya precipice – a gully crisscrossed with wild crevasses.

Moya is the birthplace of Tomás Morales, a Modernist Canarian poet. The house in which he was born and lived was converted into a museum, **Casa-Museo Tomás Morales**, in 1976. There is a permanent exhibition dedicated to the poet, which includes photographs, manuscripts and first editions of his works, displayed in rooms decorated in period style. The museum also organizes exhibitions of contemporary art.

By the entrance to the nearby catacomb cemetery, typical of the Canary Islands, stands a large stone cross – a monument to the victims of the Spanish Civil War.

Casa-Museo Tomás Morales

 Plaza de Tomás Morales
🕙 10am–6pm Tue–Sun
🌐 tomasmorales.com

---

⑩

Guía

📧 🛈 C/San José 9; 928 553 043

The only noteworthy historic building in this town is the church of Santa María de Guía, built on the site of a chapel erected between 1483 and 1509. Some parts of this triple-nave church date back to the 17th century; the façade was completed only in the middle of the following century.

Guía is the birthplace of José Luján Pérez (1756–1815), who was the most popular of the Canary Islands' sculptors during his lifetime. His works, such as the statue of Nuestra Señora de las Mercedes or St Sebastián, adorn the interior of the local church. However, Guía is perhaps best known for its cheese – *queso de flor* – made of cows' and goats' milk, with the flower of the blue thistle added. This gives the cheese its distinctive flavour and allows it to remain moist even when stored for a long time.

Some 5 km (3 miles) east of Guía is **Cenobio de Valerón**, a group of about 300 caves set into a cliff at various levels. The caves were used for grain storage and for religious services. Guanche individuals were chosen to spend years in solitude here, giving themselves to the service of the god

← The famous water feature of Paseo de Gran Canaria in Firgas

Entrance to the historic Cenobio de Valerón cave system ↑

Acoran. Their prayers were to ensure the god's protection for the island's people.

Cenobio de Valerón

 Cuesta de Silva s/n, 35458 Santa María de Guía
📞 618 607 896 🕙 Hours vary, call ahead

---

⑪

Gáldar

🛈 C/Plaza de Santiago 1, 928 880 050

At the foot of Pico de Gáldar volcano stands Gáldar, a town that was once the centre of the Guanche civilization. There are no traces left of the ancient court of their ruler Guanarteme, since, along with a Spanish fort, it was destroyed to make way for the construction of the church of Santiago de los Caballeros. This Neo-Classical church has three naves and was designed by Antonio José Eduardo. The works started in 1778 and were not completed until the mid-19th century.

Inside the church is the *pila verde* – a baptismal font brought from Andalusia in the late 15th century and, since the island's conquest, used for baptizing the local population. Other noteworthy features are the statues of Christ and the Virgin Mary, both the work of Luján Pérez.

On the square, opposite the town hall, grows the oldest dragon tree (*p24*) in Gran Canaria, planted in 1719.

The star attraction of Gáldar is the **Parque Arqueológico Cueva Pintada**. Discovered in 1873, the cave is decorated with rock paintings consisting of geometric patterns. After conservation work between 1970 and 1974, the cave was closed to prevent the paintings from being destroyed by the increased humidity. The archaeological park features a museum. A replica of the cave can be seen at the Museo Canario in Las Palmas (*p61*).

Just 2 km (1 mile) north of Gáldar is Túmulo de la Guancha. Discovered in 1936 during agricultural works, this Guanche cemetery dates from the late 11th century and consists of 30 round tombs, built of vast lava blocks. These were the burial places of members of the Andamanas royal family, who ruled this region.

At 6 km (4 miles) west, Sardina del Norte is a fishing village and diving centre. Flanked by high cliffs, it tempts swimmers with its clear water and golden sands, as well as its excellent seafood.

Parque Arqueológico Cueva Pintada

 C/Audiencia 2 🕙 Hours vary, check website 🌐 cuevapintada.com

⑫
Puerto de Mogán

ℹ️ C/General Franco; 928 158 804

Easily accessible by car, via an extension of the motorway GC1, this picturesque town and yachting marina lie at the end of the green Mogán Valley, at the foot of a rocky plateau. Canals and bridges linking the marina to the fishing harbour have earned the town the nickname "Little Venice".

The old fishing port lies adjacent to and behind the attractive, purpose-built marina and resort. The resort consists of a village-like complex of colourful, flower-decked apartments, prettily designed in typical Mediterranean style, lining narrow pedestrianized streets. The waterfront is home to various bars, shops and restaurants.

Swimmers will enjoy the human-made sandy beach that shelters between the cliffs. It is filled with several layers of sand imported from Africa.

A range of tourist trips are available from the town's marina. A little yellow submarine offers tourists the opportunity to glimpse the rich underwater life of the Atlantic, while small replicas of old sailing ships ferry passengers to the beaches of Puerto Rico and Maspalomas several times a day. There are also fascinating deep-sea fishing trips to catch tuna and marlin. The famous "Blue Marlin" angling competition is held at Puerto de Mogán every July.

Around 8 km (5 miles) north of Puerto de Mogán, in a fertile valley planted with such non-native crops as papaya and avocado, lies Mogán. This picturesque town is the capital of the district. There is a choice of good bars and restaurants here, including Acaymo, on the edge of town, and one of the best on the island.

GRAN CANARIA BEACHES

Gran Canaria has around 80 beaches, with those in the north rocky and the south sandy. In some places, such as the Playa del Inglés or Maspalomas, they stretch for miles and are lined with clubs, restaurants and hotels.

Playa de Mogán

Puerto de Mogán

Taurito

Taurito is home to the beach around Mogán, on a par with Playa de Cura and Arguineguín.

Near Playa del Cura, with its small beach, is one of the few campsites on Gran Canaria.

Playa del Cura

The sandy beach of Puerto de Mogán is hidden among high cliffs.

Playa de Amadores

Playa de Puerto Rico

Playa de Amadores is fringed with palm trees and has an elegant promenade.

GC500

Playa de Patalavaca

GC1

This golden beach provides excellent facilities for all kinds of water sports.

Arguineguín Beach

El Pujar

Stunning azure waters of Playa de Amadores

Arguineguín is a busy resort built up around an old fishing village.

← Traditional buildings along the waterfront of Puerto de Mogán

 Maspalomas

 Avda Touroperador Tui; 928 769 585

The biggest resort in Gran Canaria has more than 500 hotels, apartment blocks and chalets, capable of accommodating 300,000 guests at a time. Sun-seeking tourists flock here, attracted by miles of sandy beaches, as well as hundreds of restaurants, bars and shops. Maspalomas is in fact a conglomeration of three separate resorts, reached by three different exits from the south-coast motorway.

The furthest east is San Agustín. This quiet, tourist town, full of greenery, with dark-sand beaches is aimed at an upmarket clientele, rather than mass tourism. It has a number of luxurious hotels, exclusive clubs, a casino and scenic promenades.

In the middle of the Maspalomas coastline is Playa del Inglés. This is the most crowded and liveliest resort, with Yumbo, a multistorey shopping/restaurant centre, right in the middle of town.

To the south of Playa del Inglés are the Dunas de Maspalomas – a vast 4-sq-km (1.5-sq-mile) expanse of dunes and now a national park with a salt-water lake and palm grove, which can only be explored on foot or by camel. The dunes provide a natural habitat for lizards and rabbits, as well as several bird species.

Maspalomas is popular with surfers and windsurfers, as well as deep-sea fishing and diving enthusiasts. The resort offers **Aqualand,** the biggest water park on the island, with over 20 slides and two areas aimed at younger children. There is also **Holiday World** – a popular amusement park, which occupies 14,000 sq m (150,695 sq ft) and features an impressive 27-m- (89-ft-) high traditional ferris wheel.

This large, modern resort, crisscrossed with numerous palm-lined boulevards, has an excellent golf course – the biggest on the island – while spiritual needs are served by the ecumenical church – Templo Ecuménico. It also has four karaoke rooms, an escape room and restaurants featuring cuisine from all over the world.

Aqualand

Ctra Palmitos Park, km 3 10am–5pm daily (to 6pm Jul & Aug) aqualand.es/maspalomas

Holiday World

Avda Touroperador Tui Hours vary, check website holidayworld maspalomas.com

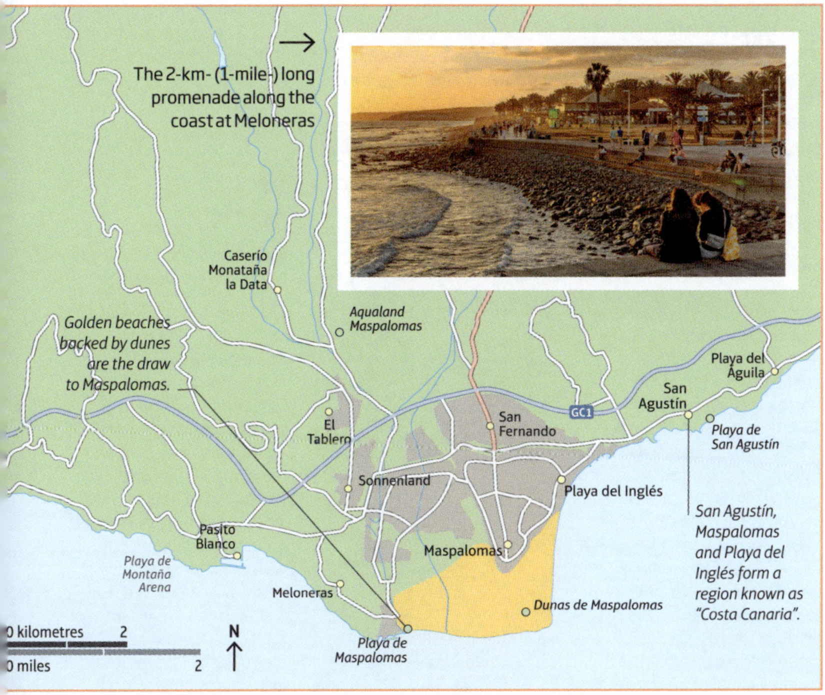

→ The 2-km- (1-mile-) long promenade along the coast at Meloneras

Caserío Monataña la Data

Golden beaches backed by dunes are the draw to Maspalomas.

Aqualand Maspalomas

Playa del Aguila

San Agustín

El Tablero

San Fernando

GC1

Playa de San Agustín

Sonnenland

Pasito Blanco

Playa de Montaña Arena

Maspalomas

Playa del Inglés

San Agustín, Maspalomas and Playa del Inglés form a region known as "Costa Canaria".

Meloneras

Dunas de Maspalomas

Playa de Maspalomas

0 kilometres 2
0 miles 2

N ↑

EAT

Bar La Candelilla

This cosy roadside bar serves delicious dishes in an informal setting.

 22 C-815, San Bartolomé de Tirajana
677 990 924

€€€

El Mirador de Tunte

Tuck into delicious regional cuisine at this casual, sit-down bar and restaurant - don't miss the spectacular views from the terrace.

 Carretera Fataga, San Bartolomé de Tirajana
928 127 432

€€€

 14

San Bartolomé de Tirajana

Founded in the 16th century by the Spanish, this little town was once a shepherd settlement. Situated in the lush green valley of Tirajana, it is known for its orchards of almonds, plums, peaches and cherries, which are used in the production of vodkas and liqueurs. The local speciality is cherry liqueur, *guinda*.

The first chapel in San Bartolomé was built in the 16th century. In 1690, work started on its site to build a much grander, triple-nave parish church, which was not, in fact, consecrated until 1922. Its noteworthy features include the Mudéjar-style wooden vaults and carved statues of the saints. It is also worth visiting the old cemetery, set on a hill, where – contrary to the Spanish tradition – the dead were buried in the soil rather than being entombed in the cemetery wall.

Some 7 km (4 miles) to the south of San Bartolomé, in a beautiful setting of tall cliffs, palms and fruit trees, is Fataga, a mountain village with old houses and the 1880 church of San José. Next to the church are reservoirs – Embalse de Tirajana and Embalse de Fataga – both of which are excellent hiking destinations.

 15

Puerto Rico

Avda de Mogán; 928 158 804

Puerto Rico lies on the coast, at the mouth of a large valley. This former fishing port has developed into a popular resort, thanks to its reputation as the sunniest place in Spain. Scores, if not hundreds, of hotels and apartments have been built on the terraces of the steeply descending slopes as a result.

One of the best features of this town, which is swamped in greenery, is its small but picturesque beach. Stretching over 280 m (900 ft) long, this popular strip is covered with sand that was originally imported from the Sahara.

↑ Palm trees lining Puerto Rico's white-sand beach

Other attractions include golf courses and a water park, featuring all kinds of amusements. Puerto Rico's numerous attractions range from water sports including water-skiing, sailing, diving and windsurfing to leisure excursions such as glass-bottomed boats and open-sea cruises for dolphin-watching. This helps to compensate for the fact that this is a rather over-built resort with limited beach space for the numbers of visitors it receives.

 16

Agaete

C/Nuestra Señora de las Nieves; www.agaete.es

The small town of Agaete lies on the northwest coast of the island, at the end of a steep ravine, Barranco de Agaete. Plantations of banana, papaya, avocado and mango flourish on the steep slopes. With its narrow streets and whitewashed houses surrounded by lush greenery, Agaete has become popular with artists and art-lovers, who have converted local houses and garages into art galleries. Despite being an old town, which was founded in 1481, Agaete has few

↑ San Sebastián Church dominating the skyline of Agüimes

historic sites. The oldest is the parish church, which was built in the second half of the 19th century.

Also in the town is a charming, small botanical garden, **Huerto de las Flores**, which features over 100 species of Canary and sub-tropical flora.

About 2 km (1 mile) to the west is a small harbour, Puerto de las Nieves, with a terminal for ferries to Santa Cruz de Tenerife. This picturesque fishing village, nestling against tall cliffs, has become popular with tourists, drawn by its craft shops, galleries and seafood restaurants.

Huerto de las Flores

 C/Huertes 📞 928 554 382 🕐 11am–4pm Mon–Fri (call ahead)

17
La Aldea de San Nicolás

🚌 ℹ️ C/Doctor Fleming s/n; 928 890 378

A fertile, green valley, crisscrossed with ravines, is the setting for this small town. It is surrounded by plantations of banana, orange, avocado, papaya and mango, and the slopes are overgrown with cacti and bamboo. The main building worth visiting is the church of San Nicolás, built in 1972, featuring sculptures by Luján Pérez. It was built on the site of an old chapel dating from the early 18th century.

A popular tourist attraction is **Cactualdea**, a park with thousands of cacti which were imported from Madagascar, Mexico, Bolivia and Guatemala; other plants include palms, dragon trees and aloe. Other features of interest include an amphitheatre, used for wrestling matches, and a Guanche Cave.

Cactualdea

🎫😊💳 🕐 10:30am–5pm
🌐 cactualdea.es

> ## Did You Know?
> ——
> Gran Canaria's Biosphere Reserve occupies nearly 50 per cent of the island's surface.

18
Agüimes

🚌 ℹ️ Plaza de San Antón; 928 124 183

The old part of this town, with its narrow streets and beautiful houses, is overshadowed by the two huge towers of San Sebastián Church, standing in the Plaza del Rosario. The basilica has three naves and a barrel vault, and was constructed between 1796 and 1808. Along with the cathedral in Las Palmas de Gran Canaria, this is one of the best examples of the Canary Islands' Neo-Classical architecture. The basilica's dome features 12 windows that symbolize the 12 apostles. The statues of saints inside the church are by Canarian sculptor José Luján Pérez (1756–1815).

Another attraction of Agüimes is the **Parque de los Cocodrilos**. This centre is home to crocodiles that have been rescued by the SEPRONA (Servicio de Protección de la Naturaleza).

The town comes to life every July during the theatre festival, Festival del Sur. Groups from Europe, Africa and South America come to participate in this lively event.

Parque de los Cocodrilos

🎫 🚗 Carretera General Los Corralillos, km 5.5 🕐 10am–5pm Sun–Fri 🌐 cocodrilopark zoo.com/es/cocodriloparks

Ingenio

This town is one of the oldest on Gran Canaria. It owes its name to the local sugarcane industry, which flourished here in the 17th century (*ingenio* means sugar mill). Later, the region turned towards rum production, but now it is a largely agricultural area, its main crop being tomatoes. Ceramics are also big in Ingenio; the **Taller Municipal de Céramica** is at once a museum featuring artisanal works from ceramics to metalwork and a workshop for ceramicists from Ingenio itself and wider Gran Canaria.

It's also worth visiting the imposing church of Nuestra Señora de la Candelaria, which dates back to 1901. Looming over the square, it's bordered by pretty houses with wooden balconies. The church's bells were made and donated by Canarian migrants in Cuba.

Taller Municipal de Céramica

🏠 Calle Nueva 7, 35250 Ingenio, Las Palmas
📞 928-783037 🕐 8am–2pm Mon–Fri

Barranco de Guayadeque

🏠 2 km (1.2 miles) N of Ingenio

A scenic, winding road runs 7 km (4 miles) along the bottom of the Guayadeque Ravine, whose name in the Guanche language means "place of the flowing waters". The stream flowing along the canyon supplies water to the neighbouring towns of Ingenio and Agüimes.

Guayadeque is overgrown with cacti, agaves, palms and Canary pines, in addition to about 80 species native to the Canary Islands. In spring, the parched, rough terrain of the ravine is softened by the blossoming almond trees.

This region is one of the most important prehistoric burial grounds, where the dead were interred in inaccessible caves. Many of these graves were plundered in the 19th century by the local population, who sold the mummies to the Museo Canario in Las Palmas. Local caves were also used by the Guanches as dwelling places, food stores and as sites used for fertility rituals.

GRAN CANARIA HIKING ROUTES

Degollada del Aserrador-Presa de Elba-Roque Nublo
This challenging 7.6-km (4.7-mile) loop takes 3 hours with an elevation gain of 380 m (1,260 ft).

Caldera Bandama
A 3.5-km (2-mile) route circling the crater, this is a 1.5-hour long hike with a gain of 211 m (692 ft).

Puerto de las Nieves-Guayedra
This moderate 6.4-km- (4-mile-) return route, with 340 m (1,110 ft) of elevation gain, takes about 2.5 hours to hike.

Today, Barranco de Guayadeque is popular with people, who, following in the footsteps of the Guanches, have made their homes in the caves. This small troglodyte population has a chapel and cave bars serving the strong local wine, bread and Temisas olives in green mojo sauce.

Guayadeque is also popular for Sunday picnics. The road

running along the ravine ends at Restaurante Tagoror. Further on, the route is impassable for cars and ends up with a narrow footpath.

 21

Santa Lucía

↑ The church of San Juan Bautista in the beautiful town of Telde

Avda de Canarias – Plaza de la Era; 928 125 260

Located in the high country, this village stands 700 m (2,400 ft) above sea level, in the fertile palm valley of Santa Lucía de Tirajana. Set on top of the hill is the church of Santa Lucía, which was built in 1898 on the site of a former 17th-century chapel.

Various archaeological finds, unearthed from the surrounding hills and dating from the time of the Guanches, can be seen in the local **Museo del Castillo de la Fortaleza**. This ethnography/archaeology museum is housed in a modern pseudo-castle with turrets and battlements. The museum also features a reconstructed bedroom, typical of a 17th-century Canarian home, and displays of pottery (including a third-century amphora), leather goods, basket-work and skeletons.

Museo del Castillo de la Fortaleza

♿ ⌂ Calle Tomás Arroyo Cardoso ☎ 928 798 310 ⏱ By appt, call ahead

 22

Telde

🚌 **Calle Conde de la Vega Grande 9; www. teldeturismo.es**

During pre-colonial times, Telde was the seat of the local king of the Guanches.

Hiking the scenic route from Barranco de Guayadeque to Caldera Bandama

Following the conquest of the island, it became known as a port for loading sugarcane.

Towards the end of the 15th century, the Spanish built a small chapel here. In 1519, work commenced on the site to build the present church of San Juan Bautista. The highlights of this basilica are the Mannerist altar and an early 16th-century Flemish triptych.

From Plaza de San Juan, home to the church, runs Inés Chemida, a street connecting San Juan with another historic part of town – San Francisco. Here, the two-storey buildings are painted white and green. The narrow streets are lined with houses adorned with balconies of wrought iron and timber.

FERNANDO DE LEÓN Y CASTILLO (1842–1918)

León y Castillo, an engineer and diplomat born in Telde, played an important role in the regeneration of Gran Canaria. It is thanks to him that the island has the Las Palmas harbour, making Gran Canaria equally as important as Tenerife. Opposed to Tenerife's domination, he was an advocate of the archipelago's division into two provinces. In 1881, he became Minister of Foreign Affairs, and also served as Spanish ambassador to France. In recognition, he was awarded the title of Marqués del Muni.

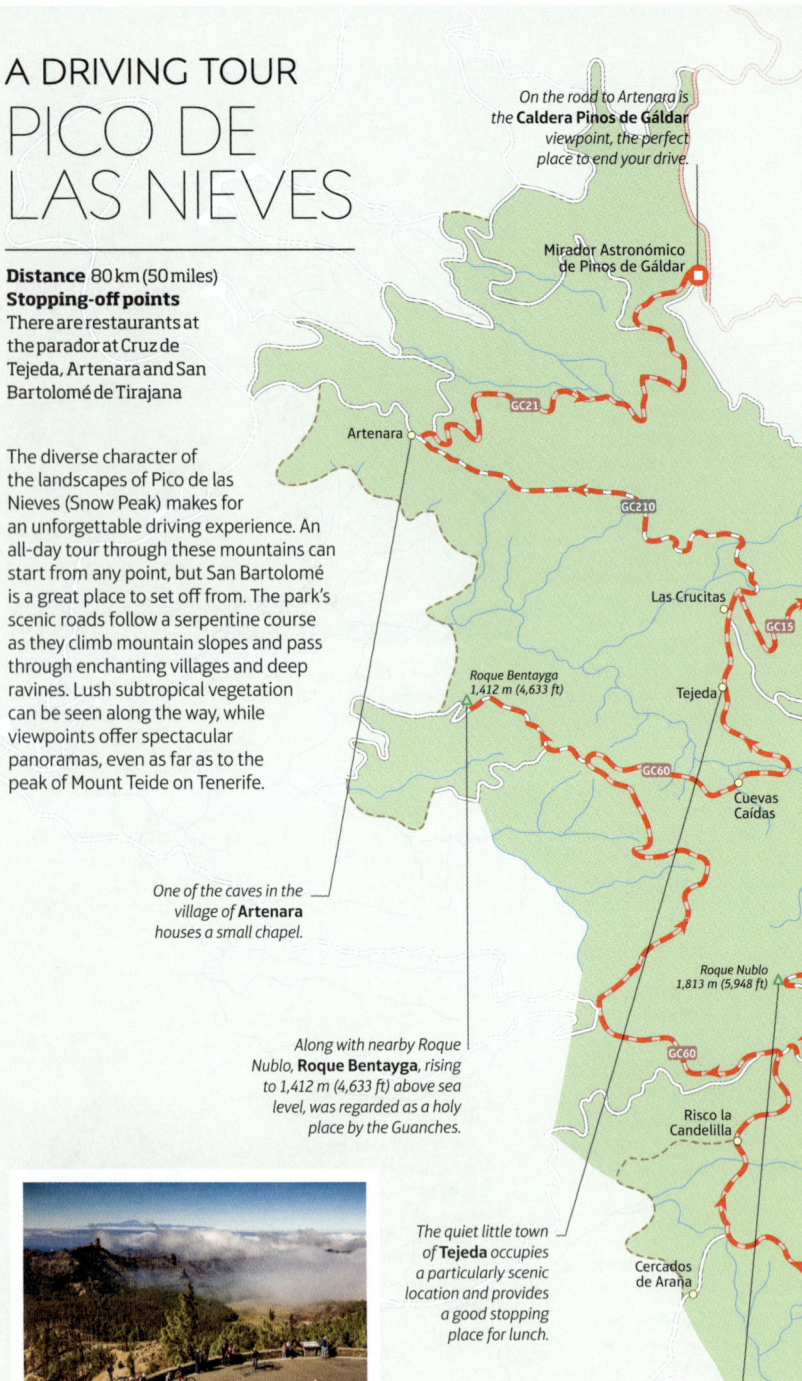

A DRIVING TOUR
PICO DE LAS NIEVES

Distance 80 km (50 miles)
Stopping-off points
There are restaurants at the parador at Cruz de Tejeda, Artenara and San Bartolomé de Tirajana

The diverse character of the landscapes of Pico de las Nieves (Snow Peak) makes for an unforgettable driving experience. An all-day tour through these mountains can start from any point, but San Bartolomé is a great place to set off from. The park's scenic roads follow a serpentine course as they climb mountain slopes and pass through enchanting villages and deep ravines. Lush subtropical vegetation can be seen along the way, while viewpoints offer spectacular panoramas, even as far as to the peak of Mount Teide on Tenerife.

*On the road to Artenara is the **Caldera Pinos de Gáldar** viewpoint, the perfect place to end your drive.*

Mirador Astronómico de Pinos de Gáldar

GC21

Artenara

GC210

Las Crucitas

GC15

Roque Bentayga 1,412 m (4,633 ft)

Tejeda

GC60

Cuevas Caídas

*One of the caves in the village of **Artenara** houses a small chapel.*

Roque Nublo 1,813 m (5,948 ft)

*Along with nearby Roque Nublo, **Roque Bentayga**, rising to 1,412 m (4,633 ft) above sea level, was regarded as a holy place by the Guanches.*

GC60

Risco la Candelilla

*The quiet little town of **Tejeda** occupies a particularly scenic location and provides a good stopping place for lunch.*

Cercados de Araña

↑ The view from the lookout point at Pico de las Nieves

Roque Nublo *is a 60-m (200-ft) monolith atop a 1,813 m (5,948 ft) peak. It's thought to have been held sacred by the Guanches.*

GRAN CANARIA

Pico de las Nieves

Locator Map

Narrow road winding its way to the pretty houses of San Bartolomé ↑

Cruz de Tejeda

*Carved in stone, the **Cruz de Tejeda** cross – from which the area takes its name – marks the central point of Gran Canaria.*

Mirador Degollada de Becerra

*The **La Degollada de Becerra** viewpoint offers a spectacular view to the west and of the Roque Bentayga peak.*

La Culata

*The best view of the highest reservoir on the island can be seen from **Presa de los Hornos**, near the summit of Roque Nublo.*

Presa de los Hornos

GC600

Pico de las Nieves
1,949 m (6,394 ft)

| 0 kilometres | 2 |
| 0 mile | 2 |

N ↑

*Also known as **Pozo de las Nieves** (the Well of Snow), the Pico de las Nieves is the highest peak on Gran Canaria at 1,949 m (6,394 ft).*

GC60

Risco Blanco

Agua Latente

Taidía

San Bartolomé de Tirajana

Rosiana Alta

*Begin your drive at **San Bartolomé de Tirajana** (p72), surrounded by orchards. The fruit is used to make liqueurs.*

FUERTEVENTURA

An island known as "Forte Ventura" first appeared on a map drawn by the cartographer Angelino Dulcert in 1339. Long before this, Indigenous groups known as Majos or Maxos inhabited the island; various dwellings and archaeological artifacts found across Fuerteventura attest to their ways of living.

Between 1402 and 1405 Fuerteventura became one of the first of the Canary Islands to be invaded by Spanish conquistadors, who landed here under the leadership of Jean de Béthencourt and Gadifer de la Salle. The village that grew up around the camp of Jean de Béthencourt, Betancuria, subsequently became Fuerteventura's capital.

Territorial expansion in the mid-17th century extended to the region of El Cotillo and included the seat of the former kingdom of Maxorata. Volcanic eruptions and sand carried from the Sahara desert, as well as frequent droughts during the 18th and 19th centuries, caused the collapse of Fuerteventura's agricultural trade, once called the granary of the Canaries. Today, most of the island's revenue comes from tourism.

FUERTEVENTURA

Must Sees

1 Parque Natural de Corralejo
2 Isla de los Lobos
3 Morro Jable

Experience More

4 Puerto del Rosario
5 Corralejo
6 El Cotillo
7 La Oliva
8 Antigua
9 Tefía
10 Ajuy
11 Betancuria
12 Pájara
13 La Pared
14 Costa Calma
15 Cofete
16 Caleta de Fuste
17 Península de Jandía
18 Gran Tarajal
19 Malpaís Chico and Malpaís Grande

Punta del
Penón Blanco

AJUY 10
Playa de los
Muertos

Playa de
Garcey

Montaño de
de Melindraga
621 m (2,037 ft)

Montaña de
Sicasumbre
528 m (1,732 ft)

Cardón
695 m (2,280 ft)

FV618

FV617

Playa de
la Pared

Morro
de la Cruzada
316 m (1,037 ft)

13
LA
PARED

Alto de
Agua Oveja
213 m (699 ft)

La Lajita

14 COSTA
CALMA

Atlantic
Ocean

Playa de
Barlovento

FV2

Playa de
Sotavento

Playa de
Cofete

Morro del Joaro
621 m (2,037 ft)

15 COFETE

PENÍNSULA DE JANDÍA

17

Playa de
Sotavento

Puerto de
la Cruz

Esquinzo

Punta de
Jandía

Playa de
las Pilas

3
MORRO
JABLE

Casas del Matorral

Gran Canaria

Lanzarote ↑

Punta de la Tiñosa

ISLA DE LOS LOBOS 2

CORRALEJO 5

El Río

Geafond

Bayuyo
272 m (892 ft)

Punta la Barra

Montaña Colorado
258 m (846 ft)

FV1

Playas de Corralejo

1

PARQUE NATURAL DE CORRALEJO

EL COTILLO 6

Lajares

FV109

FV10

Montaña Roja
312 m (1,024 ft)

Punta Paso Chico

Montaña de la Arena
422 m (1,385 ft)

FV101

Montaña de Escanfraga
529 m (1,736 ft)

FV104

LA OLIVA 7

Tindaya
401 m (1,316 ft)

FV10

Tindaya

FV103

FV102

FV1

El Time

Punta de la Tiñosa

FV10

Tetir

Casas Los Molinos

TEFÍA 9

FV10

La Asomada

San Andrés
482 m (1,581 ft)

Casillas del Ángel

PUERTO DEL ROSARIO 4

FV207

Tesjuates

FV20

FV3

Playa Blanca

Llanos de la Concepción

FV30

✈ **Fuerteventura Airport**

Valle de Santa Inés

La Ampuyenta

FV20

FV430

Playa de las Caletillas

Triquivijate

BETANCURIA 11

ANTIGUA 8

FV413

FV2

Pico de Betancuria
725 m (2,379 ft)

Morro Janana
672 m (2,205 ft)

CALETA DE FUSTE 16

Vega de Río Palmas

FV20

FV50

FV2

Casas de las Salinas

FV30

Tiscamanita

Agua de Bueyes

PÁJARA 12

Gairía
463 m (1,519 ft)

FV420

Casas de Pozo Negro

Carbón
609 m (1,998 ft)

Tuineje

19

Atalaya Pozo Negro
440 m (1,444 ft)

FV550

FV2

Punta Gorda

MALPAÍS CHICO AND MALPAÍS GRANDE

FV512

FV20

Coldera de Jacomar
437 m (1,434 ft)

Tesejerague

Vigán
464 m (1,522 ft)

Playa de los James

Caracol
468 m (1,535 ft)

FV2

FV4

Las Playitas

FV2

GRAN TARAJAL 18

Atlantic Ocean

Tarajalejo

0 kilometres   8

0 miles   8

N
↑

FUERTEVENTURA

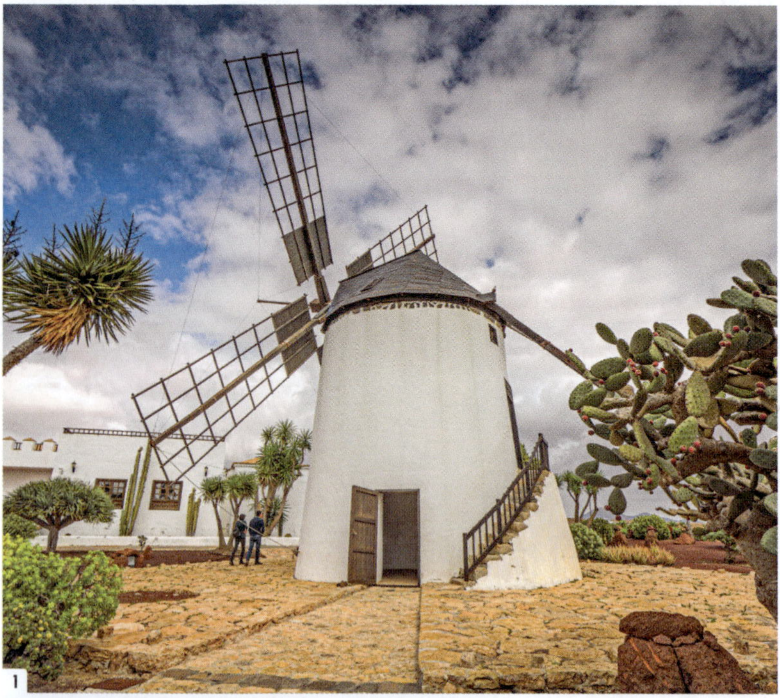

1

2

3

4

←

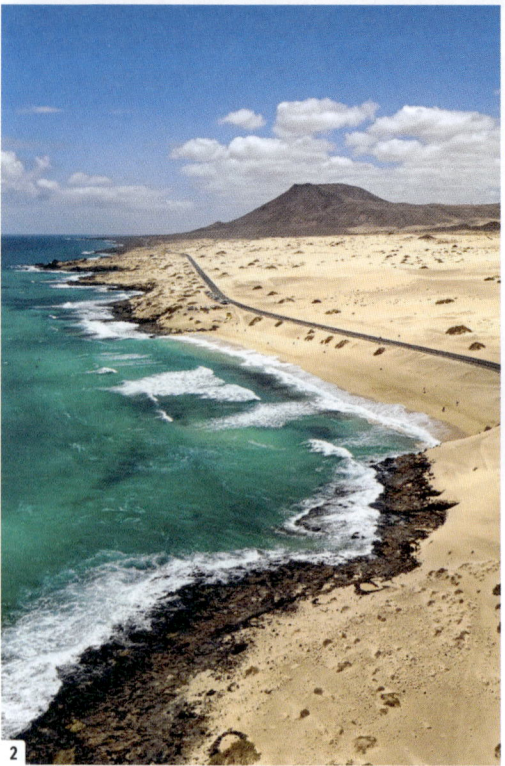

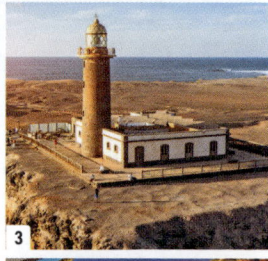

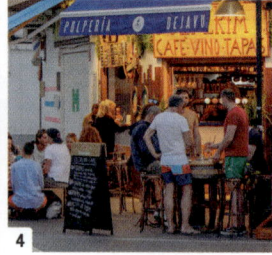

1 A windmill in Antigua.

2 The coast by Parque Natural de Corralejo.

3 The historic lighthouse of Punta de Jandía.

4 A tapas bar in Corralejo.

4 DAYS

Day 1

The town of Corralejo *(p90)* will be your starting point for this tour of Fuerteventura. Collect a rental bike from a local company like Electric Legs *(www.electric-legs.com/ebike-rental)* for the day, pack a picnic and catch an early ferry with your bike to the Isla de los Lobos *(p86)*. Cycle the dirt roads around the island, stopping off for a dip at Playa de la Concha and to see the Faro de Punta Martiño lighthouse along the way. Enjoy a refreshing drink at the only restaurant on the island, Chiringuito Lobos Antoñito El Farero *(+34 928 87 96 53)*, before catching a return ferry to Corralejo. See off the day with an evening stroll through the colourful old town here, stopping to enjoy a late dinner on one of the pleasant plazas.

Day 2

Today is all about exploring the nature of Fuerteventura. Pack snacks, swimming gear and some warm layers, before getting ready to spend the full day in the Parque Natural de Corralejo *(p84)*. Set off in a car rental and make the short drive down from Corralejo to the park. Leave your rental at one of the car parks and head out on a hike, stopping off to enjoy the long, sandy beaches and rolling dunes as you go. After a dip and a snack, make your way to the trail up the Montaña Roja volcano; the hike may be at a challenging elevation of 300 m (1,000 ft), but it's worth it for the breathtaking views of Lanzarote, La Graciosa and the town of Corralejo below. Head back down and towards the north of the park for a sunset drink at one of the beach bars here, before making your way back to the dunes for an

enchanting night of stargazing under this UNESCO Starlight Reserve. Stay in Corralejo for the night.

Day 3

Stick with the car rental for another day and get ready to town-hop. Drive over from Corralejo to La Oliva *(p91)*, a pretty town that was once the military capital of the island. After a morning stroll here, drive south to Tindaya, a mountain considered to be sacred with over 300 engravings originally created by the Indigenous Majo people of the island. Afterwards, make your way to Betancuria *(p94)* for lunch among its picture-perfect streets and plazas. In the afternoon, drive to Antigua *(p92)*, one of the oldest towns on the island, to see historic windmills once used for irrigation purposes *(p93)*, before ending the day with a light dinner.

Day 4

Make your way south from Antigua to Morro Jable *(p88)*, with its charming narrow streets winding uphill. Spend the rest of the morning strolling through the town, making time to climb up to the church to enjoy the viewpoint. Grab a light bite before heading to the Turtle Nursery, a rescue centre for marine turtles, next to the port. Back in your car, head further west to the Punta de Jandía *(p98)*, where a historic lighthouse has guided sailors since 1864; an interpretation centre for Jandía Nature Reserve can also be found on the peninsula. From here, head back north along the coast to Costa Calma *(p95)*, stopping in Playa de Sotavento before dinner at one of the many seaside restaurants in town.

❶

PARQUE NATURAL DE CORRALEJO

Parque Natural de Corralejo lies in the northeast corner of Fuerteventura, stretching 300 m (1,000 ft) south to the base of the Montaña Roja volcano. The area was declared a National Park in 1987, and has since been a magnet for kite flyers, windsurfers and wildlife watchers alike.

Corralejo Natural Park, nestled between Puerto del Rosario and Corralejo, is made up of a staggering 27 sq km (10.4 sq miles) of seemingly endless sand. Along this expanse are myriad beaches, each home to swathes of red sand, looming dunes and golden shores. Watching over it all is the looming Montaña Roja volcano, which, after trekking the elevation of 300 m (1,000 ft), rewards hikers with breathtaking views of Lanzarote, La Graciosa and the town of Corralejo.

There are plenty of ways to explore the park, but one of the best is on a local buggy safari tours, where you'll spot some of the island's 130 species of plant and bird. The park is a great place to delve into nature, and in relative peace too – even in peak tourist season, it remains a quiet spot thanks to its vastness. For those seeking more of a thrill, the park's open beaches make it a popular spot for surfing and windsurfing, with Playa El Medano offering the best conditions for both sports. Prefer to take a backseat? Every November, witness Playa el Burro covered in colourful kites for the annual kite festival.

→

The shoreline of Parque Natural de Corralejo, and *(inset)* windsurfing at the Playa El Medano

TOP 4 WAYS TO LEAVE NO TRACE

Keep to the path
Stay on designated hiking trails to protect delicate ecological environments.

Protect local species
Refrain from picking flowers or taking rocks and sand home.

Bin it
Avoid polluting the local environment by depositing your rubbish properly.

Respect the wildlife
Always observe the local wildlife from a distance.

Did You Know?
———
The biggest spread of sand dunes in the Canary Islands is found in Parque Natural de Corralejo.

Boats traversing the azure waters around the volcanic Isla de los Lobos ↑

2

ISLA DE LOS LOBOS

A small volcanic island in the El Río strait, Isla de los Lobos is a small and wild island that offers up some of the best uninhabited terrain to explore. Whether your idea of paradise involves a hike across epic landscapes or lounging with your feet in the sand, this stunning island delivers.

Little more than 6,000–8,000 years old, the oasis-like Isla de los Lobos has long been uninhabited. It owes its name to the seals – *lobos marinas* – that once made their home on its sandy shores, and nature here still abounds. Migratory birds rest in the botanical garden on the slopes of the Montaña Lobos, marine life thrives on the sea bed and rare houseleek succulents grow between rocky spots across the island.

With so much unspoiled nature and no accommodation options for overnight stays, the island is the perfect place for day trips and switching off. Take a dip in the crystal-clear waters at one of the sandy coves, or set off on one of the many walking and cycling trails.

INSIDER TIP
Permit to Visit

Visits to the Isla de los Lobos *(www. lobospass.com)* are limited and require prior authorization, which can take up to five days to process online.

ISLA DE LOS LOBOS LANDINGS

Located between Fuerteventura and Lanzarote, the island has been a landing spot for many. The French adventurer Gadifer de la Salle is said to have landed here in 1402; on the brink of starvation, he and his crew had to sustain themselves on seal meat. Around the same time, navigator Jean de Béthencourt built a hermitage on Isla de los Lobos and, later on, the island served as something of a base for pirates who were raiding neighbouring islands. By the 20th century, the population here dwindled, and by 1968 the island was entirely uninhabited.

1 Ferries are the best way to get to Isla de los Lobos.

2 The many picturesque walking trails across the island make Isla de los Lobos a hiker's paradise.

3 The unspoiled beauty of Calas del Puertito on the north coast of Isla de los Lobos.

MORRO JABLE

 928 540 776

Set amid long sandy beaches on the southern end of Fuerteventura, Morro Jable was once an old fishing village with narrow streets and lively taverns. Since then, the village has grown to become the biggest and one of the most popular resorts on the island.

Modern Morro Jable retains its past but has also welcomed in the present, and today the historic centre largely caters to tourism. There are countless hotels and apartments, shopping centres, restaurants and bars both in the town and along the harbour. With moorings for 300 yachts, the town is also the main departure point for hydrofoils and ferries connecting Fuerteventura to Las Palmas on Gran Canaria.

The undisputed highlight of the village, however, lies beyond the town centre in the natural beauty along the coast and green interior. The golden sands of the Playa del Matorral, for one, are also home to the Saladar de Jandía salt flat, where birds and salt-tolerant vegetation thrive. A path from here leads to the mid-20th-century Jandía lighthouse, which overlooks the sea to guide ships sailing around the south of the island. The area is also the gateway to the wild and unspoiled Parque Natural Jandía, which is home to the Jandía Wetlands, a site of scientific interest and ecological value. Above it all, on a hilltop to the west of Morro Jable, is the small whitewashed Parroquia de Nuestra Señora del Carmen church, from which spectacular views of the epic landscape can be enjoyed.

EAT

Restaurante Saavedra Clavijo
This seaside restaurant is known for its spectacular views and exquisite fresh produce. Try the grilled vieja fish and *papas arrugadas.*

 Avda Tomás Grau Gurrea 5 928 75 53 17

€€€

Restaurante La Puntilla Casa Menso
Enjoy traditional Canarian cuisine with a focus on fresh fish and seafood. The delicious *gofio* ice cream is a must-try dessert.

 C/ El Peatonal Balandro 1 928 54 18 02

€€€

Morro Jable's Playa del Matorral, a scenic stretch of sandy shores

1 The cactus-dotted Playa de Cofete is one of Fuerteventura's most beautiful beaches.

2 Jandía lighthouse, a great point to take in views of the island, stands tall near the coastline.

3 All manner of shops and restaurants line the picturesque seaside promenade in Morre Jable.

Did You Know?

The Saladar de Jandía salt flat is one of the main wetlands of the Canary Islands.

EXPERIENCE MORE

↑ Boats moored near the harbour of historic Puerto del Rosario

❹ Puerto del Rosario

 ✈ 🚌 🛳 **i** Avda Reyes de España; www.turismo-puertodelrosario.org

Puerto del Rosario was first established in 1797 as a port for locally produced soda and grain. The port began to grow in the mid-19th century and by 1860 had become the capital

MIGUEL DE UNAMUNO

Writer Miguel de Unamuno (1864–1936), the "Philosopher from Salamanca", played a key role in the rebirth of Spanish literature and in the intellectual life of Spain in the early 20th century. Having spoken out against the dictatorship of Primo de Rivera, he was exiled to the Canary Islands for a few months in 1924. His book *Spanish Travels and Scenes* (1922) reflects his love for his homeland.

of the island. Today, Puerto del Rosario is the largest town on Fuerteventura and home to more than a third of the island's population. It has a thriving cargo and passenger harbour, with ferries sailing to Gran Canaria and Lanzarote. It also has a yachting marina, and near the town, an international airport.

Highlights in Puerto del Rosario include the church of Nuestra Señora del Rosario, with its Classical façade. Standing opposite it is **Casa Museo de Unamuno**, which will interest lovers of Spanish literature, as it was the home of the writer and philosopher Miguel de Unamuno during his exile. Part of the house is furnished with period pieces, including the original desk used by the writer, as well as a collection of personal objects and documents. It represents a typical interior from his times.

Just 12 km (7 miles) to the west is a small village, Casillas del Angel, with pretty houses. The beautiful church of Santa Ana (St Anne), dates from 1781 and has a black, volcanic-stone façade.

Casa Museo de Unamuno

 🏠 C/Virgin del Rosario 11
🕒 8am–2pm Mon–Fri
🌐 museosfuerteventura.com

❺ Corralejo

🚌 **i** Avda Marítima 2; www.visitcorralejo.com

The northernmost town of Fuerteventura, Corralejo has a passenger harbour with ferries sailing regularly to Playa Blanca in Lanzarote. Small cruising boats also take tourists to the neighbouring Isla de los Lobos. Weather-beaten fishing boats moored at the quayside and several fish restaurants add a touch of charm to this old fishing village.

Corralejo has become one of Fuerteventura's most popular resorts, along with the Jandía peninsula. Visitors come here not so much for the town but for its setting, with striking views of Lanzarote and Isla de los Lobos and the beaches to the south of the centre. Thanks to a year-round stiff breeze, the El Río strait between Corralejo and Lanzarote is ideal for watersports. The

clear water teems with a rich variety of fish, so angling, diving and glass-bottomed boat trips are popular.

The town's most interesting sights are its modern church in Plaza de la Iglesia and the sand sculptures on a small beach by the harbour.

Located 11 km (7 miles) to the southwest, in Lajares, is the Escuela de Artesanía Canaria. The school sells craft products from all the Canary Islands.

❻ El Cotillo

📠 ℹ 609 207 967

The early days of this fishing town are associated with the Guanches, when it served as the seat of the tribal chiefs of Maxorata – the ancient kingdom that encompassed northern Fuerteventura.

The round fortified tower, Fortaleza del Tostón, dates from more recent times. A small fort, it was built around 1797 as a defence against Arab and British pirates. Thanks to restoration work, it is now well preserved. Approached via stone steps with a drawbridge, this is a two-storey structure. Originally the upper floor housed a water tank, while the lower level was used as soldiers' quarters.

The small harbour features a giant rock rising out of the water. Although picturesque, it is hard for fishers to navigate during rough weather. El Cotillo also offers scenic coves and sandy beaches.

❼ La Oliva

 ℹ 928 866 235

Situated at the northern end of Fuerteventura, La Oliva is one of the prettiest towns on the island and stands in the shadow of Montaña de Escantraga (527 m/1,730 ft). The first European settlers arrived here in the early 14th century. In 1709, the military governor of the island (the "Colonel") selected La Oliva as his seat. The town soon became the military capital of the island and, along with Betancuria, a centre of Fuerteventura's political life.

The military headquarters were at the 18th-century Casa de los Coroneles. The "House of Colonels" is an austere edifice featuring two low towers at the corners and numerous windows: it is said to have one window for each day of the year, though this is inaccurate. The nearby Casa del Capellán (Chaplain's House) is a modest single-storey building with an ornately decorated portal and window frames.

In the town centre stands the Iglesia de Nuestra Señora de la Candelaria. The white walls of this attractive church, which dates from 1711, stand in stark contrast to its square belfry, built of black volcanic stone and visible from miles away. The interior of the church houses a Mudéjar ceiling, a large painting of The Last Judgement, a Baroque altar painting and various other sculptures and paintings by the 18th-century artist Juan de Miranda.

La Oliva's Casa del Inglés dates back to the 18th century. This two-storey building is made up of rooms centred around a large courtyard. The **Museo del Grano La Cilla**, with an exhibition on grain production in an early 19th-century granary, is also worth a visit.

Museo del Grano La Cilla
🚫 🏠 C/La Orilla 5 🕐 10am–5pm Tue, 9:30am–3pm Wed–Sat 🌐 lacilladelaoliva.org

←

The Isla de los Lobos, as seen from Corralejo's shore

8 Antigua

🚐 **i** 928 163 286

In the centre of Fuerteventura at the foot of the mountains, Antigua is – true to its name, which is Spanish for "ancient" – one of the oldest towns on the island. It was established in 1485 by the settlers arriving from Andalusia and Normandy, who began cultivating the soil and breeding animals. Many windmills erected at the time were used to irrigate the fields. In 1812, Antigua was granted municipal rights and in 1835 it became the capital of the island.

Its more interesting features include the small, single-nave church of Nuestra Señora de Antigua (1785), which has wooden vaults and a high altar incorporating folk motifs.

The **Centro de Artesanía Molinos de Antigua**, situated on the town's outskirts and surrounded by a low wall, is a museum village, built under the supervision of César Manrique. It includes a craft centre, a reconstructed windmill, and a gallery and halls devoted to ethnography and archaeology.

Travel 5 km (3 miles) to the north for La Ampuyenta, a village with a 17th-century chapel, Ermita San Pedro de Alcántara. This sanctuary is surrounded by a fortification erected by Norman settlers.

About 14 km (9 miles) south is the village of Tiscamanita, with the 17th-century chapel of San Marcos. At the **Centro de Interpretación de los Molinos**, visitors can learn about the island's windmills.

Centro de Artesanía Molinos de Antigua
 C 928 878 041 ⏱ 10am–6pm Tue-Sat

Centro de Interpretación de los Molinos
 C 928 164 275 ⏱ 10am–5pm Tue-Sat

_____

9 Tefía

This tiny village on the road from La Oliva to Betancuria is home to a historic *gofio* mill Molino de Tefía. It also has an open-air museum – the **Ecomuseo de la Alcogida** – consisting of seven reconstructed traditional houses where the historic life of the islanders, and their occupations are illustrated. It also explains the process of the houses' reconstruction.

Ecomuseo de la Alcogida
C 928 175 434 ⏱ 10am–5pm Tue-Sat

_____

10 Ajuy

🔺 30 km (19 miles) SW of Betancuria

The village of Ajuy perches on the shores of a small bay and

↑ Modern windmill framed by rolling hills around Antigua

is surrounded by dramatic steep cliffs, where the old rocks of Cuevas de Ajuy can be found. Jean de Béthencourt, accompanied by Gadifer de la Salle, landed here in 1402 and embarked on the conquest of the island. For many years, the bay served as a harbour for settlers arriving in Betancuria.

Today Ajuy is a quiet little fishing village. The fishing season lasts from May until October, and during this time the simple beach-side restaurants serve up the day's catch. The dark sands of Playa de los Muertos are worth visiting. The beach gained its name, "beach of the dead", from pirate attacks. The waves on this shore can be powerful, so take care when exploring.

With its rocky seabed, vast underwater caves and shoals of darting fish, Ajuy is also a paradise for scuba divers.

Did You Know?

The Cuevas de Ajuy sedimentary rock formations were created between 100 and 150 million years ago.

WINDMILLS

Windmills of all types, driven by the steady trade winds, form an important element of the Canary Islands' landscape. Introduced in the 17th century, they came to replace the horse-driven mills – *tahonas*. The oldest type of windmill is the *molino*. Built of local stone, plastered in white and with a round body and conical roof, the *molino* has four to six sails. The 19th century saw the arrival of a second type of windmill, the *molina*, which differed from the previous design in the way its structure was exposed. There are now also wind farms all over the island, which are used for generating electricity.

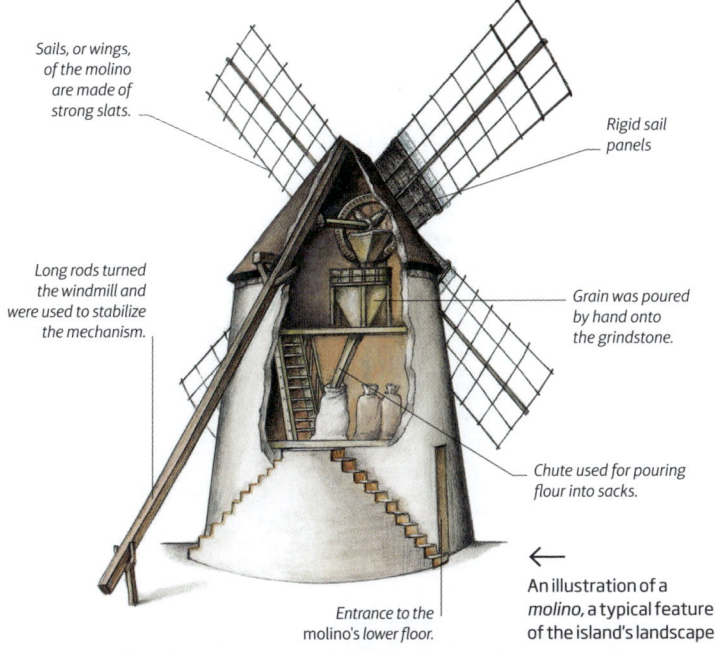

Sails, or wings, of the molino are made of strong slats.

Rigid sail panels

Long rods turned the windmill and were used to stabilize the mechanism.

Grain was poured by hand onto the grindstone.

Chute used for pouring flour into sacks.

Entrance to the molino's *lower floor.*

← An illustration of a *molino*, a typical feature of the island's landscape

↑ Observing the gear mechanism of a traditional windmill used to grind flour

11

Betancuria

C/Juan Béthencourt 6; www.aytobetancuria.org

Nestling in a volcanic crater sheltered from the winds, Betancuria lies in the central region of the island, where the rugged peaks of extinct volcanoes punctuate the wide, fertile valleys. Most of this area is within the Parque Natural de Betancuria. The highest peak, Pico de Betancuria, offers a great vantage point.

The town was founded in 1404 and was given its full name, Villa de Santa María de Betancuria, by Jean de Béthencourt. The Normans made the town the island's capital, and it remained so until 1834. Today Betancuria is the prettiest village on Fuerteventura, and one of the least inhabited, with no more than 800 residents.

At its centre stands the Iglesia de Santa María. The original church, dating from 1404, was burned by Arráez in 1593; it was rebuilt in 1620. Noteworthy features include the Baroque altar, the original stone floor, the carved stalls and the coffered ceiling. There's also a vast painting, *Nava de la Iglesia*, depicting the church as a ship, and painted by Nicolás Medina in 1730.

On the northern outskirts of the village is the Franciscan abbey of San Buenaventura – the oldest abbey on the island. Its roof collapsed in the mid-19th century, and mere scenic ruins remain today. Next to the abbey stands the Pozo del Diablo, Devil's Well. According to legend, Satan was chained to this rock and forced to carry stones used in the building of the abbey.

Betancuria has two small museums. The **Museo de Arte Sacro**, located in a former parish house, has a collection of religious art and photographs of almost every church on the Canary Islands. The other is the **Museo Arqueológico** , which has a collection dating from the time of the Guanches, as well as antique items of everyday use on display. Visitors to the restored 16th-century townhouse of Casa de Santa María can pick up souvenirs in the craft shop.

EAT

Casa Santa María

Based in a 17th-century farmhouse, this restaurant has a lovely garden and wine bar. Try the house speciality, roast kid goat in rosemary sauce.

Plaza Santa Maria 1, Betancuria Sun, PM

€€€

Around 2 km (1 mile) north of the town of Betancuria, the stunning Mirador de Morro Velosa offers a fine view over the island's lunar-like landscape.

Museo de Arte Sacro

Alcalde Carmelo Silvera s/n 928 878 003 10am-3:30pm Mon-Sat, 10am-2pm Sun

Museo Arqueológico

Roberto Roldán 12-35 928 878 241 10am-5pm Tue-Sat

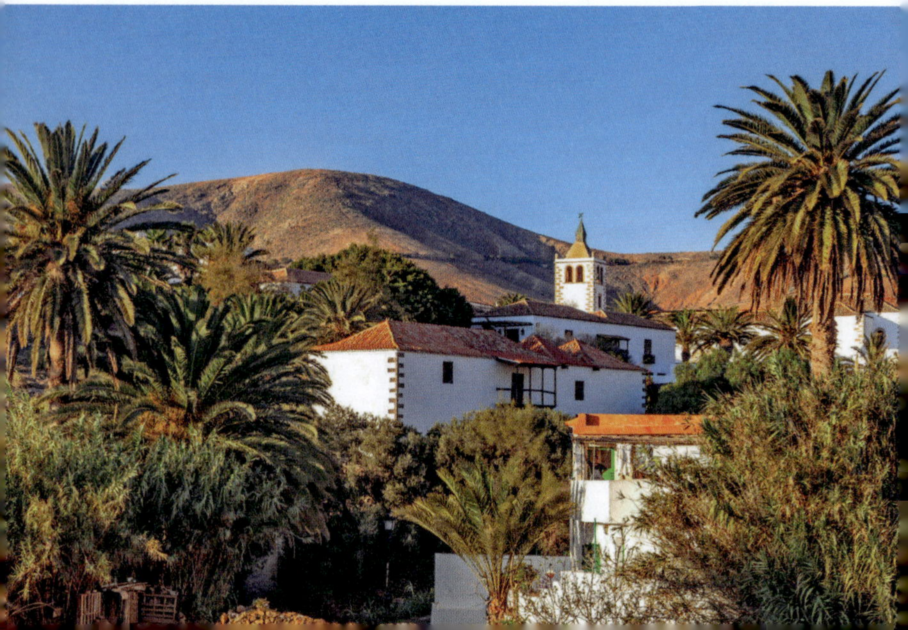

⑫ Pájara

📧 🌐 pajara.es

To the south of Betancuria lies the small town of Pájara. This is one of the oldest settlements on Fuerteventura, founded by fishers and goatherds who settled here in the 16th century.

Historic attractions include the church of Nuestra Señora de la Regla. Built in 1684, the church is worth seeing for its Latin American influences. The stone reliefs above the main portal depict stylized images of fish, lions, birds and snakes devouring their own tails. The origin of these motifs, said to be inspired by Aztec art, is unknown. The church's interior has two wooden altars, including a figure of the Madonna and Child, and one of Our Lady of Sorrows (Nuestra Señora de los Dolores), the patron saint of the island.

Some 11 km (7 miles) northeast lies Vega de Río Palmas. Here, perched among high rocks, is the hermitage of Nuestra Señora de la Peña, which features another image of Our Lady of Sorrows. Each year on the third Sunday in May a feast is held here in her honour. The 17th-century church has statues of saints, believed to have been brought here by Béthencourt for the first church built in Betancuria.

↑ Crystal-clear waters lapping the black-sand Playa de la Pared

---

⑬ La Pared

🏠 About 21 km (13 miles) S of Pájara

This small tourist resort has undergone a fair degree of development. Before the Spanish conquest, a land wall (la pared) running around here marked the boundary between two rival Guanche kingdoms, Maxorata and Jandía. Much of the wall may have been dismantled to use as building material; today no trace of it remains.

As well as its historical associations, La Pared is worth visiting for its stunning landscape. La Pared has the largest dunes in Fuerteventura and separates the Jandía peninsula from the remaining part of the island. It also forms a natural border between two contrastingly coloured beaches – the southern Playa del Viejo Rey has golden sand, while Playa de la Pared to the north consists of black sand.

A trek of several hours along volcanic formations leads to a ravine at the foot of the Risco del Pasco mountain, where it joins the road leading to Morro Jable.

---

⑭ Costa Calma

📧

Costa Calma is a modern resort distinguished by its tasteful architecture. It lies at the northern end of Playa del Sotavento, which is the longest and most scenic beach on the island, with great conditions for windsurfing. The rapid growth of Costa Calma in the 1960s and 1970s resulted in the construction of a road connecting Puerto del Rosario with Morro Jable. The building of a seawater desalination plant followed in 1986. Construction works began in the mid-1990s to provide tourist facilities.

To the southwest of Costa Calma lies Risco del Gato, which offers beautiful views of this stretch of coast. The wind farm at Cañada del Río is an interesting spot to stop at, and the prevailing winds throughout the year provide perfect conditions.

The small village of La Lajita lies some 8 km (5 miles) north. Visitors come here for the **Oasis Park**, home to 200 species of bird and mammal from around the world. A local garden centre sells specimens of tropical and subtropical flora, as well as native plants.

Oasis Park
♿ 🏠 La Lajita ⏰ 9am–6pm Tue–Sun 🌐 fuerteventura oasispark.com

> **To the southwest of Costa Calma lies Risco del Gato, which offers beautiful views of this stretch of coast.**

← The striking Iglesia de Santa María in Betancuria

 Cofete

Judging by the surroundings of this small, windswept hamlet, Fuerteventura appears to be a desert island. Only a roughly surfaced road connects it with Morro Jable (p88). At the height of Playa de Juan Gómez, the road forks: one side leads to the southwestern end of Fuerteventura; the other winds up at Cofete. The end of the line, Cofete marks the starting point for hiking trails along the ridge of Gran Valle and the pass between the peaks of Pico de Zarza and Fraile.

Beyond the village, perched below the Degollada de Cofete, is the imposing villa of Gustav Winter (1893–1971).

 Caleta de Fuste

🚌 ℹ Calle Juan Ramón Soto Morales 10; www.caletadefuste.es

Caleta de Fuste is one of the island's main holiday resorts. Though not the most attractive, it's a quiet place, and its location in the middle

---

FUERTEVENTURA'S BEACHES

Fuerteventura, one of the least populated of the Canary Islands relative to its size, features the archipelago's most beautiful beaches, which stretch for miles. The loveliest of these are on the Península de Jandía, where sunseekers will readily find peace and quiet. There are more than 150 of these remote beaches, of which some are popular with nudists.

It takes a determined effort to reach the remote and windswept beach of white sand near the village of Cofete.

Playa de las Pilas *is a small, pretty beach in an unspoiled setting. The calm sea and gentle winds attract many visitors.*

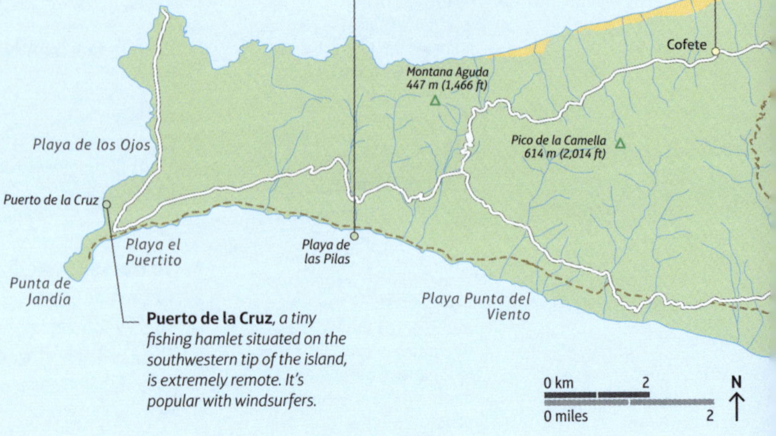

Cofete

Playa de los Ojos

Montana Aguda
447 m (1,466 ft)

Pico de la Camella
614 m (2,014 ft)

Puerto de la Cruz

Playa el Puertito

Playa de las Pilas

Punta de Jandía

Puerto de la Cruz, *a tiny fishing hamlet situated on the southwestern tip of the island, is extremely remote. It's popular with windsurfers.*

Playa Punta del Viento

0 km   2
0 miles   2

N ↑

↑ Stunning windswept golden sands of the beach at Cofete

of the eastern coast makes it convenient for the airport. It features sprawling, low-built apartments, clustered around a horseshoe bay with a safe, sandy beach. The resort is an excellent choice for visitors with small children.

At its centre is Pueblo Majorero – a modern, village-like complex of shops, bars and restaurants. One of the imposing bungalow estates, the Barceló Club El Castillo, is built round the old El Castillo watchtower near the harbour. Dating from 1741, the tower bears witness to the strategic importance of this place during the 18th century.

Around 4 km (2 miles) to the south are the Salinas del Carmen saltworks, where salt was recovered before the 1980s. Today, in the Open Air Museum, visitors can see how sea water is accumulated in small basins before evaporating, leaving salt crystals behind. In Pozo Negro, 10 km (6 miles) to the south, is the excavation site at La Atalayita. It is an ancient settlement of Indigenous Canarians, with an information centre featuring displays on the excavations that have taken place.

STAY

Elba Castillo San Jorge & Antigua Suite Hotel
One of four Elba hotels in Caleta de Fuste, ideal for a romantic getaway.

🏠 Avda José Franchy Roca, Caleta de Fuste
🌐 hoteleselba.com

€€€

Smy Tahona Fuerteventura
This three-star hotel offers freshwater pools.

🏠 C/Alcalde Marcial Sánchez Velázquez, Caleta de Fuste
🌐 smyhotels.com

€€€

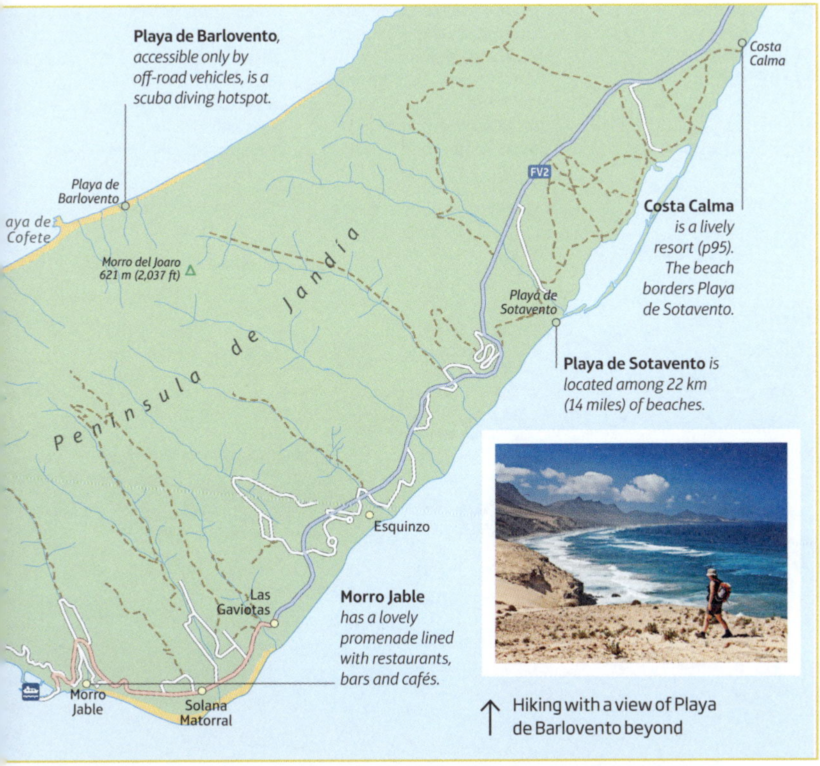

Playa de Barlovento, accessible only by off-road vehicles, is a scuba diving hotspot.

Costa Calma

Playa de Barlovento

aya de Cofete

Morro del Joaro 621 m (2,037 ft) △

 FV2

Península de Jandía

Playa de Sotavento

Costa Calma is a lively resort (p95). The beach borders Playa de Sotavento.

Playa de Sotavento is located among 22 km (14 miles) of beaches.

Esquinzo

Las Gaviotas

Morro Jable has a lovely promenade lined with restaurants, bars and cafés.

Morro Jable

Solana Matorral

↑ Hiking with a view of Playa de Barlovento beyond

TOP 4 — PENINSULA DE JANDÍA HIKES

Gran Valle – Degollada de Cofete – Cofete
A 12-km (7.5-mile) moderate hike to Indigenous structures.

Punta Pesebre – Agua Cabras – Punta Junquillo
This easy-moderate 7-km (4-mile) trek offers great sea views.

El Puertito – Caleta de La Madera
An easy 10-km (6-mile) loop across dramatic volcanic landscape.

Morro Jable – Sierra de Licanejo – Cofete
A challenging 21-km (13-mile) circular trek over rocky terrain.

 17

Península de Jandía

The Jandía Peninsula is surrounded by miles of scenic beaches with fine white sand. The longest beaches with the highest waves to be found on the island, they are particularly attractive to surfers, while the secluded beach of Barlovento, on the north-western shore, is popular with scuba divers.

The area around Puerto de la Cruz, near Punta de Jandía – the southwestern headland of the island with rocky shores and a solitary lighthouse – is a haven for caravanning holiday-makers. In this remote region, it's easy to escape all of the noise and bustle of nearby towns and switch off deep within nature.

A considerable part of the peninsula, with its rugged hills, is a conservation area and forms part of the Parque Natural de Jandía. Covering 140 sq km (54 sq miles), it features many species native to the island. In the remote mountain valleys, it is still possible to see herds of wild goats and donkeys in their natural habitat.

During World War II, this was a closed area and belonged to the German industrialist Gustav Winter (1893–1971). Rumour has it that he ran a secret submarine base in southwest Fuerteventura during the war, and stories about spies and buried Nazi treasure persist to this day.

 18

Gran Tarajal

📟 ℹ️ 928 162 723

The second-largest town on Fuerteventura, Gran Tarajal is one of the busier towns on the island. It once had a 15th-century fortress, a testament to the place's past strategic importance during this period of privateering and navigation. Since the 20th century, the town has also developed into a key trade centre on the island.

Aside from its role in trade, Gran Tarajal is also a favourite spot for a dip thanks to its long, Blue Flag beach. There are also many local spots to enjoy Canarian dishes and festivities in town. Historical sights may be few and far between, but the single-nave church of Nuestra Señora de la

→
Hiking in the
Malpaís de la Rasca
natural reserve

Candelaria, built in 1900, is a notable older structure here.

A detour 6 km (4 miles) to the east leads to a small fishing village – Las Playitas. The peaceful atmosphere contrasts with that of the bustling, crowded resorts. Instead of vast hotels and apartments, guests are invited to stay in old fishers' cottages, clad with bougainvillaea and peppers, boasting fantastic sea views. Local bars and restaurants serve fresh fish daily and there is a small stony beach near the harbour.

Some 6 km (4 miles) to the east is Punta de la Entallada, the very tip of Fuerteventura, which is also the closest point to Africa. It is reached by a narrow, winding road. On top of the staggering 300-m- (1,000-ft-) tall cliffs here stands a remarkable lighthouse. Built in 1950, it resembles a fortress. The site offers a splendid view across the mountainous part of the island and the Atlantic.

Malpaís Chico and Malpaís Grande

The inhospitable regions of Malpaís Chico and Malpaís Grande bear witness to the island's volcanic past, and occupy the south-central part of Fuerteventura. As a result of its historic volatility, this area has remained uninhabited over the years, and there are no roads connecting the different parts of this region, either.

The bleak but beautiful landscape is traversed by two hiking trails. One of the trails leads around Malpaís Chico, which was formed by lava flowing from the Caldera de Gaíra. The other, leading to Malpaís Grande, passes through the Malpaís de la Rasca national park, declared a conservation zone in view of its unique geological features. Wildlife is scarce; one of the few intriguing creatures to inhabit this desert area is the Egyptian vulture.

Did You Know?

The extensive lava fields at Malpaís Grande were formed over 26,000 years ago.

←
Courtyard of the lighthouse of Punta de la Entallada

LANZAROTE

Lanzarote's name is said to originate from the name of the Genoese sailor Lanzarotto (or Lancelotto) Malocello, who first arrived on the island in 1312. Like other islands in the archipelago, Lanzarote later became part of Spain, after its conquest by Jean de Béthencourt in 1402. Due to its location near the African coast, the island was vulnerable to frequent pirate attacks, with Algerian and Moroccan pirates often targeting Teguise, its capital at the time. In the 16th and 17th centuries, these raids were compounded by assaults from English and French pirates. Alongside these invasions, years of drought and catastrophic volcanic eruptions very nearly depopulated the island.

Lanzarote's inhabitants have long relied on agriculture and fishing, with large plantations of prickly pear and vineyards still flourishing today. The arts are important, too: the late 20th century saw a cultural revival, driven by renowned local architect and artist César Manrique, who promoted the integration of architecture with Lanzarote's natural environment. His visionary works, designed to preserve the island's beauty, can still be seen today. In recognition of the island's efforts to safeguard its unique landscape, UNESCO declared Lanzarote a Biosphere Reserve in 1993 – efforts to preserve the island for the future continue.

LANZAROTE

Punta Gaviota

Caldera Blanca
149 m (489 ft)

Montana de Mazo O Negra
329 m (1,079 ft)   LZ67

PARQUE NACIONAL
DE TIMANFAYA   1   Pico Partido
                        517 m (1,696 ft)

EL GOLFO   19   Montana
                 Tremesana   Montana del Valle
                 328 m (1,076 ft) de la Tranquillidad
                                   436 m (1,430 ft)
                                        LZ67
Los Hervideros   LZ704   LZ30
                           YAIZA
                            18
                             Uga
SALINAS   LZ2   Montana
DE JANUBIO   20   del Medio   LZ2
                        440 m (1,443 ft)
                  LZ703   Pico Nago
             Las   415 m (1,361 ft)
             Breñas   Caldera
                       de Maslan   22 FEMÉS
                       362 m (1,188 ft)
                                          Playa
                       LZ2   Quemada

              M3403

PLAYA BLANCA   21
                     Castillo de
                     las Coloradas
                  Playa de las
                  Mujeres

                  Punta del
                  Papagayo

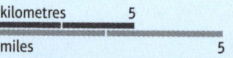

0 kilometres   5

0 miles   5

N ↑

Roque del Este

Montaña
Clara

Playa de
las Conchas

Playa Lambra

**LA
GRACIOSA**

⑪

Caleta del Sebo

Playa de la
Cantería

**MIRADOR
DEL RÍO** ④

⑩ **ÓRZOLA**

LZ203

LZ204

⑨ **MALPAÍS
DE LA CORONA**

LZ1

GUINATE ⑬

Monte Corona
609 m (1,998 ft)

LZ201

Máguez

**CUEVA DE
LOS VERDES** ③

② **JAMEOS
DEL AGUA**

HARÍA ⑫

LZ10

Punta de
Mujeres

A t l a n t i c
O c e a n

Arrieta

LZ207

Playa de
Famara

Peñas
del Chache
674 m (2,211 ft)

Mirador
de Haría

La Isleta

**CALETA
FAMARA** ⑮

Mala

La Santa

Famara

LZ10

LZ1

LZ42

LZ67

LZ2401

Montaña
de Guenia
358 m (1,175 ft)

⑧ **GUATIZA**

LZ402

TEGUISE ⑯

La Caldera
O Tinamala
323 m (1,060 ft)

Tinajo

LZ404

TIAGUA ⑭

Guanapay
446 m (1,463 ft)

LZ46

LZ20

Tao

LZ30

Mancha
Blanca

LZ409

LZ1

Mozaga

Monumento
al Campesino

LZ20

⑦ **TAHICHE**

Madasche

⑰ **SAN BARTOLOMÉ**

⑥ **COSTA
TEGUISE**

Montaña
Blanca

LZ1

LA GERIA ㉓

LZ30

LZ20

Argana

LZ3

Conil

LZ35

LZ301

⑤ **ARRECIFE**

LZ502

LZ2

Mácher

César Manrique-
Lanzarote Airport

Playa
Honda

LZ740

Punta
Montañosa

**PUERTO
DEL CARMEN** ㉔

Playa Blanca

LANZAROTE

Fuerteventura ✓   Gran Canaria ✓

1

3

7 DAYS

in Lanzarote

Day 1

The best place to start a tour of Lanzarote is on the southern tip of the island in Playa Blanca *(p121)*. Armed with a picnic, start with an easy, but long, 9-km (5.5-mile) walk along the beach. Along the way, stop at sights like the imposing Castillo de San Marcial de Rubicón de Femés *(C/Castillo del Águila 33)*. Enjoy your picnic beside the famous white sands of Playa Papagayo, one of the best beaches in Lanzarote, and take a dip after, before heading back to Playa Blanca for dinner and a rest.

Day 2

From Playa Blanca, make the scenic drive into the heart of Parque Nacional de Timanfaya *(p106)*. Your first stop is the Mancha Blanca visitor centre, where you'll learn all about the park and its landscapes, flora and fauna. From here, head to the Islote de Hilario centre and join a bus tour of the park's Montañas del Fuego. Tour over, enjoy a late lunch at Restaurante El Diablo *(p107)*, where the food is cooked over a 5-m- (16-ft-)

deep hole in the volcano, reaching temperatures up to 300°C (572°F). Then make your way to La Hoya, a town just outside the park's southern edge, to see a view of the salt flats before dinner.

Day 3

You're in Lanzarote, where the winds are always blowing, so give surfing a go today. Head out to Playa de Famara *(p119)*, where you'll find many surf schools and shops renting out boards and wetsuits. If you're a seasoned surfer, drive a short way south to the small fishing village of La Santa, where you'll find more challenging waves. Stay at Club La Santa *(www. clublasanta.co.uk)*, where a whole host of sports activities are included with board and will keep you busy well into the evening.

Day 4

Start the day with a one-hour drive to Órzola *(p116)*, a small fishing village on the northernmost tip of the island's mainland. Enjoy a late breakfast here before catching the ferry to the island of La Graciosa *(p117)*.

1 The volcanic landscapes of Parque Nacional de Timanfaya.

2 Surfers hitting the waves.

3 A seafood restaurant in the fishing village of Órzola.

4 Wine barrels inside the El Grifo Wine Museum of La Geria.

After the 30-minute journey, disembark at Caleta del Sebo and hail a taxi or rent a bike to make your way to the ancient volcano, Montaña Amarilla. Explore the area and the nearby beaches before catching an afternoon ferry back to the main island. Drive to the Mirador del Río (p112) to enjoy the views from one of the highest points of Lanzarote at sunset, and return to Órzola for a freshly caught seafood dinner.

Day 5

After breakfast in Órzola, make the short drive to Cueva de los Verdes (p110). Join a tour of this giant lava tube, which was created by the ancient eruption of Monte Corona. Next, drive to the Jameos del Agua (p108) to enjoy this paradisiacal oasis of natural lakes and have lunch in the on-site restaurant. Sated, spend the afternoon making your way to Haría (p118) for a visit the Casa Museo de César Manrique and see where the artist spent the last years of his life. After dinner in Haría, head to the Peñas del Chache viewpoint for an evening of spectacular stargazing before bedding down back in Haría.

Day 6

Today is all about the history of Lanzarote. Begin your day with a 30-minute drive to the town San Bartolomé (p120). After a bite to eat, visit the Casa-Museo del Campesino (Ctra Arrecife a Tinajo 8) to learn about Lanzarote's farming history. From here, drive over to the nearby El Grifo Wine Museum (Lugar de El Grifo) and spend the afternoon touring vineyards in this renowned wine region. When you get hungry, head over to the island's capital, Arrecife (p114), for dinner along the seafront.

Day 7

On your final morning, make the drive to Puerto del Carmen (p213) and spend some time snorkelling in the clear waters here. Head back to Arrecife for the afternoon, enjoying a tasty lunch beside the Charco de San Gines lagoon (p114) before visiting the contemporary art museum in Castillo de San Jorge (www.miaclanzarote.com). See off the day – and your trip – with a stroll along the 5-km (3-mile) coastal promenade in nearby Costa Teguise (p114).

PARQUE NACIONAL DE TIMANFAYA

🅘 **Centro de Visitantes e Interpretación de Mancha Blanca: Ctra Yaiza-Tinajo, 10 km (6 miles) from Tinajo; open 9am–4:30pm daily; www.cactlanzarote.com/centro/montanas-del-fuego**

Stretching over 200 km (120 miles), the landscapes of the Parque Nacional de Timanfaya are some of the island's most epic. The result of six-year long volcanic eruption, what remains today is a fascinating spectacle of lunar vistas, volcanic craters and lava flows.

Between 1730 and 1736, the Montañas del Fuego – or Fire Mountains – belched forth smoke and molten lava, burying entire villages and turning the island's fertile lowlands into a sea of solidified lava, grey volcanic rock and copper-coloured sand. Today, the lava remains are Lanzarote's greatest attraction. Situated to the southwest, they have become the heart of the Parque Nacional de Timanfaya, which was established in 1974.

> INSIDER TIP
> **Guided Bus Tour**
>
> Bus tours operate regularly from the El Diablo restaurant in the park complex and are an excellent way to explore the park. Grab a seat on the right side of the bus for the best views of the spectacular volcanic landscape.

↑ Lava rocks set across the lunar-like
landscape of the national park

Exploring the Park

While the small village of Femes offers superb views of the Fire
Mountains, it's only at close range that you can fully appreciate
the landscape. One of the best ways to get up close to the
lava fields is on foot with a guide or by coach. The Ruta de
los Volcanes hiking tour is great for views of one of the
most impressive geysers on the island, the Islote de Hilario.
It has the highest underground temperature in the park,
reaching 600° C (1,112° F) at a depth of 12 m (40 ft). The
park is currently quite safe, though lava still bubbles
away under the surface, and a whiff of sulphur
hangs in the air.

Must See

EAT

El Diablo
Taking advantage of
the 300° C (572° F)
temperatures, this
incredible restaurant
uses volcanic grills
to cook meat.

⌂ Montaña del Fuego,
Carretera general Yaiza-
Tinajo s/n

€€€

← Parque Nacional de
Timanfaya and *(inset)*
a signpost by Lanzarote-
born artist César Manrique

2 🏄 🎨 🖥 🍴 🛍

JAMEOS DEL AGUA

🏠 Carretera de Órzola 🕐 10am–6pm daily (last adm: 5:15pm)
🌐 cactlanzarote.com/en/centre/jameos-del-agua-guide

This series of volcanic caves, located in the northern tip of Lanzarote, has been transformed into a centre for art and culture. The complex is remarkable for its harmonious, sustainable architecture, which blends seamlessly with the natural surroundings.

Home to everything from a nightclub to an exhibition centre, Jameos del Agua is not your average cave complex. In the 1960s, César Manrique *(p115)* had the idea to turn this volcanic tunnel – a remnant of the eruption of the Volcán de la Corona – into an art, culture and tourism centre.

Manrique's design incorporates the natural setting at every turn. Above the caves is the Jameo Grande, a picturesque, irregularly shaped pool (swimming is prohibited), surrounded by artistically arranged tropical flora. From here, a cascading stone staircase leads down to a cavernous underground restaurant and, further on, to a giant cave, 62 m (203 ft) long, 19 m (62 ft) wide and 21 m (69 ft) high. There's also a salt lake on-site, connected to the ocean. Aside from the natural features, there's an exhibition on volcanoes, an auditorium that takes advantage of the incredible acoustics of the cave, and at night, a nightclub opens in one of the caves.

↑ Relaxing by the Jameo Grande pool above the complex

↑ A lecture being held inside one of the volcanic caves

EAT

Restaurante Jameos del Agua
This spot serves tasty contemporary dishes. Don't miss the soirees on Wednesdays and Fridays (book ahead).

🏠 Carretera Arrieta, Órzola s/n
📞 901 20 03 00

 €€€

Tahoyo
A charming family-friendly restaurant, Tahoyo serves simple, traditional food with a special focus on fresh grilled fish.

🏠 C/Pared del Agua 14, Punta Mujeres
📞 928 17 75 77

 €€€

Did You Know?

Jameos del Agua is a sanctuary for endemic *jameitos* – tiny, blind, albino crabs.

← The deep waters of the salt lake at Jameos del Agua

3

CUEVA DE LOS VERDES

⌂ 26 km (16 miles) N of Arrecife ☎ 928 848 484 🕐 Summer: 10am–7pm daily; winter: 10am–6pm daily

This extraordinary underground volcanic tunnel was created by the eruption of the nearby Monte Corona more than 5,000 years ago, formed from a tube of solidified lava. One of the world's longest volcanic tunnels at 7 km (4 miles), it's open for visitors to explore.

Cueva de los Verdes: the cave's name has nothing to do with any green colour, but instead derives from the name of a shepherd family, the Verdes (Greens), who inhabited it in the 18th and 19th centuries. The cave's walls and vaults are in fact red and ochre due to iron oxidation and water seeping from the surface.

From the 17th century, the cave was used by the local population as a shelter from pirates and slave traders. In 1964, lighting was installed, and 2 km (1 mile) of the cave was opened to visitors. The tour of the tunnel takes about an hour and a special highlight is the visit to a small lake inside one of the caves; although only 20 cm (8 in) deep, it appears far deeper due to the stone vaults reflected in the water. Part of the Cueva de los Verdes but closed to visitors, the underwater Túnel de la Atlantida nearby is the longest lava tube in the world.

↑ Cueva de los Verdes's clear waters creating an optical illusion

↑ Wooden sign guiding visitors to the Cueva de los Verdes

The cave's name has nothing to do with any green colour, but derives from the name of a shepherd family, the Verdes (Greens), who inhabited it in the 18th and 19th centuries.

ESCAPING PIRATES

The Canary Islands, and the island of Lanzarote in particular, were subject to frequent Amazigh pirate invasions from north Africa throughout the 16th and 17th centuries, following an increase in European expeditions to the Americas from the late 15th century onwards. The island's local population at first fiercely resisted these pillages, but they were ultimately forced to seek refuge during the ongoing attacks during this period. The cavernous Cueva de los Verdes, with its labyrinth of interconnected lava tunnels, became an ideal hideout and continued to be used by some local families after.

4 🔹 🍴

MIRADOR DEL RÍO

🕐 10am–5pm daily (last adm: 4:40pm) 🌐 cactlanzarote.com/en/centre/mirador-del-rio

The most famous panoramic viewpoint on Lanzarote is situated at the northernmost point of the island, 470 m (1,560 ft) above sea level. This spot, hidden among rocks, looks out over the high cliffs of the northern shore.

Mirador del Río is a stunning viewpoint, designed by César Manrique *(p115)* in the 1970s; at the entrance stands a distinctive sculpture designed by the artist. In 1973, the site of a 19th-century gun emplacement was transformed by Manrique to create this viewpoint, which combines nature and art in a unique and influential architectural design.

Today, visitors stop here to enjoy stunning panoramas of Lanzarote and landmarks beyond it, like Montaña Clara, Alegranza and the island of La Graciosa. Built into the rock and painted white, the viewpoint structure has an enormous window stretching the length of the room from which to enjoy the vistas. The only significant decorations inside are the mobiles crafted by Manrique, decorating the bar and restaurant here. The function of these sculptures is not merely decorative; they are also meant to soften noise, because of the poor acoustics of the space.

Sculpture by local artist César Manrique beside the viewpoint ↑

> In 1973, the site of a 19th-century gun emplacement was transformed by César Manrique to create this viewpoint, which combines nature and art in a unique and influential architectural design.

↑ Patrons enjoying the view while dining at the complex's restaurant

Did You Know?
———
The sculptures created by César Manrique are made of upcycled scrap metal and recycled material.

← Looking over La Graciosa's volcanic landscape from Mirador del Río

EXPERIENCE MORE

Arrecife

⛵ 🚌 *i* Parque
José Ramírez Cerdá;
www.arrecife.es

Arrecife is full of Spanish character. With modern houses and a palm-lined promenade, it has been the capital of Lanzarote since 1852, as well as the island's main seaport and commercial centre. Though not quite as picturesque as the rest of the island, it's home to some interesting sights and no high-rise apartment blocks; instead, the one-storey houses are built in the traditional style.

The first harbour, protected by small islands and reefs, existed here as early as the 15th century. Two forts, the Castillo de San Gabriel and Castillo de San José, were built to protect Lanzarote from seaborne raiders and have survived to this day.

The Castillo de San Gabriel is situated on a small island just off Arrecife's bay, accessible by two bridges. It was destroyed during a pirate attack in 1586 but was later restored by renowned Italian engineer Leonardo Torriani.

In 1976, the San José fortress was restored by César Manrique and turned into a modern art gallery, the **Museo Internacional de Arte Contemporáneo**. Four rooms are used for temporary exhibitions of artists like Pablo Picasso, Joan Miró, Oscar Dominguez or Manrique himself, while music recitals are held in the concert hall.

Also worth visiting are the Casa de la Cultura Agustín de la Hoz and Casa de Los Arroyo, dating back to 1749 and featuring a courtyard with wooden galleries and a well at its centre.

Outside of its historical sites, Arrecife's attractive main shopping street, León y Castillo, has goods at much cheaper prices than at the major tourist resorts, as well as many cafés and restaurants.

Quite different in character is the area around Charco de San Ginés, with its pretty cottages overlooking a small lake that connects to the sea. Its Iglesia de San Ginés is dedicated to the patron saint of Arrecife. This triple-naved church with timber vaults features late-Baroque statues of San Ginés and the Virgen del Rosario, which were brought from Cuba.

Museo Internacional de Arte Contemporáneo

 🏛 Castillo de San José, Carretera de Naos 🕐 11am–6pm daily 🌐 miaclanzarote.com

---

Costa Teguise

🚌 *i* Avda Islas Canarias; www.turismoteguise.com/en

This is the third-largest resort on the island, after Puerto del Carmen and Playa Blanca (*p121*). Just 9 km (6 miles) northeast of Arrecife, Costa Teguise dates back to 1977, when the Gran Meliá Salinas hotel was built here with the assistance of Manrique.

It's a large resort, with low-rise holiday developments of white bungalows, a golf course, a marina and a shopping centre. It also has some pleasant sandy beaches, of which Playa de las Cucharas is the largest and most scenic. Smart and modern, Costa Teguise once attracted an elite clientele (there's even a royal residence here),

TOP 4 SNORKELLING SPOTS

Veril de Costa Teguise
A local favourite, Veril de Costa Teguise is a popular snorkelling spot.

Playa del Jablillo
This beach is a great spot to learn, as the water is not too deep.

Montaña Amarilla
The charming Playa de la Cocina is a calm spot for snorkellers.

Playa de Papagayo
The coves around Papagayo, including Playa Mujeres, Playa del Pozo and Playa Puerto Muelas, are known for their underwater views.

↑ Swathes of golden sand line the shores of Costa Teguise's Playa de las Cucharas

though it is now fairly similar to other resorts on the island.

7

Tahiche

 8 km (5 miles) N of Arrecife ▭

Just outside of Arrecife, on the lava fields created by the 1730–36 volcanic eruptions, stands Taro de Tahiche. This house was built in 1968 by Manrique, who lived here until 1988. Upon moving to Haría, he donated Taro de Tahiche to the **Fundación César Manrique (Tahiche)**. Founded by himself and a circle of his friends, this organization aims to promote architecture that is in harmony with the natural environment.

In keeping with this goal, Manrique built his house amid the island's characteristic blue-black lava flows. The cubic forms above ground draw on the traditional style of the island, though the space is opened out with contemporary touches such as large windows and wide terraces. Below ground, the design becomes more startling still. The lower floor features five volcanic "bubbles" – interconnected by tunnels. These vast compartments, 5 m (16 ft) in diameter, were formed by solidifying lava.

Each of the "bubbles" has its own basalt staircase leading from the lower floor to the upper level. In one of the rooms, the upper and lower spaces are linked by a fig tree, which rises from the lower floor and into the drawing room above. The house, which became the embodiment of the artist's dream to live in harmony with nature, now houses a modern art museum, which has examples of Manrique's own works and project designs. It also exhibits other works by other artists, including Pablo Picasso, Antonio Tàpies, Joan Miró and Jesús Soto.

Fundación César Manrique (Tahiche)
⊘ ⌂ Taro de Tahiche, C/Jorge Luis Borges, 16
🕐 10am–6pm daily
🌐 fcmanrique.org

CÉSAR MANRIQUE (1919–92)

Painter, sculptor, art restorer, architect and town-planner César Manrique was born in Arrecife. Having volunteered in the Spanish Civil War, he later devoted himself to art. His abstract paintings were exhibited across Europe as well as in Japan and the United States. Manrique died in a car accident in 1992, but he left his mark on Lanzarote, both in terms of his bold designs and in the restrained way traditional island life has adapted to tourism.

← Bridges leading to the historic Castillo de San Gabriel in Arrecife

8
Guatiza

**17 km (11 miles)
NE of Arrecife**

The small town of Guatiza, in the northeast of Lanzarote, is home to the 19th-century chapel of Santa Margarita and, more famously, vast plantations of prickly pear. The plant is host to the cochineal insect – a source of vermilion or crimson dye.

At the centre of the cactus fields is the **Jardín de Cactus**, designed by César Manrique in 1990. At the entrance to the garden stands an 8-m- (26-ft-) tall metal statue of a cactus.

HIDDEN GEM
Rofera de Teseguite

Southwest of Guatiza, Rofera de Teseguite is an extraordinary landscape worth seeking out. The site is made up of volcanic rocks which have been shaped over time into mysterious silhouettes.

The garden was built in an enormous pit, originally dug by the villagers, who were excavating volcanic ash to fertilize their fields.

The Jardín de Cactus is arranged in the form of an amphitheatre, dominated by a white windmill. Growing on the terraces are about 4,500 specimens, representing over 500 varieties of cactus. There is also a good restaurant on the grounds.

Jardín de Cactus
Carretera General del Norte, s/n 10am–5pm daily cactlanzarote.com

9
Malpaís de la Corona

These volcanic badlands bear testimony to the extreme volcanic activities that shook this northernmost point of the island some 5,000 years ago. This wild terrain occupies 30 sq km (12 sq miles) between the village of Órzola and the headland of Punta de Mujeres, near Arrieta.

On the western end of Malpaís, visible from far and wide, stands the mighty Monte Corona volcano. This measures 1,100 m (3,600 ft) in diameter at its base, 450 m (1,475 ft) at its top section and 600 m (2,000 ft) high. The eruptions of this volcano produced the wide belt of strange lava formations (the Malpaís de la Corona), which include the Cueva de los Verdes and Jameos del Agua.

10
Órzola

lanzarote.com/en/discover-lanzarote

This fishing village at the northern tip of Lanzarote is a haven of peace. It is known for its excellent seafood restaurants, which stretch along the coastal seafront.

Órzola is also famous for the picturesque Playa de la Cantería. However, this beach is not suitable for bathing, as strong sea currents create unfavourable conditions.

A frequent ferry service provides links with the

 La Graciosa's Playa de las Conchas, stretching across the island's northern shore

La Graciosa

 visitla graciosa.com

The smallest inhabited island of the archipelago covers an area of just 27 sq km (10 sq miles) in total. Separated from Lanzarote by the straits of El Río, it was dubbed the "gracious island" by Jean de Béthencourt. An ideal place for scuba divers, anglers, hikers and those looking for a quiet rest, La Graciosa plays to its strengths and offers a slow pace and a minimum of amenities. The island is fringed by beaches of golden sand dunes.

The most beautiful of these is Playa de las Conchas. It is regarded as one of the most picturesque of all the beaches of the archipelago and provides a good view of the uninhabited smaller islands: Montaña Clara, Roque del Este and Alegranza.

There are no hotels on La Graciosa itself, but the village of Caleta del Sebo,

> **The smallest inhabited island of the archipelago, La Graciosa covers an area of just 27 sq km (10 sq miles) in total.**

linked by a ferry service to Órzola, has a few guest-houses and restaurants.

Guinate

Situated at the foot of the Monte Corona volcano, Guinate is a small village that is popular with bird lovers.

The **Guinate Tropical Park**, spread out on terraces, features serene waterfalls, ponds and gardens. Here you can see some 1,300 birds, representing about 300 species, as well as many small apes. The park also has a penguin pool with an underwater viewing area.

Guinate Tropical Park
⊕ ☎ 928 835 500 🕙 10am–5pm daily

neighbouring island of La Graciosa. From here, you can travel by fishing boat as far as the islands of Montaña Clara and Alegranza. You won't be allowed to explore, however, as these two small and uninhabited islands form part of the national park, which was founded in 1986 and is off-limits to visitors.

→ A pretty church in the village of Caleta del Sebo, La Graciosa

Shoppers exploring the bustling weekend market at Teguise

⑬ Haría

 ℹ Plaza de la Constitución, s/n; 928 835 2541

Cubic, whitewashed houses, reminiscent of North African architecture, along with numerous palms, give this picturesque village an almost Middle Eastern flavour. The stunning valley in which Haría is situated, known as the "valley of a thousand palms", was once home to far more of these lovely tropical trees. Many of them were burned during a pirate attack in 1856.

The shady, tree-lined Plaza León y Castillo is surrounded by restored historic houses. At one end of the square stands the main church of the village, the Nuestra Señora de la Encarnación.

Not far south of Haría is the popular viewpoint of Mirador de Haría. A winding road leads to this mountain pass, providing a fine view over the village, the surrounding volcanoes, the high cliffs, and Arietta. Ermita de las Nieves, on the road to Teguise, also offers wonderful views over the village of Los Valles.

⑭ Teguise

 ℹ Plaza de la Constitución, s/n; www.turismoteguise.com/en

Teguise is one of the oldest towns on Lanzarote. It was founded in 1418 by Maciot – nephew and successor of Jean de Béthencourt – who, it is said, lived here with Princess Teguise, the daughter of the Guanche king, Guadarfía.

Spacious squares and well-kept cobbled streets lined with beautifully restored houses are testimony to Teguise's former glory. A good time to visit is on Sundays, when there is a craft market and folk dancing.

For centuries, the town was one of the largest and richest on the island. Until 1852, it was its capital city. The fame and the wealth of Teguise, bearing the proud name of La Villa Real de Teguise (the Royal City of Teguise), attracted pirates who raided it repeatedly. The Callejón de la Sangre ("Street of Blood") owes its name to the worst of these raids and commemorates the victims of the massacre that took place in 1596.

The eclectic church of Nuestra Señora de Guadalupe stands in the town square. Since its construction in the mid-15th century, it has been rebuilt many times. The interior furnishing is Neo-Gothic and features a statue of the Virgin Mary of Guadalupe. On the opposite side of the square stands the **Casa-Museo del Timple Palacio Spínola**. This beautiful residence, with its small patio and a well, was built between 1730 and 1780. The reconstruction work, supervised by Spanish artist and sculptor César Manrique, has restored the palace interiors to their former glory. The museum showcases the Canarian equivalent of the ukulele – the *timple*.

Also of interest are two conventual churches. The 16th-century Convento de San Francisco, better known as La Madre de Miraflores, was used as a burial site for the most prominent citizens of Lanzarote, and is now a venue for cultural events.

 TOP 3 | **LANZAROTE SURF SPOTS**

Famara
This scenic spot is ideal for beginners and more experienced surfers alike.

Caleta del Mero
Intermediate surfers can enjoy this spectacular spot on the east coast.

La Santa
Only for expert surfers, La Santra hosts several prestigious international competitions.

Inside the 17th-century Convento de Santo Domingo is the original main altar. Now the abbey houses an interesting modern art gallery – the Centro Arte. Towering over the town is the Castillo de Santa Bárbara. The castle was built in the early 16th century on top of the 452-m- (1,483-ft-) high Guanapay peak, and provides a view over almost the entire island.

Casa-Museo del Timple Palacio Spínola

Plaza de la Constitución, s/n Winter: 9am–4pm Mon-Sat, 9am–3:30pm Sun; summer: 9am–3pm Mon-Sat, 9am–2pm Sun & public hols casadeltimple.org

La Caleta de Famara

 35 km (22 miles) N of Arrecife

A small fishing village, with a handful of restaurants and one of the most beautiful beaches on Lanzarote, Playa de Famara is popular with visitors. Urbanización Famara, situated to the north, is a cluster of holiday chalets.

The beautiful 3-km- (2-mile-) long sandy beach stretches along the base of tall cliffs formed during the most recent volcanic eruption in 1824. Behind the beach, which provides a wonderful view over La Graciosa, runs a long band of dunes. This is a popular surfing beach, though the strong currents can be dangerous. The village also attracts quite a few painters and has been declared a conservation area.

Club La Santa, 13 km (8 miles) west, offers around 400 apartments

and some 30 sports, so it is popular with professional sportspeople in off-season.

Tiagua

This village offers visitors an insight into local history and tradition. The main highlight is the **Museo Agrícola El Patio**, which offers insight into past agricultural practices. The complex is on the site of a farm dating back to 1845, when a group of farmers began to cultivate the land. A century later, it was the biggest and best-run estate on the island.

Some 5 km (3 miles) to the west, in Mancha Blanca, stands the church of Nuestra Señora de los Dolores, where the Madonna is said to have brought lava streams to a halt on two occasions.

Museo Agrícola El Patio

928 529 134 10am–5pm Mon-Fri, 10am-2pm Sat

← Exhibition hall in the Museo Agrícola El Patio and *(inset)* its façade

⓱ San Bartolomé

 W sanbartolome.es

Known to the Guanches as Ajei, San Bartolomé has some fine examples of traditional Canary architecture, including the 18th-century Casa Perdomo, with its beautiful courtyard and tiny chapel of Nuestra Señora del Pino. Today it houses the **Museo Etnográfico Tanit**. Various exhibits, such as musical instruments, agricultural tools, furniture and wine-production equipment, illustrate the island's economic history. In the town centre is a large, stylish square, containing the parish church of San Bartolomé (1789).

A short way north, towards Mozaga, stands the imposing Monumento al Campesino (Peasant's Monument). This 15-m- (50-ft-) tall construction was designed by César Manrique, and built in 1968 by Jesús Soto. Made of old water containers once used on fishing boats, the monument is devoted, in Manrique's own words, "to the nameless farmers, whose hard work helped to create the island's unique landscape". The nearby **Casa-Museo Monumento al Campesino** houses workshops devoted to various crafts, illustrating former rural life on Lanzarote. Its restaurant is good for lunch.

Museo Etnográfico Tanit
⊕ 🏠 C/Constitución 1
🕐 10am–2pm Mon–Sat
W museotanit.es

Casa-Museo Monumento al Campesino
⊕ 🏠 Carretera Arrecife
🕐 10am–6pm daily
W cactlanzarote.com

⓲ Yaiza

 🛈 Calle Limones 1, Playa Blanca,; 928 518150

Nestling at the foot of the Montañas del Fuego, Yaiza is regarded, along with Haría, as one of the most picturesque towns on the island. In the 19th century, rich merchants settled here, and to this day some houses with palm-shaded façades bear evidence of this former wealth.

The parish church of Nuestra Señora de los Remedios dates from the 18th century. This triple-naved church was built on the site of a former chapel dating back to 1699 and has a number of fine 18th-century paintings.

The Baroque vault decorations, which incorporate folk elements, give the church its unique atmosphere. Numerous shops along the main street sell embroidery, pottery and other craft items.

Just 2 km (1 mile) east of Yaiza, Uga is the departure point for trips across the volcanic landscape.

⓳ El Golfo

 🏠 8 km (5 miles) NW of Yaiza

The quiet hamlet of El Golfo is home to a small crater lagoon, Lago Verde, which was created by an underwater volcano. Its emerald-green colour is due to the sea algae that thrive in it. El Golfo's restaurants make it popular with tourists, while the presence of olivine (an olive-green semi-precious stone) attracts geologists and jewellery makers to the area.

Taking the path from the village, you get the best view of the lake, which is surrounded by dramatic volcanic rocks resembling a petrified wave, and separated from the ocean by a narrow strip of black volcanic sand.

South of El Golfo are Los Hervideros ("the kettles"). As the name suggests, the waves "boil" inside the vast caves of the 15-m- (50-ft-) high cliffs.

⓴ Salinas de Janubio

 🏠 9 km (6 miles) N of Playa Blanca

The greenish waters of a natural lagoon are used to produce salt at this sea-salt plant. Long used to preserve fish, the salt is still extracted by the traditional method of

← Exploring the grounds of the Casa-Museo Monumento al Campesino, San Bartolome

← Salt evaporation pans at the sea-salt plant in Salinas de Janubio

evaporation. The sea-salt plant is believed to be the largest operating on the archipelago and currently produces about 2,000 tonnes of salt per annum. While many years ago, the water was pumped into the lagoon with the help of wind power, today the pumps are electrically driven.

Local salt is still bought by fishers, with a small portion sold as table salt. Each year, during the Corpus Christi festival, locals use dyed salt to create magnificent decorations for the streets and squares.

 21

Playa Blanca

 Plaza de Los Remedios 1; 928 836 220

A former fishing village, today the scenic Playa Blanca is one of the largest resorts on the island, with regular ferry links to the nearby island of Fuerteventura.

One of the best beaches is situated near the centre, with clear water and wonderful views over neighbouring Fuerteventura and Isla de los Lobos. The Playas de Papagayo beaches, situated just 4 km (2 miles) south of Playa Blanca, are also popular for sunbathing and swimming, due to their sheltered location and calm waters.

The Castillo de las Coloradas, in Punta del Águila, is a watchtower dating from 1741–8. Between here and Punta de Papagayo is a string of scenic coves with sandy beaches: Playa de las Mujeres, El Pozo and Papagayo. The fine sand and warm, clear waters of these shores attract an ever-increasing number of visitors.

This area is a part of the Los Ajaches nature reserve, created in 1994. Among the highlights here is a bird protection zone. There is an entrance charge and the only access from Playa Blanca is by a minor road. Nearby, perched on the very edge of a cliff, are the remains of the island's first Norman settlement, San Marcial del Rubicón, which was founded in 1402 by the French explorer Jean de Béthencourt.

> **INSIDER TIP**
> **Birdwatching**
>
> The Salinas de Janubio is an Area of Special Protection for Birds. Bring your binoculars to see a surprising variety of bird species, such as the black-winged stilt and the Mediterranean short-toed lark.

STAY

Hotel Casa del Embajador

This family-run hotel offers great views of the Bay of Playa Blanca.

 C/ Bienvenida Martín La Practicante 58, Playa Blanca
Ⓦ **hotelcasadel embajador.com**

€€€

Calas Lanzarote Suites Hotel

The suites at this adult-only, stylish boutique come with great views.

 C/ La Comoda, Playa Blanca
Ⓦ **calalanzarote suiteshotel.com**

€€€

MYND Yaiza

A modern hotel, MYND Yaiza caters to families looking for fun and couples wanting rest and relaxation.

 C/ Janubio 3, Playa Blanca
Ⓦ **myndhotels.com**

€€€

Femés

Overlooked by the incredible 608-m- (1,995-ft-) high volcanic peak of Atalaya de Femés, this village was once home to one of the island's oldest religious buildings – the Ermita San Marcial del Rubicón cathedral, devoted to the patron saint of the island and destroyed in the 16th century by pirates. The present church, built on the site in 1733, is devoted to the same saint. Its walls are decorated with models of sailing ships, testimony to the seafaring heritage of the Canary Islands. Today, the church is open only during services.

Located in the centre of Femés, just by the side of the road, is a fine viewpoint, which provides a stunning panorama of Montaña Roja as well as the ocean. The opposite side of town overlooks the panorama of Montañas del Fuego.

La Geria

Stretching on both sides of the road from Masdache to Uga, the valley of La Geria is the main vine-growing area on Lanzarote. Set within this black cinder landscape that once featured only the occasional palm tree, the vineyards look as if they have been transplanted wholesale from another planet. They occupy 52 sq km (20 sq miles) and have been declared a protected area. The valley, right up to the volcanic slopes, is dotted with small hollows, sheltered from the drying wind by low, semicircular walls. Each hollow is covered with volcanic cinder that absorbs dew at night and maintains the required humidity. Each contains a single vine. There are over 10,000 such hollows here.

The grapes are used to produce the very sweet and aromatic Malvasía – an excellent-quality wine for which Lanzarote is famous. This, as well as other brands of local wine, can be purchased cheaply in one of the many local *bodegas* (wine shops). All visitors coming to *bodegas* may sample the wines on offer before buying.

The vineyards tend to be small. El Grifo, situated at the northern end of La Geria, is a good example. Its outbuildings house a wine museum, the **Museo del Vino de Lanzarote**, arranged in

> **Stretching on both sides of the road from Masdache to Uga, the valley of La Geria is the main vine-growing area on Lanzarote.**

LANZAROTE'S BEACHES

Lanzarote's 250-km (155-mile) long shoreline offers 30 km (19 miles) of sandy beaches. In contrast to the long beaches of Fuerteventura, these are usually fairly small and consist of golden or white sand. Particularly beautiful beaches are found north of Arrecife.

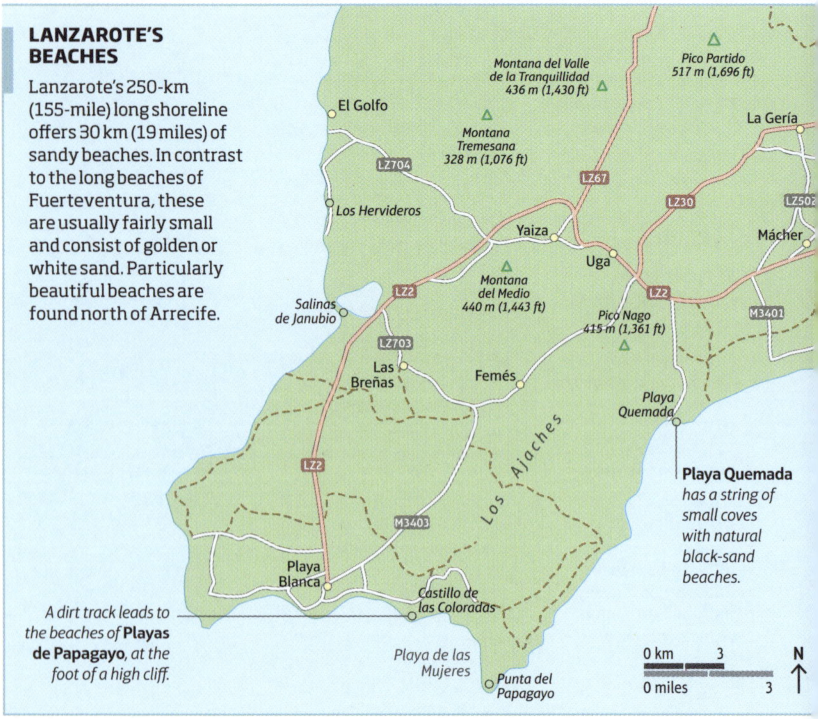

Pico Partido
517 m (1,696 ft)

Montana del Valle
de la Tranquillidad
436 m (1,430 ft)

La Gería

El Golfo

Montana
Tremesana
328 m (1,076 ft)

LZ704

LZ67

LZ30

LZ502

Los Hervideros

Yaiza

Mácher

Uga

LZ2

Montana
del Medio
440 m (1,443 ft)

Salinas
de Janubio

LZ2

Pico Nago
415 m (1,361 ft)

M3401

LZ703

Las
Breñas

Femés

Playa
Quemada

LZ2

Playa Quemada
has a string of small coves with natural black-sand beaches.

Los Ajaches

M3403

Playa
Blanca

Castillo de
las Coloradas

A dirt track leads to the beaches of **Playas de Papagayo**, *at the foot of a high cliff.*

Playa de las
Mujeres

Punta del
Papagayo

0 km   3
0 miles   3

N

an old *bodega* dating from 1775. Apart from the old equipment used in the production and storage of wine, the museum has a library with more than 1,000 books, plus several 17th- and 18th-century manuscripts devoted to wine making. The area was declared an official natural park in 1987 and reclassified as a Natural Space of the Canary Islands in 1994.

Museo del Vino de Lanzarote

🕐 10:30am–6pm daily
🔲 elgrifo.com

24

Puerto del Carmen

🚌🚲 *ℹ️* Avda de las Playas; www.puertodel carmen.com

This former fishing village is now established as the island's top resort. Visitors

↑ A waterside café with white-painted houses in the distance, Puerto del Carmen

come for the beaches along the Avenida de las Playas, which are some of the island's most beautiful.

Puerto del Carmen is densely filled with a number of hotels, guesthouses and white villas, and there is no shortage of shops, nightclubs, cafés and restaurants. Tourist information points have suggestions of ways to experience the many exciting

local attractions, such as windsurfing, diving, fishing and trips by catamaran to Fuerteventura and Lobos.

Not too far, around 9 km (6 miles) north, is Puerto Calero, home to the island's loveliest marina. It offers boat rides to the Papagayo beaches and submarine trips for glimpses of life beneath the wild Atlantic waves.

The sandy beach of Las Cucharas at **Costa Teguise** *(p114) is ideal for sunbathing, windsurfing and diving.*

The island's capital **Arrecife** *(p114) and its immediate environs have fine sand beaches.*

Playa Honda *is one of the beaches situated between Puerto del Carmen and Arrecife.*

Puerto del Carmen *has several easily accessible but built-up beaches, such as Playa de los Pocillos.*

→ The rocky volcanic rock landscape that frames Arrecife's beaches

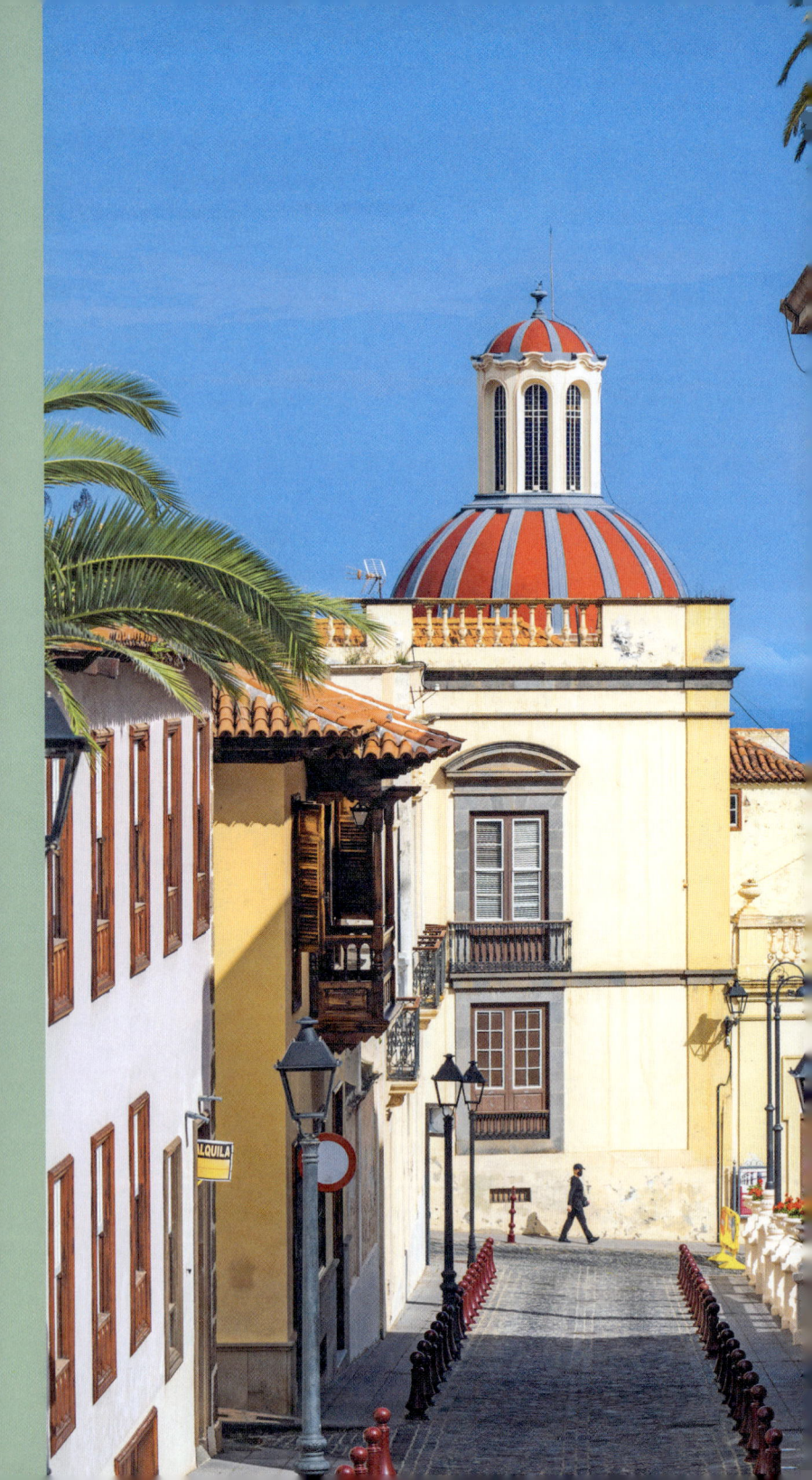

TENERIFE

First inhabited by the Guanche people, Tenerife was named after the island's imposing Pico del Teide mountain. From the 15th century, it was invaded by Spanish conquerors, who attempted to annex the island for around 30 years. In 1496, Tenerife became the last of the Canary Islands to fall to the Spanish after Castilian forces overcame the Guanche people, and imposed Spanish rule.

From the 16th century, Tenerife became a popular stopping-off point for Spanish expeditions to the Americas. Supplies were collected and new crew members were recruited for the journey ahead. This role evolved further and, by the 18th century, Tenerife was a significant link in Spanish trade with the Americas.

The island also played a key part in political changes in Spain during the 20th century. The future dictator Francisco Franco was posted to Tenerife in 1936 early on in his military career by the Republican government, which sought to reduce his influence on mainland politics. The Spanish Civil War began in the same year and the Canary Islands fell to the Nationalists early on.

Although tourists from Spain, the UK and northern Europe began to visit from the late 19th century, tourism really boomed from the 1960s. The island responded to this rise in popularity by covering its rocky southern shores with imported sand to make the coastline even more appealing to visitors. Today, the south and southwest coasts maintain these lighter and finer sand beaches, while the black-sand and pebble beaches of the northern coast are more natural for the island.

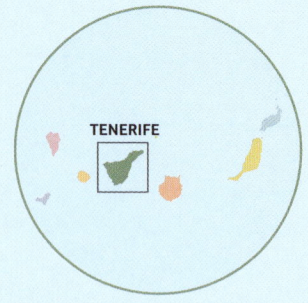

TENERIFE

Atlantic Ocean

PUERTO DE LA CRUZ 4

LORO PARQUE 7

San Juan de la Rambla

Punta del Cassado

Las Cucharas

TF5

LA OROTAVA 3

TF21

GARACHICO 11 TF42 10 **ICOD DE LOS VINOS**

Las Cruces

TF5

TF5 TF342

La vera

LOS REALEJOS 13

Cruz Santa

San José

Buenavista

El Amparo

La Guancha

Palo Blanco

TF326

Benijos

San Bernardo

El Tanque

Cueva del Viento

Teno

El Palmar

La Tierra del Trigo

TF82

Ruigómez

Baracan 1,002 m (3,287ft)

TF436

Las Portelas

Erjos

Montaña Negra 1,408 m (4,619 ft)

El Portillo

MASCA 12

Montaña de la Cruz 1,521 m (4,990 ft)

Chinyero 1,551 m (5,088 ft)

Montaña de la Carnicería 2,379 m (7,805 ft)

SANTIAGO DEL TEIDE 14

El Retamar

Tamaimo

TF375

Pico del Teide 3,718 m (1,2198 ft) 5

PARQUE NACIONAL DEL TEIDE

TF21

Acantilados de los Gigantes

TF82

Pico Viejo 3,134 m (1,0282 ft)

Teide Cable Car

Las Cañadas

Topo la Grieta 2,503 m (8,212 ft)

LOS GIGANTES AND PUERTO DE SANTIAGO 15 TF47

TF36

Los Roques de García

Morra del Rio 2,529 m (8,297 ft)

Alcalá

Chío

Guía de Isora

Guajara 2,718 m (8,917 ft)

TF463

San Juan

Tejina

Vera de Erques

Tijoco Alto

TF21

VILAFLOR 18

TF82

Taucho

Barranco del Infierno

TF28

TF47

TF1

TF567

TF51

TF563

TF21

La Gomera

Callao Salvaje

Playa Paraiso

Adeje

La Escalona

TF555

San Miguel

Granadilla de Abona

TF636

La Caleta

Arona

TF28

El Salto

TF647

TF64 TF636

SIAM PARK 17

La Camella

TF66

TF65

San Isidro

TF645

Buzanada

TF657

Aldea Blanca

PLAYA DE LAS AMÉRICAS 16

16 **LOS CRISTIANOS**

✈ **Tenerife South Airport**

Arenas del Mar

20 **EL MÉDANO**

TF66

Guargacho

El Hierro

El Palmar

TF653

Los Abrigos

TF65

TF643

Punta Roja

TF66

Las Galletas

Costa del Silencio

N ↑

0 kilometres 8

0 miles 8

TENERIFE

Must Sees

1. Santa Cruz de Tenerife
2. Parque Nacional de Anaga
3. La Orotava
4. Puerto de la Cruz
5. Parque Nacional del Teide

Experience More

6. La Laguna
7. Loro Parque
8. Tacoronte
9. Bajamar
10. Icod de los Vinos
11. Garachico
12. Masca
13. Los Realejos
14. Santiago del Teide
15. Los Gigantes and Puerto de Santiago
16. Playa de las Américas and Los Cristianos
17. Siam Park
18. Vilaflor
19. Candelaria
20. El Médano
21. Güímar

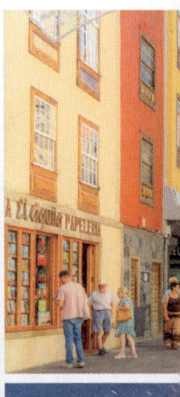

7 DAYS

in Tenerife

Day 1

Begin your tour of Tenerife exploring the island's capital, Santa Cruz de Tenerife *(p130)*. Visit Plaza de España to see the underground remains of the 16th-century Castillo de San Cristóbal, before getting stuck into the history of the Guanche people at the Nature and Archaeology Museum *(Calle Fuente Morales, s/n)*. After a light lunch on the Plaza de San Francisco, visit Palmetum Botanical Garden *(Avenida la Constitución 5)*, home to the world's largest tropical island palm collection, before returning to town for the evening.

Day 2

Leaving Santa Cruz de Tenerife, drive over to the picturesque San Cristóbal de La Laguna *(p148)* and explore its stunning Old Town – a UNESCO World Heritage Site – on a guided tour from the tourist office. Enjoy a lunch in the historic town before heading over to Parque Nacional de Anaga *(p134)* in Monte de Las Mercedes, stopping at Mirador de la Jardina for some spectacular views across La Laguna. Conditions permitting, you may even see

a rare cloud forest from here. Afterwards, head back to La Laguna to rest for the night.

Day 3

Today is all about the stunning nature of Tenerife, starting with an hour-long drive from La Laguna to the Parque Nacional del Teide *(p146)*. From Las Cañadas del Teide, take in the remarkable lunar landscapes before heading to El Portillo Visitors' Centre to learn about the park's history. Leave the car in a car park and enjoy one of the many walks here, or visit the Teide Observatory, the largest solar observatory in the world. Afterwards, take the cable car up to Mount Teide's epic 3,500-m- (11,400-ft-) high summit, where you can sip on a coffee or tuck into a snack at the base station. Head back down and drive to Icod de los Vinos *(p150)* for the night.

Day 4

Start at the Drago de Icod de los Vinos botanical garden *(C/Arcipreste Ossuna 1)*.

1 Santa Cruz de Tenerife's Palmetum Botanical Garden.

2 The pretty Old Town of San Cristóbal de La Laguna.

3 The Teide Observatory in the Parque Nacional del Teide.

4 One of La Laguna's bars.

Here, you'll see the iconic thousand-year-old dragon tree, an important Canarian plant. Afterwards, head to the nearby Cueva del Viento (C/Los Piquetes 51) and take in the sight of one of the world's largest lava tubes, formed by the Pico Viejo eruptions in 1798. Head back to town for lunch before following the coast around by car to the nearby town of Garachico (p151). Spend the afternoon here swimming in the natural volcanic rock pools, which formed when the eruption of the Trevejo volcano in 1706 buried much of the town. Ready to relax? Return to Drago de Icod de los Vinos to reset for the next day.

Day 5

Start early with a drive down to Puerto de Santiago (p153), making it in time to join a boat tour to the massive cliffs of Los Gigantes. See the sight from the water; while you're there, look out for the beautiful Masca Valley (p152) nearby and, with luck, dolphins and whales in their natural habitat. After disembarking from this day trip, stop off for a bite to eat at one of the restaurants in Santiago del Teide before making your way over to the Mirador de los Gigantes (C/El Pino 50) to witness some spectacular sunset views with drinks.

Day 6

Set off by car from Puerto de Santiago to Finca Las Margarita (Av la Calma, s/n). Spend time here exploring a banana plantation and learning about one of the island's biggest global exports. Then it's time to flop on the beach: bring snacks and water, a good book and plenty of sun-cream and prepare to laze on Playa de las Americas (p154) for the rest of the day.

Day 7

The last day of your time on Tenerife is all about fun. Spend the morning at Siam Park (p154) hitting the water slides and pools. After a spot of lunch nearby, drive to Playa del Confital for an afternoon watching surfers catch some epic waves – and maybe get inspired to try it for yourself.

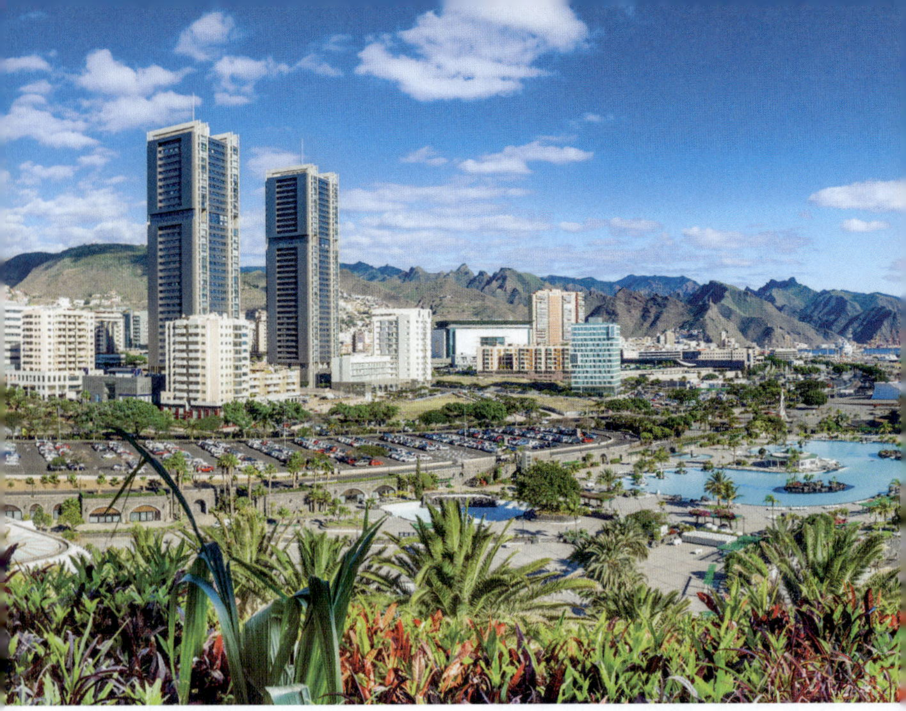

1

SANTA CRUZ DE TENERIFE

Plaza de España, s/n; 922 281 287

Santa Cruz de Tenerife took its name from the Holy Cross, erected by the Spanish navigator Alonso Fernández de Lugo upon landing here in 1494. Today, it's home to a deep-water harbour, which supports this former fishing village's economy and can accommodate luxury liners, tankers and container ships.

CARNIVAL IN SANTA CRUZ

Santa Cruz de Tenerife's spectacular carnival is among the world's largest. Each year, a new theme is chosen and participants are urged to follow. Don't miss the selection of the Carnival Queen and the grand parade that culminates in the Burial of the Sardine. Dates change each year, with the festival ending on the seventh Tuesday before Easter.

①

Museo de la Naturaleza y Arqueología

C/Fuente Morales, s/n 9am-7pm Mon-Sat, 10am-5pm Sun & public hols 1 & 6 Jan, Shrove Tue, 24-25 & 31 Dec museosdetenerife.org

The fascinating natural history museum occupies a Classical building that was once a military hospital. The exhibition is a colourful multimedia show dedicated to the geology, archaeology, and flora and fauna of the Canary Islands. In addition to the ever-popular mummies and skulls of the Guanches, it also displays a small collection of artifacts (including pottery, African carvings and pre-Columbian art) as well as fossils from around the world.

②

Museo Militar

C/San Isidro 2 922 298 557 9am-3pm Mon-Fri, 10am-2pm Sat

Founded in 1988, the Military Museum occupies the former site of the Cuartel de Almeida, a fortress dating back to 1884. The display features ancient weapons of the Canary Islands,

←

Santa Cruz, the capital of Tenerife, and its bustling harbour

④

Museo Municipal de Bellas Artes

🏠 C/José Murphy 12 🕐 10am–8pm Tue–Fri, 10am–3pm Sat, Sun & public hols 🌐 santacruz detenerife.es

Founded in 1898, this fine arts museum holds works from the Prado, including works by Old Masters. There are pieces by Spanish painters from the 17th and 18th centuries, and collections of coins and armour. There is also a display of works depicting local events and landscapes, such as *Santa Cruz Harbour or Landscape around Laguna*, by Valentín Sanza y Carta (1849–98).

⑤

TEA (Tenerife Arts Centre)

🏠 Avda de San Sebastián 10 🕐 10am–8pm Tue–Sun 🌐 teatenerife.es

Housed in a modern building, the TEA showcases contemporary photography, painting and sculpture exhibitions, both temporary and permanent. It also hosts regular movie screenings.

Many visitors come to Santa Cruz with the sole purpose of spending a few hours in the shops in and around Calle Castillo.

17th-century Spanish militaria and weapons dating from the 19th century. Banners, uniforms and the belongings of famous soldiers form a major part of the exhibition. One section is devoted to the July 1797 battle against the British fleet under Nelson. The most famous exhibit, El Tigre, is a cannon that fired the grapeshot that tore into Nelson's arm during the attack on Santa Cruz.

③

Calle Castillo

Many visitors come to Santa Cruz with the sole purpose of spending a few hours in the shops in and around Calle Castillo, the main pedestrianized shopping precinct. The street is busy – with bargains on electronic goods, watches or designer label clothes to be found in the local shops that line it – except during the siesta, which takes place between 1 and 4:30pm. There are also many handicraft centres selling embroidery, wickerwork and pottery here.

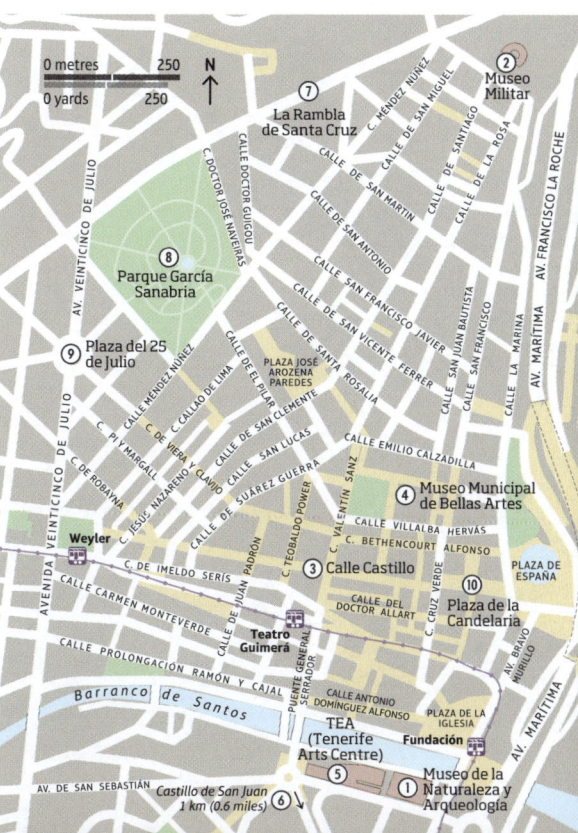

SHOP

Mercado de Nuestra Señora de África

Built in a North African architecture style, this bustling market was first established in 1946. Today, the iconic building is home to stalls that plenty of sell fresh local produce. As well as shopping for fish, poultry and cheese, visitors can also pick up fresh flowers.

⌂ Avda de San Sebastián 51
🕐 Market: 6am-2pm Mon-Sat, 7am-2pm Sun

⑥
Castillo de San Juan

Situated on the attractive waterfront, the protective fort of Castillo de San Juan was built in 1641. One of its functions was to guard the safety of the port, once central in the trade of enslaved people from Africa that was carried out on the Los Llanos wharf. The nearby small chapel of Nuestra Señora de Regla dates from the same period. Now both these buildings are overshadowed by the colossal edifice of the **Auditorio de Tenerife**, one of the island's leading performing arts venues. Every year on 25 July, a re-enactment of the Battle of Santa Cruz de Tenerife is held, marking Admiral Nelson's unsuccessful attempt to take the city.

Auditorio de Tenerife
⌂ Avda de la Constitución 1
🆆 auditoriodetene rife.com

La Rambla de Santa Cruz

This is one of the most elegant streets in Santa Cruz, stretching from the Plaza de la Paz to Avenida de Anaga. With its smart houses, numerous restaurants and cafés, this pretty street sweeps in a semi-circle through most of the city. Visitors can also explore the many local businesses that have set up shop along it.

Its wide central reservation, exclusively for use by pedestrians, separates two busy traffic lanes. Planted with tall palms, Indian laurel trees and lilac jacaranda, it is a veritable "art boulevard". Modern sculptures are set amid the trees, which are illuminated at night and bear plaques with the names of famous artists from around the world, including Michelangelo, Vermeer, Piranesi, Warhol and Pollock. Every Sunday, a lively antiques fair takes place here.

8
Parque García Sanabria

🏠 C/ Méndez Núñez, s/n
📞 922 60 60 99

Established in the 1920s, this attractive and peaceful park was named after the mayor of Santa Cruz. The park is full of lush tropical plants and has a wonderful collection of trees. It has since been improved by the addition of a fountain and modern sculptures. Besides being a good place to cool off, the park provides a brief lesson in Tenerife's history. Three benches depict the arrival of the conquistadors, the daily life of the Guanches and their defeat at the second Battle of Acentejo.

← One of the original stone benches, a highlight of Plaza del 25 de Julio

Did You Know?

The Swiss clock with flowers in Parque García Sanabria was a gift from the Danish consul in 1958.

9
Plaza del 25 de Julio

The 25th of July Plaza is a green oasis at the centre of the crowded, buzzing city. Its charm is enhanced by the central fountains and landscaped areas of trees and shrubs. The place, popular with the inhabitants of Santa Cruz, has a circle of original benches made of stone imported from Seville. Note the backrests of benches decorated with ceramic tiles featuring old advertisements.

10
Plaza de la Candelaria

Laid out in 1701 and adjoining the Plaza de España on the west, the Plaza de Candelaria is a popular local meeting place and promenade. Its official name is Plaza de la Constitución. The monument standing at its centre – El Triunfo de la Candelaria – depicts the patron saint of the island. Carved in white Carrara marble and unveiled in 1787, it is the work of the Italian master Antonio Canova. Another landmark on the square is the Palacio de Carta (1742). It now contains a branch of the Banco Español de Crédito. It is worth seeking out for its fine example of a traditional Canarian patio.

GREAT VIEW
Opera House

Head to the rooftop bar of AC Hotel Tenerife *(Calle Candelaria 31),* just off pretty Plaza de la Candelaria, for views of the gorgeous Calatrava-designed Opera House and the harbour.

← The Auditorio de Tenerife, home to the Symphony Orchestra of Tenerife

②
PARQUE NACIONAL DE ANAGA

ⓘ **Centro de Visitantes, Cruz del Carmen; 922 633 576**

A picturesque range of volcanic peaks, Parque Nacional de Anaga is a hiker's paradise. Narrow tracks lead through craggy, hard-to-reach valleys, and wind among steep rock faces and dense forests.

The Parque Nacional de Anaga is a stunning national park, home to a lush and verdant landscape thanks to its cool, wet climate. The evergreen vegetation of this region, including laurel and juniper trees, and heather, ferns and herbs, gives the air its spicy scent.

The main highlights of the park are the impressive paths for hiking and cycling; these can be challenging, with many of them narrowing as they lead through forested valleys and volcanic peaks. The effort is worth the reward, though: stunning coastal views and diverse wildlife, especially through the moss-overed Túnel de las Hadas, await. Climbers get their kicks here, too, especially on the epic Roque Negro, with a peak over 730 m (2,390 ft) high. For those seeking the beach, there's the park's picturesque Playa de las Teresitas for sunbathing or paddle surfing.

Punta del Hidalgo

Tenejías
811 m (2,660 ft)

Bajamar

Las Montañas

Casa del Río

Tejina

Túnel de las Hadas

Tegueste

Las Mercedes

*Known as the gate to the Anaga Mountains, **the road to La Laguna** runs from Mirador Pico del Inglés, through the plateau of Las Mercedes.*

0 kilometres   2

0 miles   2

N ↑

↑ Hiking in the laurel forest of Anaga, a UNESCO biosphere reserve

💬 INSIDER TIP
Barranco de las Huertas

This three-hour hike ends at a spectacular 200-m- (660-ft-) high waterfall. Only 40 people are allowed in per hour, so you must book ahead *(www. barrancodelinfierno.es).*

Tall, rugged cliffs, running west of Taganana, create picturesque nooks and inlets. They are best admired from a boat.

The road leading from the El Bailadero Pass to **Chinobre** is where, according to folk legend, witches used to hold their sabbaths.

The bay and the rocky beach at **Roque de las Bodegas** are popular with surfers.

From Chamorga, one of the loveliest villages on Tenerife, a steep path 2 km (1 mile) long runs to the **Anaga lighthouse**.

The enchanting village of **Taganana** lies at the foot of the mountains, amid palm trees.

*Atlantic
Ocean*

Faro de Anaga
Roque Bermejo

El Draguillo

Benijo
Chamorga

TF134
Almaciga

Taganana

Chinobre
910 m (2,985 ft)

TF123

El Bailadero

TF12

Mirador Pico
del Inglés

TF12

Igueste de
San Andrés
Punta de
Antequera

El Penico de
Valle Marcos
275 m (902 ft)

The locals of **Igueste de San Andrés** grow mangoes, avocados and bananas in plantations that stretch to the ocean.

San Andrés

Playa de las Teresitas

The sand on **Playa de las Teresitas** was imported from the Sahara.

Santa Cruz
de Tenerife

The former fishing village of **San Andrés** is now a resort. It is justly famous for its great selection of seafood restaurants.

The road from San Andrés to El Bailadero runs along the bottom of the **Barranco de las Huertas** ravine.

The capital of Tenerife, **Santa Cruz de Tenerife** (p130) is the start of the two motorways – del Norte and del Sur.

→

A winding mountain road in the scenic Parque Nacional de Anaga

3

LA OROTAVA

C/Calvario 4

The town of La Orotava first belonged to Taoro, the richest of the Guanche kingdoms on Tenerife. After the Spanish conquest, settlers from Andalusia populated the Orotava valley and built the first churches and residences in the 16th century. Take in their wooden decorations among La Orortava's historic streets, which make it one of the most scenic towns of the islands.

① Plaza del Ayuntamiento

During Corpus Christi, this pleasant square, which is situated at the very heart of the old town and towered over by its Neo-Classical town hall, becomes the focus of religious celebrations. At this time, the paving stones of the tree-lined square are covered with unusual, colourful "carpets", created from volcanic ash, soil and sand. It's easy to take home images of these fleeting works of art: they're recorded on colourful postcards that can be found on sale throughout the town all year round.

② Palacio Municipal

Plaza del Ayuntamiento, s/n laorotava.es

The town's administration centre is the *ayuntamiento* – the town hall, built in 1871–91 in a late Neo-Classical style with a modest façade virtually free of decoration. Its vault is painted with the heraldic arms of other towns on Tenerife, and with wall carvings depicting allegorical figures, which represent agriculture, history, morality and the law. Its patio once featured the oldest and largest dragon tree in the islands, which was destroyed during a storm in 1868.

③ Calle Carrera Escultor Estévez

La Orotava is one of the best-preserved old towns on Tenerife. Among its defining features is the chain of streets, including Calle Doctor Domingo González García, Calle San Francisco and Calle Carrera Escultor Estévez, which run in a semi-circle through the old part of the town. Lined with houses built mostly in the second half of the 19th century, the streets wind up the hill towards the Plaza del Ayuntamiento. The tourist office at Calle Carrera Escultor Estévez 2 can supply free town maps indicating the must-see sights along this street. One interesting stopping-off point is El Pueblo Guanche (*C/Carrera 7*), an ethnographic museum in a renovated townhouse. The museum has a shop selling handicrafts and food products and also a restaurant.

④ Hijuela del Botánico

C/Tomás Pérez
9am–2pm daily

La Orotava's charming botanical garden was established in 1923 using shoots and cuttings taken from the Jardín Botánico in Puerto de la Cruz (*p145*), which is famous throughout the Canary Islands. This process gave the garden its name, Hijuela del Botánico, meaning "daughter of the botanical garden". Today, this relatively small but stunning garden

---

CORPUS CHRISTI

Apart from the widely observed feast day of Epiphany, Corpus Christi is the most celebrated religious festival in the Canary Islands. In Tenerife, extravagant festivities are held in La Orotava and La Laguna, which try to outdo each other in the splendour of the occasion. The streets are lined with floral decorations, and the Plaza del Ayuntamiento is adorned with stunning pictures and temporary decorative floor designs made of volcanic sands, which can take several months to prepare. The remarkable size of the carpets has been recognized by the Guinness World Records.

↑ Red poinsettias lining the cobbled Calle San Francisco

is blooming and features many species of tropical and subtropical plant.

Rodríguez – who together produced this fine example of Canary Baroque architecture. The building takes much of its inspiration from the sacral structures of Latin America. In 1948, the iconic church was listed as a national monument.

> GREAT VIEW
> **Villa Arriba**
>
> This village, once a working class neighbourhood, has some astounding views of La Orotava.

⑤
Iglesia de la Concepción

📍 Plaza Casañas 🕐 Daily

The Iglesia de la Concepción, or Church of the Immaculate Conception, located in Plaza Casañas has a truly unique atmosphere. Its magnificent interior, with wooden sculptures by several local artists, including Fernando Estévez and José Luján Pérez, is enhanced by recordings of Mozart's music, which are played here almost all day long.

The original church, built in the 16th century, was destroyed by earthquakes in 1704 and 1705. The present triple-naved church is the result of restoration work carried out between 1768 and 1788 by two architects – Diego Nicolás and Ventura

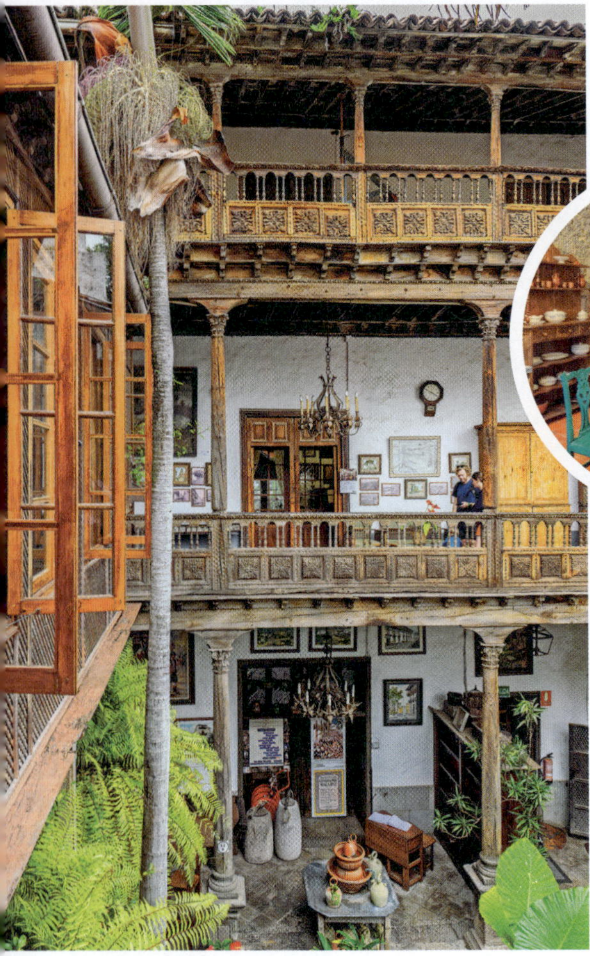

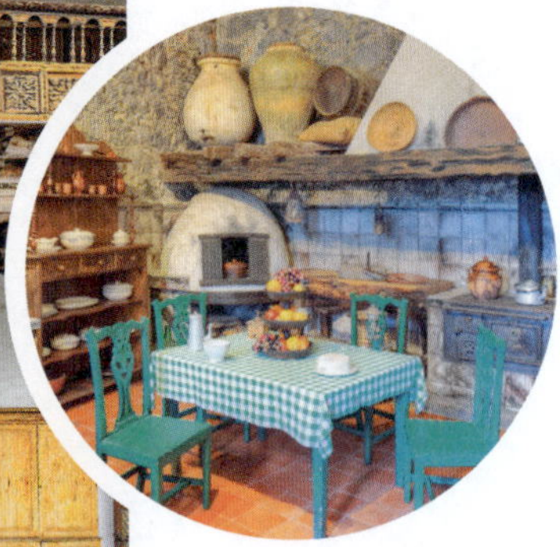

←

The ornate balconies of Casa de los Balcones, and *(inset)* the traditional kitchen of the building

6

Casa de los Balcones

C/San Francisco 3
8:30am–7pm daily (from 9am Sun)
casa-balcones.com

The striking three-storey "House of Balconies", also known as the Casa de Fonseca, is a major landmark of La Orotava. Its light-coloured façade is adorned with a heavy, carved door, smart windows and long teak balconies. The palm-shaded patio, brimming over with greenery, is surrounded by the first- and second-floor galleries, which rest on slender wooden columns. The house was built in 1632–70 by skilled specialist craftspeople. The first floor is open to the public and can be accessed through a narrow, wooden spiral staircase. Various rooms, including some of the living quarters and kitchen, can be explored. There is also has a small museum of Canary art and handicrafts. Here, visitors can view and buy a wide range of local handcrafted products, including embroidery, lace, pottery, regional costumes and other souvenirs. Don't miss the miniature balconies of La Orotava. Souvenirs can also be bought from the website of the Casa de los Balcones.

7

Iglesia San Francisco

C/San Francisco
Interior

The church of San Francisco, with its Baroque portal and rather plain interior, is located in the attractive palm-shaded Plaza de San Francisco. Next to

STAY

Orotava Casa Antigua Patrimonio Nacional

This 18th-century house has wooden balconies, a sun terrace and airy apartments, as well as an on-site restaurant.

Calle Tomás Zerolo 22, La Orotava

€€€

the church is the historic Hospital de la Santísima Trinidad (Hospital of the Holy Trinity), which has occupied the 18th-century Convento de San Lorenzo since 1884. The church now serves as the hospital chapel. Note the revolving drum on the door, where foundling babies were placed to be cared for by the nuns in the church.

 8

Gofio Mills

📍 C/Doctor Domingo González García

In the south, Calle San Francisco becomes Calle Doctor Domingo González García, a charming street of 17th- and 18th-century mills. These mills once produced *gofio* (a roasted mixture of wheat, maize or barley), and Gofio Mills is one of the last remaining ones to still be in use. Here, visitors can witness the entire process of flour production, as well as buy the end product. Inside the mill, there is a room featuring a display that sheds light on the flour production process as it once was prior to the introduction of electrical machinery.

→

Musical instruments at the Convento de Santo Domingo's museum, Calle Tomás Zerolo

 9

Plaza de la Constitución

Lined with bars and cafes, this is a great place to sit down and admire La Orotava as it comes to life in the evening. The plaza, a relic of the old town's merchant past, has a tree-lined terrace offering fine views over the buildings below. The multi-coloured roof tiles and slender church towers combine to produce a memorable panorama of the town and valley that is reminiscent of Florence.

 10

Calle Tomás Zerolo

Almost every street or alley in La Orotava offers some historic interest. Calle Tomás Zerolo, which passes through the lower part of the old town, is no exception. It features the Convento de Santo Domingo, which has a small museum of Latin American handicrafts, and opposite it stands the Casa Torrehermosa, a colonial-style house built in the 17th century for the Hermosa family. Today this residence houses the Empresa Insular de Artesanía, a small workshop and museum devoted to local handicrafts.

 11

Iglesia de San Agustín

The north side of the Plaza de la Constitución is occupied by the church and abbey of St Augustine. Dating from the 17th century, this building features a beautiful façade with a Renaissance-Baroque portal. The church has many fine historic remains and a panelled ceiling, which was renovated between 2009 and 2011. The former abbey was once a music school, then an office and is now the Casa de la Cultura.

> The Plaza de la Constitución, a relic of the old town's merchant past, has a tree-lined terrace offering fine views over the buildings below.

EAT

Liceo de Taoro Bar Restaurante

Set in the elegant Liceo de Taoro social club, this spot focuses on classical interpretations of international dishes.

🅰 C/San Agustín 6 🕒 Mon 🌐 liceodetaoro.es

Restaurante y Tasca Tapias

A lovely, rustic restaurant, Tasca Tapias offers a lip-smacking array of traditional Canarian dishes and local wines. Try the roasted duck.

🅰 Avda de Canarias 6 🕒 7:30am–midnight daily 🌐 restaurantetapias tenerife.es

---

Bar Parada Cerveceria

Enjoy delicious food with an excellent selection of wine and beer at this historic bar, with tables on the Plaza de la Constitución.

🅰 C/San Agustín 3 🌐 barparada.net

Dilecto Gastrobar

Fresh ingredients are used to prepare creative dishes at this popular fusion restaurant. Don't miss the goat meat tacos.

🅰 Plaza V Centenario 📞 922 153 744 🕒 Mon

Casa del Turista

🅰 C/San Francisco 4 📞 922 330 629 🕒 9am–7pm Mon–Fri, 8:30am–5pm Sat

Standing on the opposite side of the road to the striking Casa de los Balcones is the Casa del Turista, the former Convento Molina. This is a magnificent Canarian town house, which once belonged to a wealthy family. It was known collectively (with the 17th-century Casa Mesa and the Casa de los Lercaro) as the Doce Casas or "twelve houses". The house is built in a style similar to that of Casa de los Balcones, but is older, dating from 1509. It also offers visitors the chance to view and purchase local handicrafts.

Although the building itself is well worth a visit, the prize exhibit here is a religious scene made from coloured volcanic sand, which is on display throughout the year. This type of decoration, for which the town is famous, is usually only made during Corpus Christi. Make a detour up to the terraces at the back of the house for a fine view over the gorgeous Orotava valley.

Jardín Victoria

🅰 Plaza de la Constitución 🕒 8am–6pm daily

Bordering the grand historic building of the Liceo de Taoro school is the 19th-century Jardín Victoria, which is full of flowers and palm trees, arranged on terraces along a shallow ravine with a stream running at the bottom. The main feature of this garden is the mausoleum of Diego Ponte del Castillo, made of Carrara marble.

Museo de Cerámica-Casa de Tafuriaste

🅰 C/León 3 📞 922 333 396 🕒 10am–6pm Mon–Sat, 10am–2pm Sun

The island's passion for ceramics reached its peak before the advent of the European conquerors, and remains alive to this day, particularly among the local population of La Orotava. The traditional designs, which are based on old Guanche forms, are popular with many tourists, as are items in a more modern style.

The picturesque Jardín Victoria and the Liceo de Taoro club

balconies resting on wooden columns. These rooms are occupied by the Museo de Artesanía Iberoamericana, which opened in 1991. This ethnographic museum has an interesting exhibition of handicrafts from Spain and Latin America. The collection includes traditional musical instruments (look out for the Canarian *timple*, a kind of ukulele), pottery, textiles, wickerwork and some fine locally produced furniture.

 ⑯

Iglesia San Juan Bautista

📍 C/San Juan Bautista

The single-nave church of St John the Baptist was built in the 18th century. Its simple and modest façade, with a monumental belfry, does nothing to hint at the magnificence of its interior. Thanks to the beautiful *artesonado* – the wooden coffered ceiling – and the opulent interior decorations featuring sculptures by Luján Peréz and Fernando Estévez, the church is regarded as one of the most precious historic sites in La Orotava. The striking altars deserve special attention. In front of the church is a bust of the Venezuelan President, Rómulo Betancourt (1908–81).

 HIDDEN GEM
Lace-Making Workshop

Book a workshop at La Ranilla Espacio Artesano in Puerto de la Cruz (*www.laranilla.org*) to try lace-making. The one-day workshops also include crafts such as traditional macrame and weaving.

La Orotava's Museo de Cerámica was founded to cater for this interest. It is housed in the magnificent Casa de Tafuriaste – a much-restored 17th-century Canary town house, which is about 2 km (1 mile) west of La Orotava's old town on the La Luz–Las Candias road. The collection includes nearly 1,000 vessels from the Canary Islands and Spain. On the ground floor is a pottery workshop, where visitors can see demonstrations of how modern jugs and bowls are made. The museum's first floor has a fine display of antique ceramics. There is also a gift shop, which sells some interesting souvenirs.

 ⑮

Ex-Convento Santo Domingo

📍 C/Tomás Zerolo 34

On the outskirts of La Orotava's old town stands a 17th- to 18th-century Dominican convent, which has a triple-naved church featuring a magnificent polychromatic wooden coffered ceiling. The remaining rooms of the former convent are arranged around a patio with lovely

Iglesia San Juan Bautista's austere façade, belying its ornate interior

The bustling seaside promenade of Calle de San Telmo

4

PUERTO DE LA CRUZ

 Puerto Viejo 13 ; www.puertodelacruz.es

With its many shops, restaurants and nightclubs, as well as historic sites and a lagoon, this old port town is a popular resort. Puerto de la Cruz was once the principal port of the island and, by the late 19th century, it became a favourite destination for upmarket visitors. Today, over 100,000 visitors a year make their way here.

①

Iglesia de Nuestra Señora de la Peña de Francia

 Plaza la Iglesia

The magnificent triple-naved cathedral was built in 1684–97. Its tall tower was added in the late 19th century. In the dark interior of the church the eye is drawn to Baroque sculptures – the work of the local artist Fernando Estévez and José Luján Pérez, a well-known island artist. No less precious are the paintings by Luís de la Cruz. The cathedral's organ was brought from London in 1814. A bust of Agustín de Betancourt (1758–1824), founder of the Engineering College in Madrid, stands in front of the church.

②

Plaza de Europa

Hugging the picturesque shoreline of Puerto de la Cruz, this large square was laid out in 1992, but is based on 18th- and 19th-century European-style town planning. Its features include the town hall and the Casa de Miranda, an old townhouse, which now accommodates a restaurant specializing in local fare.

③

Calle Quintana

This charming street leads to Punta del Viento, a terrace poised on the edge of the ocean and affording a fine view over the rocky coast and Lago Martiánez. Branching off eastwards is the Calle de San Telmo, a seaside promenade with stone seats and numerous bars. The Monopol Hotel – one of the oldest hotels in Puerto de la Cruz – stands in Calle Quintana.

CANARIAN BANANAS

One of the most famous exports from the Canary islands are bananas. They were first exported in the late 19th century, and have remained popular ever since. From Puerto de la Cruz, head to bananaECOplantation to learn more about bananas cultivated in Tenerife and sample some tasty banana liquor, as well as the fruit itself, and enjoy marvellous views.

Casa de la Real Aduana

📍 C/de las Lonjas
📞 922 378 103 🕐 9am–8pm Mon–Fri, 9am–5pm Sat & Sun

This house was built in 1620 for Juan Antonio Lutzardo de Franchy and is the oldest in town. After the destruction of Garachico, it became the seat of the governor, and from 1706 to 1833 served as the customs house. The building was restored in the 1970s and now houses the Museum of Contemporary Art Eduardo Westerdahl and a shop selling local crafts. The tourist information office is here too.

Puerto Pesquero

The history of this picturesque fishing harbour, situated on a small, stony beach, goes back to the 18th century, when the town was the main exporter of the island's agricultural produce. Today you can buy freshly caught fish direct from the fishers.

Iglesia de San Francisco

📍 C/San Juan

The church of St Francis is built around the 16th-century Ermita de San Juan. One of the oldest buildings in Puerto de la Cruz, it is decorated with sculptures and paintings, from the 16th century up to modern times. Now an ecumenical church, it holds services for all Christian denominations.

Must See

💬 INSIDER TIP
Mueca Art Festival

For a dose of culture, visit in May and catch the annual Mueca Art Festival. The streets become a hotspot for live music, street performances, dance shows and street art.

↑ Iglesia de San Francisco, featuring three naves and a finely carved wooden ceiling

DRINK

The Molly Malone

This quirky Irish pub serves a good choice of beer, cider, wine, whiskey and other spirits every night of the week. Live music performances and sports screenings are regularly hosted here.

🏠 C/Las Lonjas 4

Bodega Mario

An unassuming bar with friendly staff, Bodega Mario is popular with both locals and tourists for its wide range of tasty cocktails. The nightly karaoke is a major draw, and there are regular live music nights, too.

🏠 C/Corales
🕐 Mon & Tue

Aquanama Cocktail Bar

Come to Aquanama for the stunning ocean views from its popular waterside bar; stay for the lively atmosphere, delicious bar snacks and lavish drinks served with a smile.

🏠 Playa San Telmo

La Fragata

Located just a few steps from Playa del Muelle, La Fragata is a perfect spot for lunch and an even better place for an early evening tipple. Grab a seat on the terrace and try one of the many cocktails on offer here while soaking up the ocean breeze.

🏠 C/de la Marina 5

→

The leisure park of Lago Martiánez, and *(inset)* wading in the pool around its volcanic fountain

Lago Martiánez

🏠 Playa Martiánez
🕐 10am–5pm daily, 10am–3pm 24 & 31 Dec 🕐 May
🌐 lagomartianez.es

This artificial lagoon, designed by César Manrique, was built in 1969. Conjuring up a sub-tropical paradise, it consists of a complex of seawater swimming pools and fountains, which contrast with the surrounding lava field. There is also an ultrasmart casino here.

Museo Arqueológico

🏠 C/del Lomo, 9A 📞 922 371 465 🕐 9am–3pm Mon–Fri

Opened in 1991, this small museum contains displays that showcase the vibrant Indigenous history and cultural heritage of the Canary Islands. The permanent exhibits include a collection of Guanche objects and the mummified remains of the island's original inhabitants. The museum also hosts temporary archaeological exhibitions, and puts on educational, cultural and social action programmes.

⑨

Plaza del Charco de los Camerones

Many of the town's most historic buildings can be found in the cosmopolitan Plaza del Charco, a pretty square shaded by palm and laurel trees, which were imported from Cuba. The centre of the square is occupied by a huge yam plant within a fountain. Set in the heart of the city, the plaza makes for a pleasant place to sit and watch the world go by, particularly on Sundays, when locals enjoy leisurely strolls.

> **Many of the town's most historic buildings can be found in the cosmopolitan Plaza del Charco, a square shaded by palm and laurel trees, which were imported from Cuba.**

Jardín Botánico

📍 C/Retama, 2 📞 922 383 572 🕐 9am–6pm daily 🚫 1 Jan, Good Fri, 25 Dec

The local botanical garden is one of the oldest in the world. It was established in 1788 at the request of Carlos III

↑ Admiring a huge ficus tree in Jardín Botánico

of Spain, by Alonso de Nava y Grimón. Set in the north of Tenerife, it has a pleasant, tropical climate. Carlos III had hoped that rare and non-native plants arriving from Asia and America would find the climate of the garden favourable and adapt to it before being brought to the mainland.

Today, the lush garden is crammed with over 1,000 species of plant and tree from the Canary Islands, as well as flora from all over the world. In addition, the Jardín Botánico carries out international seed exchanges and maintains an extensive herbarium. There are also research programs on the flora and vegetation of the Canary Islands and on the conservation of endemic species.

Parque Taoro

🏠 Carretera Taoro

This park is a good place to escape the bustle of town. Here you'll find cascades, gurgling waterfalls, streams crossed with charming

Did You Know?

Spain's first coffee trees were planted in the Jardín Botanico in 1788.

bridges, small ponds and several viewing terraces. At the centre of the park lies the Jardín Risco Bello Acuático, a tropical water garden that is home to varieties of fish, as well as ducks and swans.

Castillo de San Felipe

 C/Luis Lavaggi 10

This small 17th-century fort once guarded the harbour entrance against attacks from pirates and the ships of Spain's two maritime rivals: France and England. Now the fort, situated in the western part of town, often serves as a venue for temporary exhibitions. To the west of the fort are the striking black sands of Playa Jardín, the town's longest beach.

5

PARQUE NACIONAL DEL TEIDE

📷 🕘 9am–4pm daily 🚫 1 Jan, 25 Dec ℹ️ Oficina del Parque Nacional, C/ Emilio Calzadilla, 5–4a, Santa Cruz de Tenerife; www.webtenerife.com

Some three million years ago, volcanic subsidence left behind the remarkable 16-km (10-mile) Las Cañadas depression with the island's emblematic volcano, Teide, standing 3,718 m (12,198 ft) high at its centre. Since 1954, the area has become one of Spain's largest national parks.

A UNESCO World Heritage Site since 2007, the Parque Nacional del Teide is ripe for exploration. Marked paths guide visitors through the best of its wilderness of ash beds, lava streams and mineral tinted rocks.

Exploring the Park

As you head inside the park, you'll come across the observatory near the entrance. It's used primarily for solar observation and houses state-of-the-art equipment, such as the THEMIS solar telescope, drawing space enthusiasts from all around the world. Hiking up to Pico del Teide itself will require a permit, but is an unforgettable experience. Beyond this, Los Roques de García has uniquely shaped rocks rising around 150 m (490 ft) above the crater floor. Further east are Las Cañadas, seven sandy plateaux that came into being after ancient craters collapsed.

A beautiful mountain lodge, the Parador de Cañadas del Teide, has an excellent café for a refreshment while hiking here. With a central location, it makes for an ideal base for exploring the surreal and spectacular landscape of the national park.

💬 INSIDER TIP
Observatory Tour

To learn about the stars, go on a tour of the Teide Observatory. This starts with a visit to the world's largest solar observatory and ends with stargazing from the cable car base.

PICO DEL TEIDE

At 3,718 m (12,198 ft), Pico del Teide is the highest mountain in Spain, and the snow-capped peak is often visible from across Tenerife. La Fortaleza viewing platform in the park, reached by a footpath from the top cable-car station, affords views of the entire archipelago. A special permit is required if you are ascending the summit of Pico del Teide from the Rambleta mountain station *(reservas parquesnacionales.es)*. Ascending to the viewpoints at La Fortaleza and Pico Viejo does not require a permit.

The Observatorio del Teide crowning one of the park's peaks ↑

→ Alfresco dining at the scenic Parador de Cañadas del Teide café

↑ Hiking among the scenic landscapes along one of the park's many trails

Bracamonte, also known as Casa de los Capitanes, and the 18th-century Casa Mesa.

Casa Lercaro, built in 1593 by Genoese merchants, now houses the **Museo de Historia y Antropología de Tenerife**. Opened in 1993, it chronicles the history of Tenerife from the times of the Spanish conquest through to the 20th century. The collection includes old documents, tools and 16th-century paintings. Among the collection's highlights are some of the oldest maps of the archipelago.

Nearby is another striking building, the Palacio Episcopal. The bishop's palace features a beautiful stone façade dating from 1681. Of equal interest are some 19th-century buildings, such as the Casino de la Laguna (1899), whose creators drew on French designs, and the Ayuntamiento, the town hall of 1829 that houses the banner under which de Lugo fought during his conquest of Tenerife.

The present town hall, with its interior frescoes illustrating the island's history, stands in the Plaza de Adelantado. The adjacent church of San Miguel (1507) was founded by de Lugo himself. Also in the tree-shaded square is the Convento de Santa Catalina de Siena, with its original cloisters, and the Palacio de Nava – an example of Spanish colonial architecture. Behind the square is a large market hall, where fruit, cheese and flowers are sold.

To the east of the Plaza de Adelantado stands the Cathedral (1904–15). The building features a twin-towered façade dating from 1825. The main feature of the interior is the magnificent retable at the back of the altar, dating from the first half of the 18th century. Behind the

EXPERIENCE MORE

⑥
La Laguna

🚌 ℹ️ **Casa Alvarado Bracamonte, C/La Carrera 7; 922 631 194**

Officially named Ciudad de San Cristóbal de la Laguna, La Laguna is Tenerife's second-largest city and a UNESCO World Heritage Site. Situated in the middle of the fertile valley of Aguere, it owes its name to the lagoon on whose shores it stood, and which was drained in 1837.

Founded in 1496 by the conquistador Alonso Fernández de Lugo, the town was the original residence of the Adelantados – the island's military governors. Until 1723, La Laguna was capital of the island, but moving the capital to Santa Cruz has not reduced the city's importance.

La Laguna is a university city, and its academic traditions date back to the

> 💬 INSIDER TIP
> ### La Romería de San Benito Abad
>
> This agricultural thanksgiving fiesta is celebrated with song and dance in San Cristobal de La Laguna every July. It dates from a drought in 1532, and ends with prayers to St Benedict.

18th century. The University of La Laguna, still in existence, opened its doors for the first time in 1817. Since 1818, the city has been a bishopric.

The old town retains its traditional form with a network of narrow streets and alleys following a chequerboard pattern. The district also features several noteworthy houses including Casa del Corregidor and Casa de la Alhondiga (both dating from the 16th century), the 17th-century Casa Alvarado

Officially named Ciudad de San Cristóbal de la Laguna, La Laguna is Tenerife's second-largest city and a UNESCO World Heritage Site.

main altar stands the simple tomb of Alonso de Lugo.

Standing in the Plaza de la Concepción is the Iglesia de Nuestra Señora de la Concepción (1502) – an example of the architectural style dating from the time of the conquest. This triple-naved Gothic-Renaissance church has a magnificent wooden vault. Each year, in August, thousands of pilgrims flock to the Santuario del Cristo – a small church at the northern end of La Laguna's old quarter – to pay homage to a statue of Christ carved in the late 15th century. This Gothic sculpture by an unknown artist was brought to Tenerife in 1520, by Alonso de Lugo.

Museo de Historia y Antropología de Tenerife

C/San Agustín 22
9am–7pm Mon–Sat, 10am–5pm Sun 1 & 6 Jan, Shrove Tue, 24, 25 & 31 Dec museosdetenerife.org

7

Loro Parque

Avda Loro Parque s/n, Puerto de la Cruz
9:30am–5:30pm daily
loroparque.com

From the day it opened in 1972, this tropical plant complex has been hugely popular and has established itself as a firm favourite with tourists, despite recent controversy over the welfare of its orcas. It has now launched more than 240 conservation and research projects. The park is home to many species of bird, mammal and fish from around the world. Attractions include an impressive free flight aviary, where you can watch birds in their natural habitat, the children's playground "Kinderlandia," and the park's beautiful gardens of orchids and dragon trees. The entrance to the park also passes a reconstructed traditional Thai village.

Illustration of
↓ Loro Parque's extensive complex

The Penguin House simulates Antarctic living conditions..

The Tower of Fish is an illuminated glass cylinder housing vibrant fish.

Gorilla enclosure

Entrance

Jaguars are housed in a reconstructed volcanic landscape.

The aquarium for sharks has a glass-tunnel walkway.

Flamingo enclosure.

A golden pheasant (Chrysolophus pictus) in the Loro Parque

8

Tacoronte

A coastal village, set 450 m (1,476 ft) above sea level, Tacoronte dates back to the Guanche times. The town and its environs are famous for their excellent wines. When in the area, you should visit one of the many wineries to sample the fine local vintages, known as Tacoronte-Acentejo.

Tacoronte is notable for its two churches. The Iglesia del Cristo de los Dolores features a revered 17th-century statue of Christ, which during the harvest festival, is carried through the streets of the town. Also noteworthy are the Baroque woodcarvings decorating the interior. The 17th-century Iglesia de Santa Catalina has a fine wooden vault and rich furnishings.

Also famed for its wine, El Sauzal is a short way to the south. Its main attraction is La Casa del Vino La Baranda – a complex in a renovated country house, comprising a wine museum, wine-tasting

---

hall, bar and store, as well as an excellent restaurant with views of Mount Teide.

9

Bajamar

The inhabitants of Bajamar once made their living from fishing and cultivating sugar cane. It is now popular as a resort and is a well-known tourist centre for Tenerife's northern coast. The coastal cliffs and the soaring peaks of Monte de las Mercedes provide a picturesque backdrop for the numerous hotels and bungalows. The main road is lined with restaurants and cafés. Visitors who like bathing will enjoy the large complex of salt-water swimming pools.

About 2.5 km (2 miles) to the northeast is Punta del Hidalgo, a headland offering a fine view of the rocky coast and banana plantations. Strong winds create ideal conditions for windsurfing, though the currents make it dangerous for novices. Punta del Hidalgo is a starting point for a marked hiking trail to the historic cave dwellings at Chinamada.

10

Icod de los Vinos

 C/San Sebastián, 6; 922 812 123

As its name suggests, this small town is in the heart of a fertile wine-growing region. However, most tourists visit Icod to see the legendary symbol of the islands – the Drago Milenario. Reputed to be over 1,000 years old, this dragon tree is probably half

---

that age. The biggest specimen in the archipelago, it is best seen from the Plaza de la Iglesia.

At **Mariposario del Drago**, close to the dragon tree, you can learn about the life cycle of butterflies. Many tropical butterflies flutter freely here, among lush jungle vegetation and water gardens.

Another highlight, the triple-naved church of San Marcos was built in the 15th and 16th centuries. Its interior features a beautiful coffered ceiling and a silver high altar. Other interesting items include the painting of Santa Ana, attributed to Bartolomé Murillo, and a fine marble baptismal font (1696).

One of the chapels houses the **Museo de Arte Sacro**. The jewel of its collection is an enormous filigree silver cross. Made in Cuba in 1663–8, by Jerónimo de Espellosa, it is 2.45 m (8 ft) high. Weighing

→

Exploring Mariposario del Drago, and *(inset)* a resident Tree Nymph butterfly

---

EAT

Casa del Drago
This stunning garden terrace café overlooks the Drago and serves tapas, salads and juices.

C/Arcipreste Ossuna 3, Icod de los Vinos
casadeldrago.es

€€€

La Parada - Casa de Comida
A traditional restaurant serving regional fare.

Rbla Perez del Cristo 2, Icod de los Vinos
922 811 491

€€€

48.3 kg (106 lb), this gleaming filigree silver cross is thought to be the largest ever made.

Mariposario del Drago
 Avda de Canarias, s/n ⏰ 10am–8pm daily 🌐 mariposario.com

Museo de Arte Sacro
🏛 Iglesia de San Marco 📞 922 810 695 ⏰ 10:30am–1:30pm & 4–6:30pm daily

---

 ⑪

Garachico

Established in the 16th century by Genoese merchants, Garachico, on the north coast of Tenerife, is a jewel of a town, with historic buildings and traditional-style houses.

Garachico was once the most important port on the island (later developing into a centre of sugar production) until the eruption of the Volcán Negro in 1706 put an end to its prosperity. Lava buried whole districts and most of the harbour, with only a handful of houses escaping destruction, together with the Castillo de San Miguel (1577). The castle currently houses the Heritage Information Centre and guards Garachico Bay. The only portion of the former Santa Ana church to escape is the 16th-century façade. The restored interior has a Baroque font and a crucifix attributed to Martín de Andújar.

Another relic of the town's former glory includes the partially restored Palacio de los Condes de la Gomera (Palace of the Counts of Gomera), which stands in the Plaza de la Libertad. There are also several former convents, including the 17th-century Santo Domingo, now a modern art **museum**, and the convent of San Francisco Nuestra Señora de los Ángeles. A section of this 18th-century convent is occupied by a

> 🔍 HIDDEN GEM
> ### El Caletón
> The incredible natural rock pools of El Caletón in Garachico were created from volcanic activity during the eruption in 1706. The crystal-clear pools offer a unique swimming experience, great views and areas to sunbathe.

↑ The gorgeous seaside town of Garachico with its traditional houses

modest museum, Casa de la Cultura. Also in the plaza is a monument to Simón Bolívar, liberator of South America.

Every winter, Garachico is battered by Atlantic gales. The huge waves are truly spectacular, especially when the water level drops to reveal the vast Roque de Garachico.

Museo de Arte Contemporáneo
🏛 Plaza de Santo Domingo 📞 922 830 000 ⏰ 9am–1pm & 4–7pm daily

↑ Taking in the impressive mountainside view from a terrace in Masca

The shady square is idyllic and has traditional Canarian houses with wooden balconies.

 Los Realejos

A sprawling town overlooked by the peak of the Tigaiga Mountain, Los Realejos played a crucial part in Tenerife's history. It was here that the last free chieftains of the Guanches surrendered to the Spanish invaders in 1496.

Crisscrossed with steep streets, Los Realejos consists of two parts: Realejo Bajo (the lower town) and Realejo Alto (the upper town). In the upper part stands the Iglesia de Santiago Apóstol (1498). The oldest church on the island, it has a Mudéjar (Spanish-Moorish) wooden vault. Meanwhile, over at the entrance to the town, from the direction of Puerto de la Cruz, stands El Castillo de los Realejos, built in 1862. This square structure, with four almost round towers at its corners, is set in a beautifully tended garden. Unlike other fortresses on the Canary Islands, built during the 16th and 17th centuries on the ocean coast for defence, it was never used for military purposes.

 Masca

Masca, located at an altitude of 600 m (1,970 ft), is a popular destination for day trips from many of the big resorts. Just above the small village is a terrace that offers an impressive outlook, especially at sunset, towards Mount Teide on one side, and the Atlantic on the other.

Masca was once a refuge for pirates and accessible only by mule. Even today, it can only be reached via a steep, winding road. The views as the road winds through the mountains are reason enough to visit.

The village itself is charming and consists of a handful of old, red-tiled, stone houses clinging to the sides of the gorge, and surrounded by lush palm trees. Roadside vendors sell prickly pears and oranges to passers-by.

Crops are grown in small fields on terraces, which descend towards the Barranco de Masca ravine. The villagers also keep bees that gather nectar from the surrounding flowering meadows.

The village is an excellent starting point for hikers. One of the best routes leads along the Masca ravine, to the seashore. A fit mountain walker should be able to get there and back again in under four hours. Take care, however, as the return hike is steep and fairly arduous.

Past the village, the road leads north through the Macizo de Teno massif, towards the coastal flatland. Some 12 km (7.5 miles) along the route is the scenic village of El Palmar. The nearby Montaña de Talavera has had chunks cut out of it to provide soil for the banana plantations.

Another 5.5 km (3.5 miles) further on is Buenavista, the island's westernmost village, which has a small fishing harbour and a pebble beach.

A short way eastwards in the midst of banana plantations, Los Silos is a quiet little town with a compact 19th-century layout. In the town centre is a typical tree-shaded square, with a coffee pavilion.

 Santiago del Teide

🚌 ℹ Avda Marítima, Playa de la Arena; 922 860 348

Should you visit Santiago del Teide in February, when the countless almond trees are in bloom with pink and

→
Pretty resort town of Puerto de Santiago on the coast of Tenerife

Did You Know?

The famously winding road to Masca uses laybys to allow vehicles to pass each other.

white blossom, you will see it at its loveliest. The small town is surrounded by vineyards and cornfields, and nestles among the foothills of the Teno massif. La Gomera can be seen in the distance.

The pride of the town is the Baroque parish church of San Fernando, which was built in the mid-16th century and stands at the end of the main street. Its asymmetric façade is adorned with a shaded wooden balcony. A tall belfry has been added at the northern end of the church. The small, Moorish-looking domes give the building its distinctive look.

Look out for the distinctive figure in front of one of the side altars: it represents Christ on horseback, wearing a black Spanish hat and carrying a sword.

Branching off from the southern approach road to the village is a path to Camino de la Virgen de Lourdes. The path, dedicated to the Virgin Mary of Lourdes and with a shrine and an ornamental bridge, leads along the slope of the mountain to a grotto decorated with flowers.

Los Gigantes and Puerto de Santiago

The huge cliffs, known as the Acantilados de los Gigantes ("Cliffs of the Giants"), form the ridge of the Teno massif. Some 10 km (6 miles) long, this steep cliff-face plunges 500 m (1,640 ft) into the ocean. The dark rocks are best seen by boat. Trips often leave from Puerto Deportivo and usually travel further north to include a wonderful view over the Barranco de Masca.

Beneath the cliffs, the town of Los Gigantes is a typical Canarian holiday resort, the biggest on the northwest coast of Tenerife, with apartment complexes stretching over the slopes. Its yachting marina has diving clubs and offers angling trips. The town itself, with its concentrated development, gives the impression of being overcrowded. Only narrow alleys separate small hotels and apartment blocks.

A seaside boulevard connects Los Gigantes with nearby Puerto de Santiago, which has long been a resort, although on a smaller scale. The main attraction here is the dark volcanic-sand beaches, including the most popular of them, Playa de la Arena, situated to the south. Most of the fishers here have traded in their rods and nets and take tourists out for boat trips instead.

INSIDER TIP
Boat Tour

Take a boat tour of the coastline, where you can marvel at the cliffs of Los Gigantes and spot dolphins and whales in their natural habitat. There are a variety of tour options, all leaving from Los Gigantes Port.

DRINK

Tramps

Located on the vibrant Veronica's Strip in Playa de la Américas, Tramps is a local institution and a favourite with townspeople and visitors alike. It is known for all-night dancing, upbeat music and great drinks.

🅰 **Centro Comercial Starco, Playa de la Américas** 🕙 **10pm–6am daily** 🆆 **trampstenerife.com**

PJ's Bar

A Tenerife staple since 2005, this spot is popular for its excellent and reasonably priced cocktails. This great spot also serves snacks during the day.

🅰 **Avda Rafael Puig Lluvina 24, Playa de la Américas** 📞 **670 735 636** 🕙 **10am–1:30am Tue–Sun**

STAY

Hotel Spa VillAlba

This retreat, perched at 1,500 m (5,000 ft) above sea level, is set in the heart of the Corona Forestal Nature Park. The rooms offer spectacular sea views. Visitors can also explore the surrounds via a range of hiking and cycling routes of varying difficulty levels.

🅰 **Camino San Roque, s/n, Vilaflor** 🆆 **hotelvillalba.com**

Playa de las Américas and Los Cristianos

🚌 🚕 **ℹ Avda Rafael Puig Llivina 19; 922 797 668**

You would not think so to look at it now but Los Cristianos was once a quiet fishing village. Today, it is a year-round provider of fun and sun with artificial beaches, sprawling hotel-apartments, and countless bars, clubs and souvenir shops. Many people embrace the noise and kitsch good humour of the place, and Los Cristianos is one of the most popular resorts in the archipelago. It extends into the virtually identical Playa de las Américas, which merges in turn with picturesque Costa Adeje just a little further up the coastline.

A lively promenade, running alongside the more crowded beaches and the harbour wall, is home to shops, restaurants and bars. In Las Américas the promenade turns into a tranquil palm-shaded boulevard several miles long, which runs above numerous sheltered beaches. The most exclusive among them is the Playa del Duque. Ferries and hydrofoils make regular trips from Los Cristianos' port to La Gomera and El Hierro.

A short way northeast is the green space of Parque Ecológico Las Águilas del Teide, which offers a choice of activities. Visitors can enjoy stunning displays of condors in flight, pick from a range of evening variety shows and even witness feeding time at a floodlit pool full of crocodiles. Venture some 7 km (4 miles) north, and enjoy a two-hour walk from the town of Adeje, to the Barranco del Infierno, a wild gorge with an impressive waterfall.

Siam Park

🅰 **TF-1, Costa Adeje** 🕙 **Summer: 10am–6pm daily; winter: 10am–5pm daily** 🆆 **siampark.net**

Enjoy an exhilarating wet and wild experience at

Tenerife's greatest water park. Owned by the same company that runs Loro Parque *(see p149)*, this theme park offers a wealth of attractions that are aimed at giving visitors a white-knuckle ride. The Tower of Power, The Dragon and The Volcano are among the most popular with thrill-seekers. There are some more relaxing options for less adventurous visitors, such as a visit to the park's Floating Market, a stroll on the bright white sand of Siam Beach or the Mai Thai River boat ride. As well as these, there are rides suitable for the whole family, with the Lost City water slide aimed at younger children. Don't miss the Wave Palace attraction, where visitors swim among the biggest artificial waves in the world, rising up to an astonishing 3 m (10 ft) high. Head to the website to book surfing sessions at the Wave Palace. There are also several restaurants and a shop.

↑ Nave and wooden ceiling of the Vilaflor's San Pedro, built in 1550

 18

Vilaflor

Set at an elevation of 1,400 m (4,600 ft), Vilaflor is the highest village in the Canaries. In the 19th century the village became famous for its intricate and finely made lacework. Not far from the picturesque village, which is surrounded by pine forests, is "Pino Gordo", a beautiful pine tree over 70 m (230 ft) tall. In the plaza at the top of the village is the 16th-century Iglesia de San Pedro, which has a statue of the church's patron saint.

Hikers can set out from Vilaflor on a well-marked footpath, Camino de Chasma, for the so-called Paisaje Lunar ("Lunar Landscape"). It is an incredible volcanic rock formation made of striking cones of sandstone weathered by erosion over time.

←

Gorgeous sun-kissed Playa las Vistas Beach in Los Cristianos

TENERIFE'S BEACHES

The beaches of Tenerife may not be as scenic as those of Fuerteventura, but they have their own charms, especially when it comes to watersports. There are numerous diving packages on offer to visitors, from courses aimed at beginners to expeditions into the depths of the ocean. Reliable winds make the place popular with windsurfers and conditions are also good for other water sports, from paragliding to water skiing.

The beaches of black and grey sand at Playa de las Americas are covered with light imported sand.

Los Cristianos *is one of the Canary Islands' most popular resorts, with three sand beaches close to its centre.*

| 0 kilometres | 2 |
| 0 miles | 2 |

N ↑

19

Candelaria

 7 Avenida de la Constitución, s/n; 922 032 230

Candelaria is famous for its religious sanctuary, the most important in the archipelago. Every August, pilgrims come to the Basílica de Nuestra Señora de Candelaria to pray to the Black Madonna – the Canary Islands' patron saint.

According to local legend, in 1390 two fishers from a Guanche tribe found a statue that had been washed up on the beach – probably a figurehead from a shipwreck. The tribe placed it in one of the coastal caves as an object of veneration, and there it remained until 1826, when it was swept away during a violent storm. The basilica itself was built on the site of an earlier 16th-century church in 1958. The present statue of the Madonna is the work of sculptor Fernando Estévez.

The basilica adjoins the 17th-century church of Santa Ana. Both churches stand along the Plaza de la Patrona de Canaria, a square that has nine bronze statues depicting the legendary Guanche rulers, known as the *Menceyes*.

←

Bronze statue of Guanche ruler Tegueste at the Plaza de la Patrona de Canaria

Did You Know?

The Parque Eólico de Granadilla in El Médano is expanding to supply electricity to nearly 16,000 homes.

20

El Médano

 7 Plaza de los Príncipes de España; 922 176 002

El Médano, a former fishing village, is now famous for its bay, fringed by long, sandy beaches. These stretch south to the Punta Roja, towered over by the Montaña Roja volcano (now a nature reserve). The strong winds (known as *alisios*) make the place very popular with windsurfers (international competitions are held here). The winds are also utilized in the Parque Eólico de Granadilla – a wind farm,

Steps leading to the rocky beach at Los Abrigos

Tenerife South Airport

Médano Beach

El Médano

La Tejita

La Mareta

Playa del Confital

Playa de la Tejita

Playa San Blas

Los Abrigos

argacho

osta del ilencio

Los Abrigos is a fishing village next to a quiet, rocky beach.

Playa de la Tejita is one of the island's most beautiful beaches.

Playa San Blas is situated near Los Abrigos. From here a road leads to Golf del Sur.

Playa del Confital, situated between Los Abrigos and El Médano, is great for water sports.

With strong and steady winds blowing from Africa, **Médano Beach** is a magnet for windsurfers.

Costa del Silencio, as its name suggests, is quieter than many resorts, though it is right next to the airport.

---

supplying electricity to over 3,000 homes.

Some 5 km (3 miles) to the northwest, is the Cueva del Hermano Pedro – a cave converted into a sanctuary and dedicated to Father Peter, the first Canarian saint (1626–67).

㉑

Güímar

The largest town in southeast Tenerife, Güímar is home to the 18th-century church of San Pedro Apóstol. The town is known for the pyramids, made from uncut stone found in the suburb of Chacona in the 1990s. They can be seen in the fascinating **Parque Etnográfico Pirámides de Güímar** museum.

Parque Etnográfico Pirámides de Güímar

🏠 C/Chacona, s/n 🕙 10am-6pm daily 🚫 1 Jan & 25 Dec
🌐 piramidesdeguimar.es

→ The stone pyramids and cacti at Parque Etnográfico Pirámides de Güímar

LA GOMERA

La Gomera was home to the Guanche people for many centuries before the time of Spanish colonization. During the 1488 Rebellion of Los Gomeros, the Castilian ruler of the island, Hernán Peraza the Younger, was killed by Indigenous people, which ultimately led the Castilian rulers to repress and fully conquer the island.

In 1492, navigator Christopher Columbus and his caravels stopped off in San Sebastián de la Gomera, the island's capital, on their way to the Americas. La Gomera has been sometimes referred to as "Isla Colombina" as a result ever since.

A smaller and more mountainous island, La Gomera did not see the same level of trade and tourism as its neighbouring islands in the years that followed. However, it has drawn tourists seeking peaceful, unspoiled nature since the 1960s. This interest was in large part thanks to the Parque Nacional de Garajonay, a huge UNESCO-protected park in the centre of the island. In 2012, some 20 per cent of the park tragically burned down in forest fires; it could take up to 30 years for the forest to return to its former glory.

LA GOMERA

Punta de los Roques

Los Órganos

Playa de
Vallehermoso

Guillama

Arguamul

TF712

Ville Abajo

Las Rosas

Tazo

VALLEHERMOSO ④

Roque Cano
650 m (2,133 ft)

GM1

Punta del Viento

CV16

Cruz de Tierno

La Pálmita

CV5

Alojera

Epina

Los Chapines

El Tión

Playa de Alojera

CV16

Macayo

Rosa de
las Piedras

Meriga

Banda de
las Rosas

Mirador de
Vallehermoso

Tejeleche
618 m (2,028 ft)

GM2

Quemado
1,136 m (3,727 ft)

Los Aceviños

CV5

PARQUE

Roque
de Mona
547 m (1,795 ft)

GM1

NACIONAL

Arure

Las Hayas

CV18

Montaña
de la Asomada
1,227 m (4,026 ft)

DE

GARAJONAY

Playa de
Heredia

Mirador
del Santo

CV18

La Laguna
Grande

①

Alto de Cherelepin
1,360 m (4,462 ft)

Lomo del Balo

EL
CERCADO ⑥

Garajonay
1,487 m (4,879 ft)

Chipude

GM1

CV17

Igualero

CV17

GM2

Playa del
Inglés

⑤

CV12

La Fortaleza
1,050 m (3,445 ft)

La Calera

VALLE GRAN REY

CV13

La Playa

Gerián

Imada

La Puntilla

CV7

Erquito

Lo del Gato

Vueltas

CV17

Agalán

CV11

Guarimiar

CV20

ALAJERÓ ⑦

Arguayoda

Colvario
806 m (2,644 ft)

Antoncojo

La Dama

Quise

Roque
del Becerro
618 m (2,028 ft)

CV11

Playa de la Rajita

Punta Falcones

Punta del
Becerro

La Palma

*Atlantic
Ocean*

LA GOMERA

Must See

❶ Parque Nacional de Garajonay

Experience More

❷ San Sebastián de La Gomera
❸ Agulo
❹ Vallehermoso
❺ Valle Gran Rey
❻ El Cercado
❼ Alajeró
❽ Hermigua

GM1

❸ AGULO

Playa de Hermigua

Playa de la Caleta

CV3

Las Heyetas

Las Poyatas

Punta Majona

❽ HERMIGUA

Punta Gaviota

El Cedro

Mirador de Carbonera

Tunel de la Cumbre

Ermita de Nuestra Señora de Guadalupe

Punta Llana

GM1

△ Roque de Ojila 1,171 m (3,842 ft)

La Laja

Barranco de la Villa

El Molinito

Playa de Abalo

CV1

GM2

Vegaipala

CV10

SAN SEBASTIÁN DE LA GOMERA

❷

GM2

Tenerife →

Las Toscas

Tejiade

Playa de la Guancha

Pastrana

El Cabrito

GM3

Barranco de Santiago

Punta Gorda

La Gomera Airport

Playa de Tapahuga

Playa de Santiago

El Hierro ↙

| 0 kilometres | | 3 |
| 0 miles | | 3 |

N ↑

←

1 The village of Vallehermoso.

2 A path in Parque Nacional de Garajonay.

3 The Torre del Conde.

4 Inside Vallehermoso's San Juan Bautista church.

24 HOURS
in La Gomera

▎*Morning*

After arriving by ferry at the port of San Sebastián de La Gomera *(p166)*, stretch your legs with a visit to the small but mighty Torre del Conde *(Parque de la Torre del Conde, s/n)*. This 15th-century fortress famously served as a refuge for the 15th-century Castilian courtier Beatriz de Bobadilla while evading the Gomeros Rebellion. From here, grab a coffee in the pedestrianized Calle Real before dropping by the Church of the Asunción further down the road, with its eclectic mix of Mudéjar, Gothic and Baroque architecture. Driving is the best way to get around the rest of the island, so hop into a rental car and head inland on the GM-2. There are numerous lookout points from where you can enjoy some of the amazing natural views: stop at either the Mirador de La Lomada del Camello, with spectacular views of the San Sebastián de La Gomera and the neighbouring island of Tenerife beyond, or the Mirador del Sombrero, for views of the stunning terraces built to support harvests on the steep slopes. From here, it's another 10-minute drive to see an incredible sweep of Canary palms from the Mirador Degollada de Peraza.

▎*Afternoon*

Continue your drive and head into the Parque Nacional de Garajonay *(p164)*, heading towards the village of El Cedro, located inside the park. Stop off here and enjoy a walk through the ancient laurel forests of this beautiful UNESCO World Heritage Site. Stop for lunch at Las Vistas restaurant *(Calle el Cedro 52)* for a traditional, home-cooked meal before making your way along the GM-1 towards the rural village of Vallehermoso *(p167)*, located in the north of the island. Along the way, make time for the Chorros de Epina mountain springs, believed locally to hold mystical properties, as well as the huge, looming rock formation known locally as Fortaleza de Chipude. At just over 1,200 m (4,000 ft) above sea level, this stunning natural monument can be seen from all around La Gomera. Climb the path to the top for gasp-worthy views of the palm-dotted landscape below it.

▎*Evening*

End the day trip in the village of Vallehermoso. Start by recharging after the afternoon's walk with some cake and a tipple from the cosy Lucia Cosas de Verdad café in the main square *(Plaza de la Constitución 4)*. With a new burst of energy, spend the evening taking a relaxing stroll around the characterful old town, which is centred around the imposing church of San Juan Bautista *(Calle Iglesia)*. As day draws to a close, make your way down to the beach and walk along some of the more than 25 km (15 miles) of coastline here for stunning sunset views to see off your tour.

Did You Know?

—

Alto de Garajonay is the highest point of La Gomera, soaring 1,500 m (4,600 ft) above sea level.

Hiking through the densely forested Parque Nacional de Garajonay ↑

PARQUE NACIONAL DE GARAJONAY

❶ La Palmita, Agulo; 922 800 993

Covering an area of 40 sq km (15 sq miles), La Gomera's national park is the largest intact area of ancient woodland in the archipelago, despite one-fifth of it being destroyed by forest fires in 2012. So precious is this region that it has been declared a UNESCO World Heritage Site.

The unique weather conditions here, caused by the constant flow of mist produced when the cool Atlantic trade winds encounter warm breezes, ensure constant dew and humidity conducive to the growth of some 450 species of plant and tree. The vegetation often reaches unprecedented sizes, providing an idea of what a Mediterranean forest looked like before the last Ice Age.

One of the best ways to experience the park is by taking one of the many walking trails. The village of El Cercado, enjoying a scenic position and easily reached by bus, provides a starting point for these walks. Along these are viewpoints such as the Mirador de Vallehermoso and Mirador el Bailadero. Just inside the park boundary and surrounded by dense heather, you can see the expanse of the national park and the north side of the island. The park is also crisscrossed by a number of densely wooded ravines, which provide shelter for numerous species of rare bird, including the long-toed Canary pigeon.

Often shrouded in mist, La Laguna Grande is a good stopping-off point, with a restaurant, a children's playground and a picnic area. The excellent visitor centre, near Las Rosas within the park, offers craft workshops and features an exhibition on Gomeran handicrafts, a well-labelled garden and a restaurant specializing in Canarian cuisine.

ANCIENT VEGETATION

The term *laurisilva*, meaning "laurel grove", is used to describe the ancient laurel forest at the heart of the park. These evergreen trees grow to 20 m (66 ft) and shroud large areas of the park with a thick ceiling of green, which keeps in mist and provides enough shade to keep walkers cool on the hiking trails through the forest. As well as laurel trees, the park has dense tree heather and juniper groves.

→ Engaging with the exhibits at the park's informative visitor centre

← Roque de Agando, a huge rock formation, as seen from the Mirador el Bailadero

EXPERIENCE MORE

❷ San Sebastián de La Gomera

 🅸 C/Real 4;
922 141 512

With the daily arrival of tourists on the Tenerife ferry, the island's quiet capital and main harbour come alive. The road from the harbour into town passes through the laurel-shaded Plaza de las Américas, which is lined with street cafés.

To the west of the square stands the Torre del Conde. This Gothic tower was built in 1447 by the first Spanish governor of La Gomera, Hernán Peraza the Elder. Restored in 1997, it is the only remaining fragment of the town's fortifications. The Torre del Conde is a reminder of a tragic uprising in the town. In 1448, Beatriz de Bobadilla, wife of Hernán Peraza the Younger, barricaded herself within its walls after her husband was killed by a Guanche in revenge for his illicit affair with an Indigenous princess. When help arrived from Gran Canaria, Beatriz avenged herself by putting almost every male Guanche on Gomera to death.

The island's main church is the Iglesia de la Virgen de la Asunción in Calle Real. The foundations were laid in the mid-15th century and Christopher Columbus is said to have knelt down to pray in the church's dim interior before continuing on his first voyage. Casa de Colón, at Calle Real 56, is where Columbus allegedly stayed before setting off for the Americas, while the Pozo de Colón, a well standing in the courtyard of a former customs building, has the inscription "With this water, America was baptised." Another sight to look out for is the small Ermita de San Sebastián. Built around 1450, this is the oldest church on the island; it is dedicated to La Gomera's patron saint.

Heading towards Mirador de la Hila, which offers stunning views over the whole of San Sebastián de La Gomera, the road leads to the Parador de San Sebastián. This comfortable hotel was

> **With the daily arrival of tourists on the Tenerife ferry, the island's quiet capital and main harbour San Sebastián de La Gomera comes alive.**

built in 1976 and is a modern replica of an older Canarian colonial mansion.

Some 4 km (2 miles) north, the gravel road divides: one route descends towards the quiet beach at Playa de Abalos; the other leads to Ermita de Nuestra Señora de Guadalupe – every five years a statue of the Virgin Mary is carried to San Sebastián from here.

---

❸ Agulo

The 17th-century town of Agulo lies in the northeastern part of the island. It is set high above the sea and at the foot of a natural rock amphitheatre, which is surrounded by verdant banana plantations. Together with the nearby hamlet of Lepe, inhabited by little more than a handful of crofters, this is a picturesque little place and a popular destination for sightseers around La Gomera.

One unique feature of Agulo's architecture is the Neo-Gothic Iglesia de San Marcos (1939). Located in the centre of the town in the Plaza de Leoncio Bento, the church is Moorish in design and features four white domes, which are visible from far away. The town's best-known Indigenous son is the painter José Aguiar (1895–1976) who was born in Cuba of Gomeran parents and spent his childhood in Agulo.

A steep, twisting road leads upwards from Agulo to the Mirador de Abrante. This stone terrace offers a splendid view over the rocky coast and the ocean and is a fine spot to appreciate Mount Teide on Tenerife. The viewpoint also features a spine-chilling glass box that hangs over thin air and a charming café-restaurant.

A little further along the road, at the end of a wooded ravine, is the delightful

 The pretty town of Agulo overlooking the Atlantic

village of La Palmita, renowned for preserving its traditional lifestyle.

4

Vallehermoso

🚌 **ℹ️ Plaza de la Constitución; 922 800 000**

Vallehermoso translates as "beautiful valley," and the surrounding agricultural landscape is evidence of the island's fertile soil. About 15 km (9 miles) along a winding road from Agulo, this compact town, with its bustling centre (including shops, a post office, a bank and a petrol station), is a good starting point for sightseeing and walking tours around this pleasant region.

At the centre of the town is the Iglesia San Juan Bautista, which was designed by the Tenerife architect Antonio Pintor. There's also a small park with groups of roughly hewn sculptural figures.

Facing the sea lies the Castillo del Mar. This former banana offloading station dates back to 1890. After restoration, cultural events are scheduled to take place here. See the website for more detail (www.castillo-del-mar.com).

 Iglesia de la Virgen de la Asunción, San Sebastián de La Gomera

A short way to the north is Playa de Vallehermoso, which is good for windsurfing. Less adventurous visitors can relax in the swimming pool next to the pebble beach.

Some 4 km (2 miles) north is Los Órganos – a section of steep cliff that can be seen only from the sea, on cruising trips from Valle Gran Rey, Playa de Santiago or San Sebastián. This basalt wall, 80 m (260 ft) high and 200 m (660 ft) wide, resembles the pipes of an organ and is one of the most unusual (and least accessible) attractions on La Gomera.

Just 2 km (1 mile) to the east is the Roque Cano. This 650-m (2,132-ft) high fang-shaped rock was created by erosion of a volcanic peak.

Situated 11 km (7 miles) from Vallehermoso, Las Rosas is a popular stopping place for coach tours. It has a restaurant where tourists are treated to demonstrations of El Silbo – the island's famous whistling language (p169).

 GREAT VIEW
Roque Cano

The volcanic rock formation of Roque Cano towers over Vallehermoso. Once a sacred spot for the Guanches, it offers stunning views. Hike to the summit for an unforgettable experience.

5 Valle Gran Rey

 C/El Caidero 16; www.vallegranrey.es

The centre of tourism on the island, Valle Gran Rey ("Valley of the Great King") was known before the Spanish conquest of La Gomera, when it was named "Orone" after a Guanche leader. Today Valle Gran Rey is a complex of several seaside villages – La Calera, La Playa, La Puntilla, Borbalán and Vueltas. Their collective growth is a measure of the tourism boom that has even reached La Gomera. The estates throughout Valle Gran Rey offer the opportunity to enjoy a relaxing stay in a more remote setting, close to nature. The place attracts many visitors, who come not only for the idyllic scenery, but also for the excellent guesthouses and restaurants. The magnificent Atlantic waves will satisfy even the most demanding of surf fans.

La Calera, with its charming setting in the midst of banana plantations, is an upmarket part of La Gomera, thanks to its small boutiques and cosy restaurants. It is regarded as one of the archipelago's prettiest towns, and the house prices here are some of the highest on the island. Like La Playa, it also has a small beach.

The harbour at Vueltas offers hydrofoil links to Los Cristianos on Tenerife, as well as short cruises along the coast of La Gomera and to Los Órganos. It is also used by fishing boats and numerous yachts. Several restaurants tempt visitors with tasty dishes of freshly caught fish. The most scenic road on the island is surrounded by massive basalt rocks and runs through the valley, renowned for its fertility. Local crops include dates, bananas, papayas, avocados, mangoes and tomatoes. Small fields, cutting into the valley slopes in the form of terraces, are similar to Balinese rice fields.

For hikers there are several walking trails, representing various degrees of difficulty. Above the town, right at the entrance to the valley, is a viewpoint made according to a design by César Manrique, and featuring one of the island's best restaurants.

Perched above the valley, 11 km (7 miles) to the north, is the village of Arure, which, prior to the island's conquest, used to be its main centre. Today the place has a desolate look about it and is known mainly for its excellent *miel de palma* – "palm honey". The palms from which the honey is made have flanges fitted around their trunks to protect them against hungry ants.

Around 8 km (5 miles) northeast of Arure lies the sources of Chorros de Epina, surrounded by beautiful expanses of heather and a forest. The nearby Mirador del Santo offers a splendid

 INSIDER TIP
Whale Watching

The waters around La Gomera and Tenerife have been declared the first Whale Heritage Site in Europe. See these gentle giants on a boat trip from Valle Gran Rey (*www. whalewatchng-gomera.com*).

Admiring the massive cliffs and azure waters in the Valle Gran Rey

view over the ravines and on to the tranquil islands of La Palma and El Hierro.

6
El Cercado
Chipude

This small village is best known for its handicrafts, especially earthenware products that are made of dark Gomeran clay, without the use of a potter's wheel. Local traditions are also being upheld by a small number of bars offering traditional cuisine.

Some 3 km (2 miles) to the south, at the foot of La Fortaleza – a massive basalt rock that is almost as flat as a table top – lies Chipude. At 1,050 m (3,445 ft) above sea level, this is the highest village on La Gomera. It is known for its 16th-century church, the Iglesia de la Virgen de la Candelaria. Like El Cercado, Chipude is renowned as a pottery village. A steep country road that later becomes a walking trail leads from El Cercado to La Laguna Grande, an information point at the entrance to the vast Parque Nacional de Garajonay (p164).

Some 17 km (10.5 miles) to the south is La Dama. Surrounded by banana plantations, this small village is poised high above the ocean.

7
Alajeró
 928 895 650

A typical Gomeran village, Alajeró sprawls along a mountain road in the southern part of the island. Most of the village's inhabitants make a living by growing bananas.

EL SILBO GOMERA

Long before the invention of the telephone, La Gomera's inhabitants needed a way of communicating across the island. A unique whistling language known as El Silbo was the solution, wherein two distinct whistles replaced the five Spanish vowels and four whistles replaced the consonants. Modulating the whistle by changing finger positions produced many different sounds, which could be transmitted up to 4 km (2 miles). Today the whistle is not used as often, but the local Guanches once relied on it when threatened or during hunting expeditions. The whistle has been deemed of important cultural heritage and is taught to children in school.

The 16th-century Iglesia del Salvador is one of the few remains of the village's historic past.

From Alajeró a path leads westward, along a very deep ravine, to La Manteca. Though many of the people who were born here have left in search of a better life, this ghost village, set in a very picturesque spot, is one of the few villages to be totally abandoned.

In Agalán, 2 km (1 mile) north of Alajeró down a cobbled road, is the island's only surviving dragon tree (p24). The Drago de Agalán was planted in the mid-1800s.

8
Hermigua

A winding road leads from San Sebastián to Hermigua. Along the route, the scenery is attractive and varied with weathered rocks, forests of willow and laurel, juniper groves, deep ravines and lush green valleys.

Hermigua, known as Mulagua during the Guanche times, was once an important town but is today little more than a village. The fertile soil in the lower regions of Barranco de Monteforte still allows cultivation of grapes, bananas and dates.

Today the only evidence of the past is a handful of old buildings and the Convento de Santo Domingo de Guzmán in the Valle Alto district. Dating from the 16th century, the church features a 19th-century image of the Madonna by Fernando Estévez.

Hermigua is famous for its handmade rugs and other woven products. These can be seen and purchased in Los Telares, the local handicraft centre. Nearby is Playa de Hermigua – covered with shingle, it is not the most beautiful of beaches and is subject to rough weather.

An hour's hike along the footpath, to the northeast of Hermigua, brings you to Playa de la Caleta, one of the island's best black-sand beaches.

↑ The striking Convento de Santo Domingo de Guzmán, Hermigua

A LONG WALK
MIRADOR CÉSAR MANRIQUE ROUND

Distance 8 km (5 miles) **Walking time** 4 hours
Elevation 700 m (2,300 ft) **Terrain** Hilly

The Mirador César Manrique is at the heart of one of the most popular hiking routes of La Gomera. This viewpoint offers spectacular views across Valle Gran Rey, named after the Indigenous king who fought against Spanish occupation in the 15th century. To reach it, start off in the town of Los Granados and make your way around this moderate, circular route. En route, you'll pass beautiful palms, reservoirs and towns before reaching the viewpoint. The terrain can be challenging; for an easier option, it's also possible to drive it.

*The **Mirador César Manrique** offers spectacular views. Don't miss the gardens, home to native plants like the Canary palm tree.*

↑ Mirador César Manrique, with views over a gorge of the Valle Gran Rey

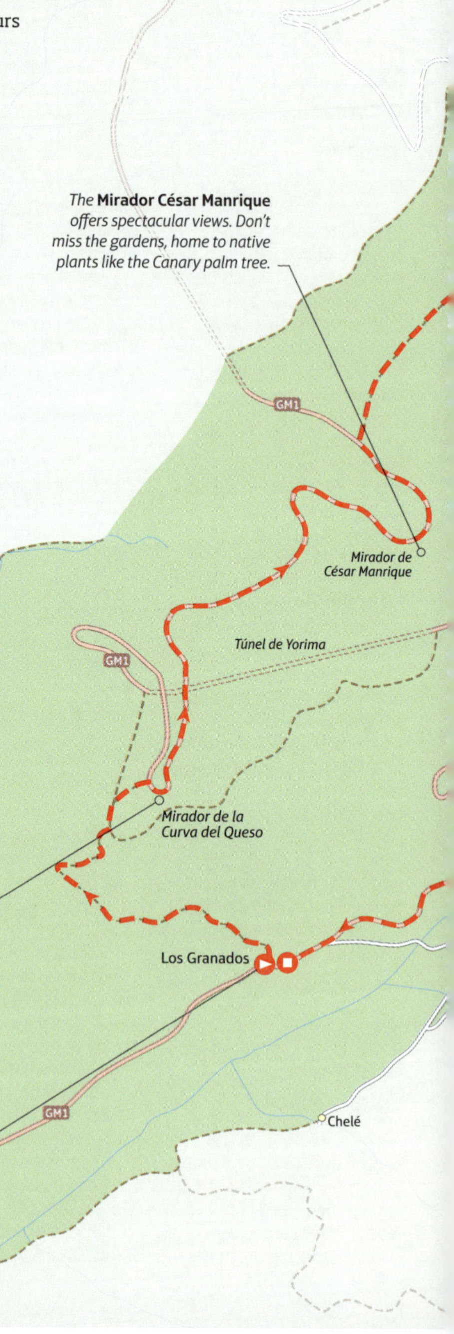

GM1

Mirador de César Manrique

Túnel de Yorima

GM1

Mirador de la Curva del Queso

*After 15 minutes of walking, you'll reach the **Mirador de la Curva del Queso**, which has breathtaking panoramic views of Valle Gran Rey.*

Los Granados

GM1

Chelé

*Set off on the hike from the small, picturesque town of **Los Granados**, surrounded by the characteristic crop terraces and green vegetation of the area.*

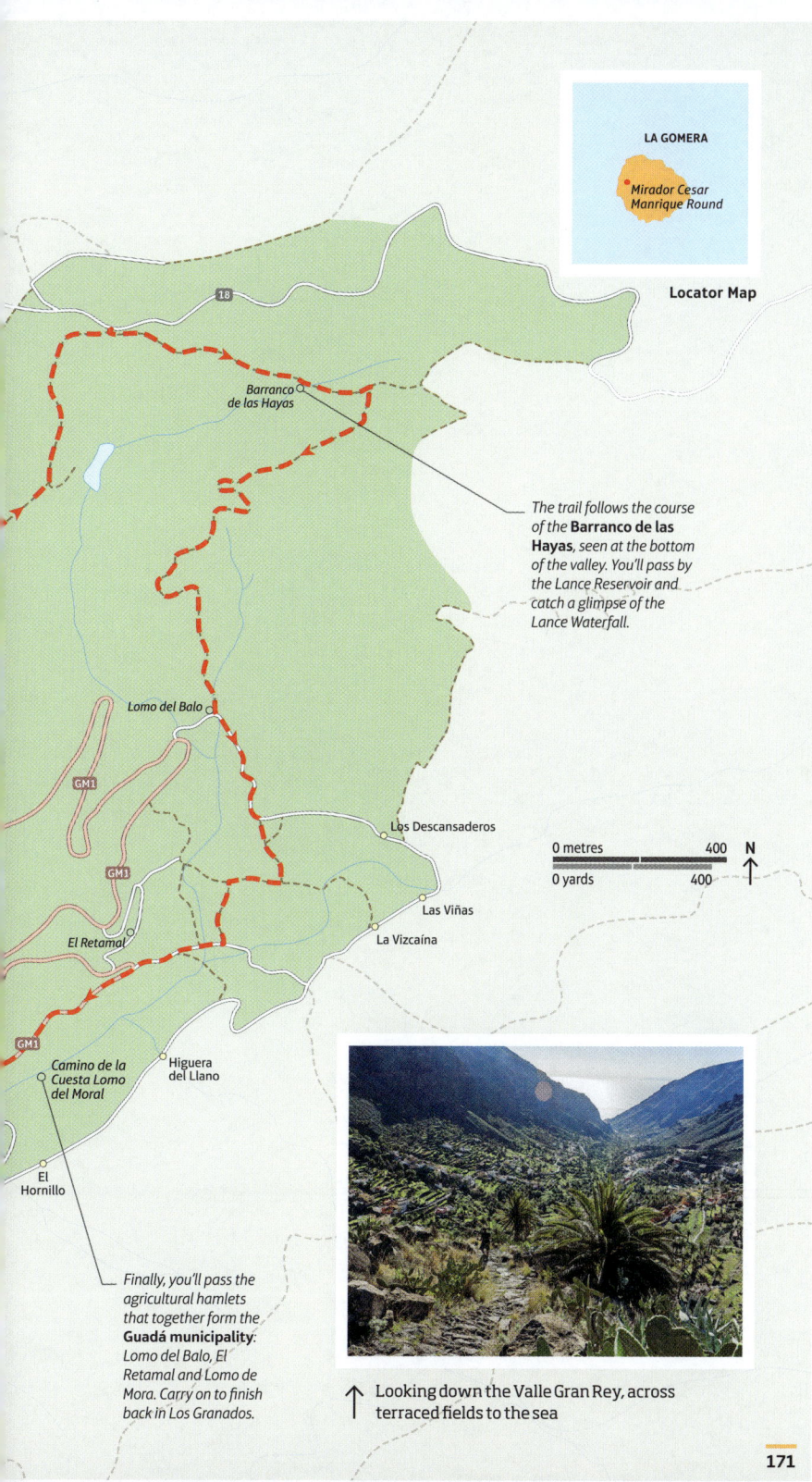

LA GOMERA

●Mirador Cesar
Manrique Round

Locator Map

18

Barranco
de las Hayas

*The trail follows the course
of the* **Barranco de las
Hayas**, *seen at the bottom
of the valley. You'll pass by
the Lance Reservoir and
catch a glimpse of the
Lance Waterfall.*

Lomo del Balo

GM1

Los Descansaderos

0 metres   400   N
0 yards   400   ↑

GM1

Las Viñas

El Retamal   La Vizcaína

GM1

Camino de la   Higuera
Cuesta Lomo   del Llano
del Moral

El
Hornillo

*Finally, you'll pass the
agricultural hamlets
that together form the*
Guadá municipality:
*Lomo del Balo, El
Retamal and Lomo de
Mora. Carry on to finish
back in Los Granados.*

↑ Looking down the Valle Gran Rey, across
terraced fields to the sea

EL HIERRO

The island of El Hierro came into being some 50,000 years ago, its shape the result of a strong earthquake that struck the island. The island is thought to have eventually been inhabited in around the 2nd century CE by an Indigenous population of Bimbache tribes.

After the Spanish invasion of 1403 and later conquest at the end of the same century, many Bimbache people fell victim to slave traders, while their land was appropriated by Norman and Castilian settlers. A feudal system was introduced which survived until the mid-19th century. Like the other islands of this archipelago, El Hierro was visited by navigators heading for the Americas, including Christopher Columbus on his second voyage in 1493.

Over the subsequent centuries, the island saw a number of significant weather events and eruptions. The most recent volcanic eruption on this mountainous island was in 2011, when an underground volcano spewed magma 20 m (66 ft) into the air. Today, the population lives mainly off agriculture, growing grapes and bananas, as well as almonds, peaches, potatoes and tomatoes. As elsewhere, fishing is another key element of the local economy, particularly on the southern coast.

EL HIERRO

Atlantic Ocean

El Golfo

Punta de la Sal

Playa de
Arenas Blancas

Playa de
los Bucios

Playa de
Verodal

HI500

HI551

Pozo de la Salud

El Chijo

Los
Llanillos

Mirador
de Basco

La Caldereta
152 m (499 ft)

HI50

SABINOSA 4   HI50

EL SABINAR

HI108

SANTUARIO DE NUESTRA
SEÑORA DE LOS REYES

Punta de
los Reyes

HI500

6

Montaña Tenaca
625 m (2,051 ft)

Tajusara
1,275 m (4,183 ft)

Tanganasoga
1,384 m (4,541 ft)

Malpaso
1,500 m (4,921 ft)

Montaña
Tembárgena
900 m (2,953 ft)

HI500

Montaña del
Tomillar
991 m (3,251 ft)

HI45

Punta del
Barbudo

HI503

HI400

Orchilla
238 m (781 ft)

Faro de
Orchilla

El   Julán

Playa de
las Coloradas

Playa de
los Mozos

Playa del
Cuervito

Cala del
Tacorón

EL HIERRO

La Gomera ↗

Punta del
Guanche

Pozo de
las Calcosas   HI100   HI151
                              HI150

Montaña   Echedó   Playa de
Bermeja   Adentro
346 m (1,135 ft)   HI100
Playa de   Tamaduste
Agache   HI100
                    HI101   El Hierro
Roques de Salmor   Mocanal   HI15   Airport ✈
                              HI5   HI3
                    HI10   Tesbabo   La Caleta
Playas del   VALVERDE ❶ 310 m (1,017 ft)
Cantadal   HI5   Guarazoca   HI2
                    Jarales   Las Montañetas   HI1
              HI10   La Montaña   HI2   La
        Mirador   HI110   839 m (2,753 ft)   Caleta
        de la Peña   Ventejís
Playas   HI10   1,139 m (3,737 ft)
del   Casas   Tiñor   PUERTO
Mulato   de Guinea ❸ LAS PUNTAS   HI10   DE LA ESTACA ❿
                        HI120   Montaña del Jablito   Playa de
        HI555   1,176 m (3,858 ft)   Tijeretas
              HI55   ❾
FRONTERA   Mirador de   SAN   La Cuesta   Tenerife →
        ❷   Jinama   ANDRÉS
Tigaday   HI1   Montaña la Gotera   Los Llanos   Punta de
        HI1   1,325 m (4,347 ft)   Tijimiraque
              Montaña del Fraile   La Torre
              1,304 m (4,278 ft)   Tajace
        HI4   ❽ ISORA
Tenerife   HI30
1,419 m (4,656 ft)   HI40   Mirador de
HI1   Isora
Montañita del   Mirador de   Punta de Ajones
Guanche de Abajo   las Playas
1,235 m (4,052 ft)   Roque de la Bonanza
Mercadel   Las
1,251 m (4,104 ft)   Playas
HI453
        HI400   Las Casas
Tanajara   El Pinar   Parador del Hierro
911 m (2,989 ft)
        Taibique
                    Venticota   Atlantic
El Río   648 m (2,126 ft)   Ocean
        Tembárgena
        774 m (2,539 ft)   Playa de Miguel

Tecorón
303 m (994 ft)   Playa del Pozo
HI410

HI4   Punta del Miradero
        Restinga   0 kilometres   2   N
Bahía de Naos 198 m (650 ft)   0 miles   2   ↑
        ❼ LA RESTINGA

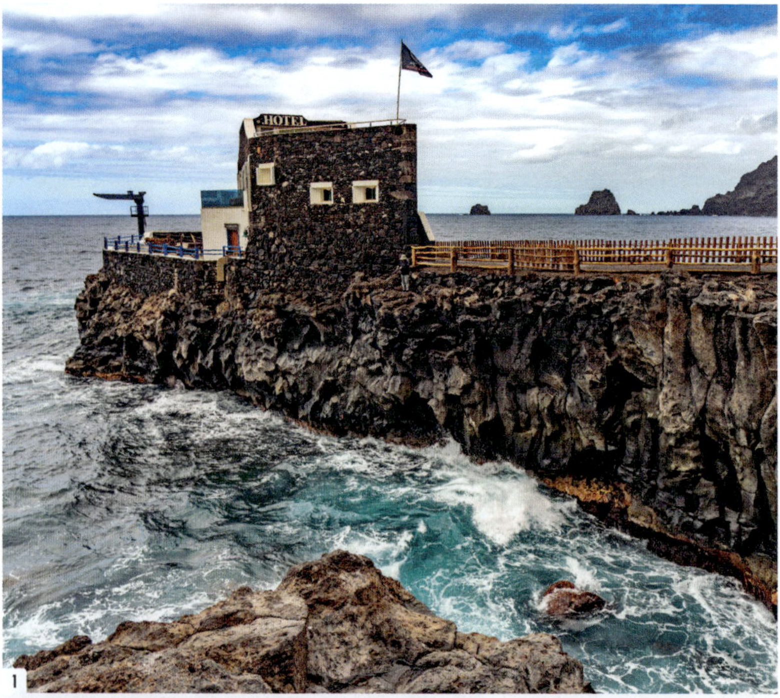

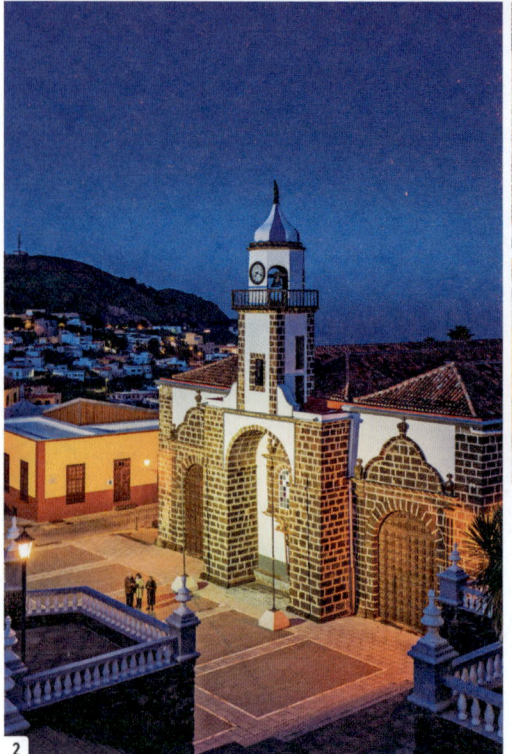

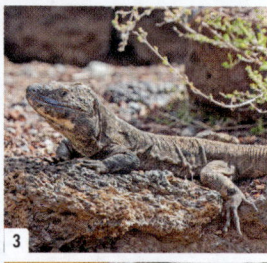

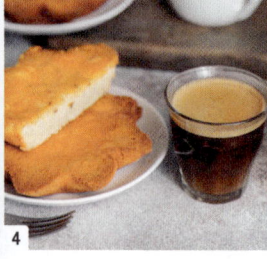

1

2

3

4

←

1 The Hotel Puntagrande facing the coast.

2 Valverde's Iglesia de Nuestra Señora de la Concepción.

3 The El Hierro giant lizard.

4 A traditional *quesadilla*.

24 HOURS
in El Hierro

Morning

Begin your day in El Hierro's capital, Valverde *(p178)*, with a leisurely stroll through this quiet town on a green hill. Make your way to the Iglesia de Nuestra Señora de la Concepción *(Calle Gral. Rodríguez y Sánchez Espinosa 1)* in the heart of town. The church has an impressive belfry, which houses a large Parisian clock donated to the church in the 19th century. Continue the historical theme of the day and visit the nearby Centro Etnográfico Casa de Las Quinteras *(Calle Armas Martell)*, a small museum showcasing the history of trade and industry on the island. After that, grab a snack from the La Fábrica de Quesadillas Adrián Gutiérrez e Hijas *(Calle Veintidós de Febrero 2)*, which specializes in the island's renowned cheesecake-like pastries known as quesadillas (not to be mistaken for the savoury Mexican treat of the same name).

Afternoon

Pick up a rental car for the afternoon and head along the winding road over to Las Puntas *(p179)*. Enjoy a light midday meal from one of the many cafés in the town, before setting out to see what was once the world's smallest hotel on the coast, the Hotel Puntagrande *(Calle Las Puntas)*. From here, head west along the coast, stopping off at Mirador Punta del Pozo for sweeping views of El Hierro's rugged coastline. Make your way over to the Ecomuseo de Guinea *(Calle Gral. las Puntas, s/n)*, to learn more about island life since the time of the Indigenous Bimbache tribes to the present day. Attached to this site is the Lagartario, a recovery centre for the critically endangered subspecies of Simony's giant lizard, known as the El Hierro giant lizard. Driving south, zigzag up the mountains, where the pine forests contrast with the volcanic coastline. Alongside the road, stop at Mirador La Llanía and Mirador de las Playas *(p182)* for stunning views of the island.

Evening

End your day with dinner in the town of La Restinga *(p181)*, the southernmost point in Spain (and Europe). Once night falls, it's time to wrap your time on El Hierro with a memorable experience: suit up and join a guided nocturnal dive in the protected Coastal Reserve Punta Restinga, an area with very calm waters into which any level of diver can delve. Much of the marine life in these waters comes alive at night, making for a once-in-a-lifetime end to the trip.

EXPERIENCE MORE

1

Valverde

 C/Dr Quintero 4; www.elhierro.travel

The full name of the island's capital is La Villa de Santa María de Valverde. Unlike the other island capitals, Valverde has no harbour. The small town is located a few kilometres inland and poised on the slope of an evergreen valley (hence the name, "green valley"). It is extremely quiet and often rather foggy.

The only noteworthy local historic sight is the Baroque Iglesia Santa María de la Concepción. Built in 1767 on the site of a former 16th-century chapel, this vast church was erected in thanksgiving for the repulse of a pirate attack. The belfry includes a large clock brought from Paris in 1886. The main highlights of the interior are the ornate altar, an image of the Virgin of La Concepción, the patron saint of the town, and a fine Genoese sculpture, *Santísimo Cristo a la Columna (Christ at the Column)*. The town hall, standing opposite the church, took 30 years to build (1910–40) and is in the local style.

Tamaduste, located around 10 km (6 miles) to the north-east, is one of the more popular resorts, and has a quiet cove with a pleasant beach.

Charco Manso, 8 km (5 miles) to the north, is a complex of natural pools set in volcanic rock. These are reached by a narrow road with hairpin bends. The sea here can be dangerous, and swimming is not advisable.

Meanwhile, Pozo de las Calcosas, 8 km (5 miles) to the northwest, is a good place to swim and features pools similar to those of Charco Manso. It also has many black stone huts on the ocean shore, all reached by steep steps.

An unforgettable view over El Golfo bay and the Roques de Salmor is to be had from

---

BAJADA DE LA VIRGEN DE LOS REYES

In the early 18th century, during a period of drought, the Madonna was carried down from the Nuestra Señora de los Reyes sanctuary by villagers to Valverde. It rained thereafter, and ever since, a feast has been held every four years on the first or second Saturday in July. The next feast will take place in 2029. The statue of the Holy Mother follows the same route along unmade country lanes - the Camino de la Virgen - and is carried on a litter to Valverde. The ceremony, which begins at 5am and goes on till late, is accompanied by a week of merriment, with many villagers dressed in red and white costumes.

↑ The Iglesia Santa María de la Concepción complex in Valverde

→

Hotel Puntagrande
standing on the edge of
the Arco de las Puntas

the stone-walled Mirador de la Peña, 8 km (5 miles) to the west of Valverde. The small restaurant here was built in 1988 following a design by César Manrique.

Frontera

Many of the inhabitants of the island's second-largest town make their living by growing grapes. Frontera's rolling vineyards are the source of Viña Frontera – wines famous throughout the archipelago. More recently, the cultivation of pineapples has also become popular here, and El Hierro has emerged as one of the largest producers of this tropical fruit in Spain. A variety of cheeses are also produced in Frontera and feature in local dishes.

The Iglesia de la Candelaria, standing on the outskirts of the town, was built in 1818 and occupies nearly the entire square. The interior, covered with a wooden ceiling, features a striking, gilded altar. Standing above the church, on a hill of red volcanic ash, is a belfry that is visible from afar.

Tigaday, 1 km (half a mile) to the west of Frontera, is a relatively large village and

a great wine-producing centre. It is the starting point for the road to Las Puntas.

Las Puntas

Standing on the old wharf, where until 1930 ships arrived bringing supplies, is the Hotel Puntagrande, which was once recognized as the world's smallest hotel. It began life in 1884 as a harbour building, until it was transformed into a hotel. It has four rooms, a bar and a restaurant. Although it is difficult to get a room here, it is still worth coming in order to admire the beautiful sunset and enjoy a swim in one of the rocky coves.

Another local landmark is the Roques de Salmor. These scenic rock formations rise from the sea, and are home to one of the island's most important bird colonies.

A little to the south, Poblado de Guinea is an old Norman settlement dating from the early 15th century. Along with Las Montañetas, it claims to be the oldest village on El Hierro. Today it houses the **Ecomuseo Poblado de Guinea** – a complex of former shepherds' huts that have been restored and kitted out with furniture from different periods. A small

  PICTURE PERFECT
Arco de las Puntas

The Arco de las Puntas in Las Puntas is one of the most stunning volcanic stone arches in the archipelago. Strike a pose at this long, dramatic arch, which stretches over rocky coves.

site known as **Lagartario**, above the museum, is used to provide natural breeding conditions for a rare species of lizard from Salmor, found only in El Hierro. The giant, 1.5-m (5-ft) lizards eventually disappeared from the island in the 1930s, and were believed to be entirely extinct, until some surviving subspecies were found in 1974. A project to save the region's endangered species from extinction commenced in 1975.

Ecomuseo Poblado de Guinea
⊕ 🏠 C/Gral de Las Puntas
📞 922 555 056 🕐 10am–6pm daily

Lagartario
⊕ 🏠 C/Gral de Las Puntas
📞 922 555 056 🕐 10am–2pm & 4–6pm Tue–Sat, 11am–2pm Sun

Sabinosa

Swamped with vibrant flowers, Sabinosa is pleasantly remote, with picturesque, narrow streets. Poised high up on a slope, overlooking almost all of El Golfo bay, it is known for its "well of health" – Pozo de la Salud – which can be found by the sea below the town. The water, drawn from a well, is highly radioactive and is believed to be something of a cure-all for a number of ailments. The Balneario Pozo de la Salud, a hotel catering to the needs of health-seeking visitors, is the only one of its type in the Canary Islands.

Playa de Arenas Blancas, 6 km (4 miles) to the west, is a sandy beach, popular with tourists and locals alike. Some 10 km (6 miles) to the west is Playa de Verodal. This small, scenic, windswept beach, with its rust-coloured volcanic sands, lies at the foot of a high cliff. Accessible via a bumpy, coarse-gravel road, it is generally considered to be the most beautiful beach on El Hierro.

East of Sabinosa, a road leads through banana and pineapple plantations to Los Llanillos, a tiny village with a small chapel built of blocks of volcanic rock. Standing by the roadside is a workshop producing all shapes and sizes of birdcages. A little further along, the road reaches Charco Azul, where scenic rocky coves with turquoise water tempt visitors to swim.

El Sabinar

The name of this upland, swept by Atlantic winds and crossed by a gorge, derives from the local word *sabina* (juniper). It features a tranquil forest filled with striking white-trunked juniper trees that have bent and twisted into bizarre shapes by strong winds.

El Sabinar is reached by a road that starts as asphalt and later becomes a dirt track running among pastures and crossing cattle gates. It's located just under 4 km (2 miles) from the sanctuary of Nuestra Señora de los Reyes, the patron saint of the island.

The **Mirador de Basco**, 3 km (2 miles) to the north, offers breathtaking views (on sunny days) not only of El Golfo, but also of La Palma, La Gomera and Tenerife.

Santuario de Nuestra Señora de los Reyes

🅰 4 km (2 miles) S of El Sabinar 🕐 Jul & Aug: 10am–5:30pm Tue–Sun; Sep: 10am–6pm Tue–Sun

Set among wooded hills in the western part of the island, surrounded by a low wall, is the pilgrim sanctuary of the Holy Mother of the Kings (Magi) – the patron saint of El Hierro. Inside is a statue of the Madonna, kept on a silver litter. Every four years, in the course of a ceremonial procession known as the Bajada de la Virgen de los Reyes, the statue is carried to Valverde (*p178*).

Legend has it that a French ship was becalmed near the shores of the island, and the crew were only able to survive thanks to the help of El Hierro's inhabitants. Having no money to pay for food and water, the captain presented the islanders with a statue of the Virgin Mary. On the same day, 6 January 1577, the day of the Epiphany, a strong wind sent the ship on her way.

> **Poised high up on slope, overlooking almost all of El Golfo bay, Sabinosa is known for its "well of health" - Pozo de la Salud - which can be found by the sea below the town.**

← Santuario de Nuestra Señora de los Reyes, and *(inset)* the altar, adorned with statues of the Madonna

The towering Faro de Orchilla lighthouse is 7 km (4 miles) to the southwest. In 150 CE, the Greek geographer Ptolemy declared this western end of the island to be the end of the world. In 1634, the zero meridian was drawn through this point and was recognized as such until 1884, when it was moved to Greenwich. Even so, El Hierro still refers to itself as "Isla del Meridiano", and visitors can buy a certificate confirming that they have crossed the zero meridian.

7

La Restinga

La Restinga is a small fishing harbour and yacht marina, situated on the sunnier, southern end of the island. It is also one of the most popular resorts on El Hierro. There's a large hotel and a small apartment complex, and the coastal road – the Avenida

← Wind-twisted juniper tree, El Hierro's official symbol, in El Sabinar

Marítima – features a variety of shops, bars and restaurants. This is a good place to sit out and watch the world drift by.

In the centre is a small black-sand beach that is sheltered by the large harbour. Though generally rather quiet, La Restinga has plenty of facilities for watersports, including diving. The local waters around here have protected status and feature rich marine fauna and flora combined with underwater gullies and interesting rock formations to explore. Diving centres are open all year round and offer trips and night-time expeditions.

A short way to the northwest is Bahía de Naos – which is known principally as the place where Jean de Béthencourt landed in 1403.

Some 10 km (6 miles) to the northwest is Cala del Tacorón – a number of small coves carved into the volcanic shore of Mar de las Calmas. Here, swimmers find the clear waters and steps down to the sea particularly inviting.

Cueva Don Justo, 2 km (1 mile) to the north, within the Montaña de Irama massif, is a great attraction to pot-holers, with its 6-km (4-mile) labyrinth of volcanic tunnels.

EAT

Tasca La Restingolita
Seafood, fish and rice are the specialities at this family-friendly, beachfront restaurant.

⌂ Avda Marítima, La Restinga **☏** 822 09 61 30 **☒** Wed

€€€

Restaurante El Sorchante Del Hierro
This restaurant offers great value for money and a wide range of traditional dishes.

⌂ Avda Marítima, La Restinga

€€€

Restaurante El Refugio
Freshly caught fish and excellent meat dishes are served at this family-owned spot.

⌂ C/La Lapa, La Restinga **☏** 922 55 71 30

€€€

Taking in the majestic
views at the Mirador
de Isora

Isora

Situated in the eastern
part of the island, Isora
is a picturesque assembly
of several hamlets, and
is best known for its long
history of cheese production.
Another attraction
is the famous *lucha canaria*
contests, when feats of
Canary-style wrestling take
place at the local stadium.

It's well worth trying to
arrive in Isora at dawn to
admire the magnificent
sunrise. The area has
a number of stunning
viewpoints to be enjoyed,
including the 1,000-m-
(3,330-ft-) high Mirador de

INSIDER TIP
Isora Hike

For a scenic hike that
offers marvellous views
of the Atlantic Ocean,
head to Mirador de Isora.
From here, the fairly
easy 7-km (4-mile)
return route ascends
143 m (470 ft) to reach
the vistas at La Cuesta.

Isora, about 1 km (half a mile)
to the south, at the edge
of the mountain range of
El Risco de los Herreros,
offering enchanting
panoramic views over
the ocean.

A scenic walk leads down
from Mirador de Isora to
Las Playas on the coast.
Known as the Camino de
Isora, this narrow footpath,
some 4 km (2 miles) long
and at an incline of around
830 m (2,700 ft), is considered
to be one of the island's more
challenging descents, but it's
worth it for the wonderful
views on the way down.

About 3 km (2 miles) to
the south is the Mirador
de las Playas – a high viewpoint, set among Canary
pines. The broad terrace
provides magnificent panoramic views over Las Playas
bay, from Roque de la
Bonanza up to the parador.

El Pinar, 6 km (4 miles) to
the south, is the collective
name often used to describe
two villages, Las Casas and
Taibique – which has a main
street featuring bars, restaurants, shops, a hotel and
bank. The local Artesanía
Cerámica sells ceramics and
handmade jewellery. There
is also a small church, Iglesia
de San Antonio Abad.

San Andrés

A heady 1,100 m (3,610 ft)
above sea level, the prickly
pear and fig trees of San
Andrés are often shrouded
in cold, damp mist for hours
on end, and especially at

night. This small agricultural
town tends to be very hot in
the summer, but winters are
cold, and often battered with
strong winds.

Its inhabitants live mainly
off the land, cultivating crops
and grazing sheep and goats.
Despite the fertile soil, the
unfavourable weather
conditions cause many
of them to leave this
extremely rough and
inhospitable terrain.

To the north, an asphalt
road a little under 4 km
(2 miles) long, which later
becomes a footpath, leads
to Árbol Santo, the holy
Bimbache tree, known to
locals as the Garoé. According to local folk legend,
water once flowed from the
tree to give the island its
entire supply (in fact the
pine tree's needles had
the ability to accumulate

The charming town of
San Andrés, overlooking
the bay of El Golfo

and hold large quantities of water). The ancient and revered tree was destroyed in 1949 by a hurricane. Today, in its place grows a beautiful laurel tree, planted here in 1957.

Some 2 km (1 mile) to the southwest of Isora is the Mirador de Jinama. It is reached by road through fields divided by dry stone walls. In clear weather, the viewpoint provides a fine panorama over the bay of El Golfo.

Puerto de la Estaca

Until 1972, when the airport opened, this small, isolated harbour, cut off from the land by high volcanic cliffs, was El Hierro's only link with the world. The name of the harbour, which was originally built in 1906, is derived from the word *estaca*, a type of wooden pile, to which fishermen tied their boats.

The imposing Roque de la Bonanza, or "Rock of the Silent Ocean," is found in Las Playas bay. A bare basalt rock, it rises vertically from the depths of the sea, just a few steps from the shore, 9 km (6 miles) to the south of Puerto de la Estaca. The amazing rock formation is considered a symbol of the island. It can be reached via a picturesque coastline road that lies in the shadow of a steep volcanic slope.

Take care: at one point the road passes through a single-lane tunnel with intermittently functioning traffic lights.

Did You Know?

In terms of its energy needs, El Hierro is the first self-sufficient island of the archipelago.

Some 2 km (1 mile) further south stands the elegant and spectacularly located Parador del Hierro. The most comfortable hotel on the island, it has an isolated waterfront location, affording wonderful views of the cliff walls round the bay. The hotel was built in the Castilian style in 1976. Its opening was delayed by five years, due to the slow building of the road that terminates here.

↑ Rock formations in the pristine waters at the Roque de la Bonanza

A BOAT TOUR
THE VOLCANIC COAST

Duration 2–10 hours, depending on the tour company
Stopping-off points La Restinga for snorkelling; Charco Azul and Charco Manso for swimming **Information** To book a boat tour, visit www.sereaexcursiones.es

A boat trip around El Hierro is the best way to discover its volcanic coastline. With cliffs peaking over 200 m (660 ft), few of the island's scant beaches are only accessible by boat. Departing from the ports at La Estaca and La Restinga, tours range in duration and can offer access to some hard-to-reach beaches. Along the way, you may spot marine life, snorkel in Mar de Las Calmas or splash in Charco Manso's natural pools, depending on the tour.

EL HIERRO

The Volcanic Coast

Locator Map

Often the first stop is **Cala de Timijiraque**, *one of the island's largest stretches of sand.*

Pozo de las Calcosas *provides a marvellous spot for bathing, a perfect way to end your tour.*

Roque Grande, the largest rock of **Los Roques de Salmor**, *is 100 m (330 ft) tall.*

Perched at the historic zero meridian, the beams from **Faro de Orchilla** *reach 24 nautical miles.*

Charco Manso

FINISH

Pozo de Las Calcosas

Roques de Salmor

Montaña Bermeja
△ *346 m (1,135 ft)*

5

Ventejís
1,139 m
(3,737 ft)
△

START

Puerto de La Estaca

Montaña del Jablito
1,176 m (3,858 ft)
△

San Andrés

55

Playa de Timijiraque

551

Frontera

553

Tajusara
1,275 m
(4,183 ft) △

Tanganasoga
1,384 m (4,541 ft) △

1

4

Roque de la Bonanza

500

45

400

Mercader
1,252 m (4,108 ft) △

Faro de Orchilla

Mar de las Calmas

Mar de Las Calmas, *a protected reserve, has a rich marine life as well as warm, tranquil waters.*

4

La Restinga

The volcanic dike **Roque de la Bonanza** *is a symbol of El Hierro. Swim around the wall to see marine life.*

0 km — 4
0 mile — 4

N ↑

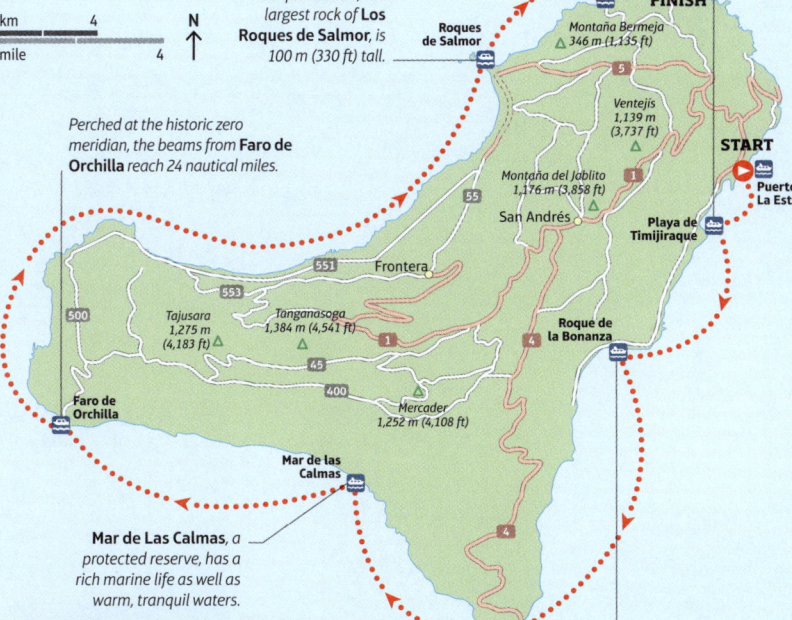

←
Passengers enjoying an atmospheric boat excursion

LA PALMA

Like its neighbouring islands, La Palma was inhabited by Indigenous groups for many years. They referred to the island as Benahoare, and so were known by the same name. Remnants of Benahoare life still visible on La Palma today include the carvings of spirals, circles and linear figures found at the archaeological site of La Zarza, in the north of the island.

The island soon became one of the many stopping-off points across the archipelago for expeditions en route to the Americas from the end of the 15th century. La Palma was colonized by the Spanish in 1492, although they first arrived on the island almost a century before that. During this time, the ways of the Benahoare people were replaced by new traditions and legends.

Known as "the beautiful island", La Palma drew tourists seeking to explore its stunning nature from the 19th century onwards. The island's dramatic scenery is the result of its volcanic roots. In 2021, La Palma saw its most recent volcanic eruption, which lasted 85 days and caused great destruction in the southwestern half of the island. Black lava fields and a new volcano – known as Tajogaite and now part of the Cumbre Vieja volcanic rift – were created by this latest eruption.

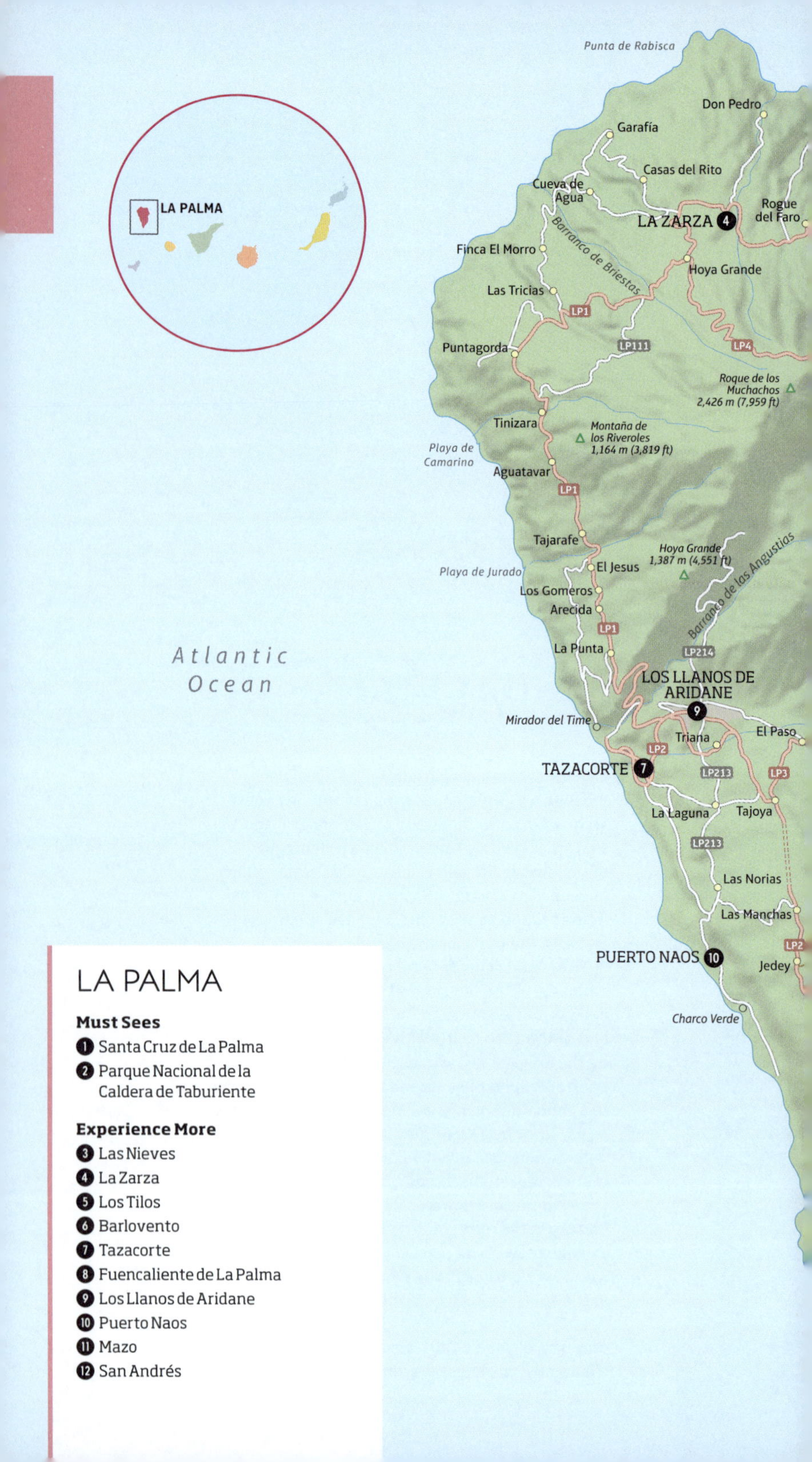

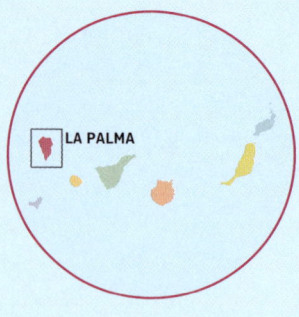

LA PALMA
Punta de Rabisca
Don Pedro
Garafía
Casas del Rito
Cueva de Agua
LA ZARZA 4
Rogue del Faro
Finca El Morro
Barranco de Briestas
Hoya Grande
Las Tricias
LP1
Puntagorda
LP111
LP4
Roque de los Muchachos
2,426 m (7,959 ft)
Tinizara
Montaña de los Riveroles
1,164 m (3,819 ft)
Playa de Camarino
Aguatavar
LP1
Tajarafe
Hoya Grande
1,387 m (4,551 ft)
Barranco de las Angustias
Playa de Jurado
El Jesus
Los Gomeros
Arecida
LP1
La Punta
LP214
Atlantic Ocean
LOS LLANOS DE ARIDANE 9
Mirador del Time
Triana
El Paso
LP2
TAZACORTE 7
LP213
LP3
La Laguna
Tajoya
LP213
Las Norias
Las Manchas
LP2
PUERTO NAOS 10
Jedey
Charco Verde

LA PALMA

Must Sees

1. Santa Cruz de La Palma
2. Parque Nacional de la Caldera de Taburiente

Experience More

3. Las Nieves
4. La Zarza
5. Los Tilos
6. Barlovento
7. Tazacorte
8. Fuencaliente de La Palma
9. Los Llanos de Aridane
10. Puerto Naos
11. Mazo
12. San Andrés

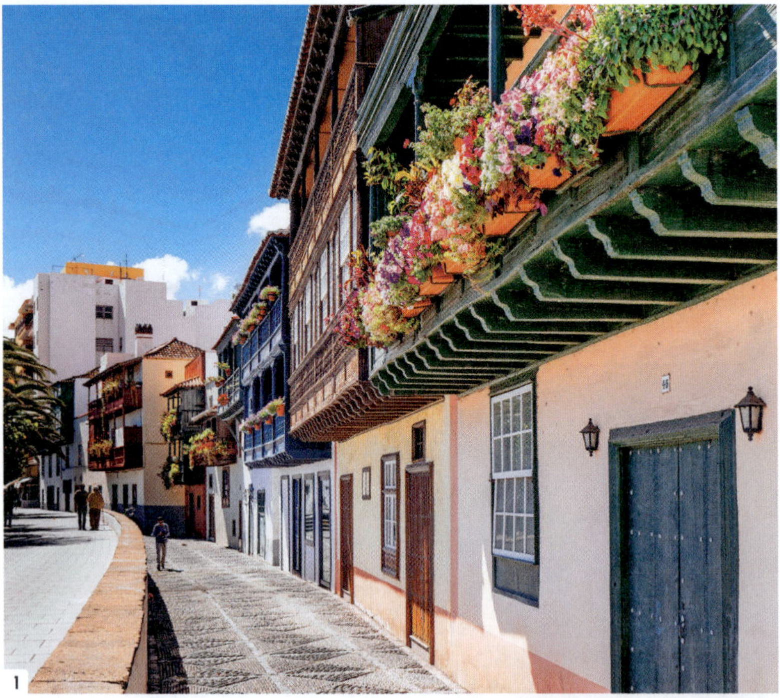
1

2

3

4

←

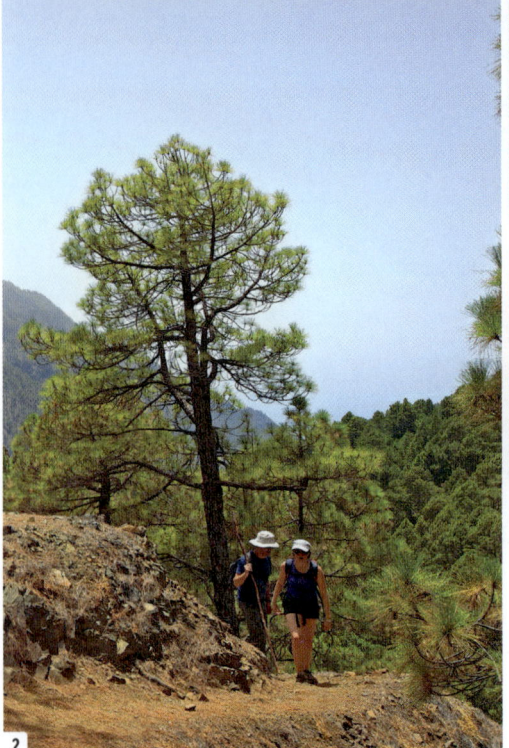

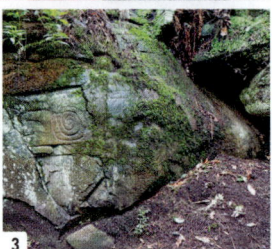

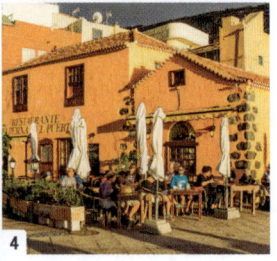

1 The Avenida Marítima.

2 A trail to volcanic Tajogaite.

3 Petroglyphs at Parque Cultural La Zarza.

4 A restaurant in Puerto de Tazacorte.

5 DAYS

Day 1

Commence your trip to La Palma in Santa Cruz de la Palma (p192). Grab a breakfast on the go before strolling along the picturesque Avenida Marítima, adorned with pretty wooden balconies typical of the islands. Parallel to this is the Calle O'Daly, where you can spot more historic houses (and shops). After a spot of lunch, explore the Plaza de España, making time to check out the Iglesia del Salvador. Then, it's over to the Museo Naval to learn all about La Palma's maritime history. Come evening, wander to the Castillo de Santa Catalina (Calle el Castillete 10) to watch the sunset before enjoying dinner at one of the many seaside restaurants.

Day 2

Pick up a rental car and drive from Santa Cruz de la Palma to the lush Caldera de Taburiente Parque Nacional (p196) for a day in nature. Hit the winding LP-3 mountain road up to the visitor's centre (LP-3- Carretera General Padrón 47, El Paso). From here, get information on trails and enjoy displays about the protected area, geology and animal life. Enjoy an early picnic near the centre before heading out on one of several hiking routes; these vary in length and difficulty, but all offer stunning views. After an active afternoon, head to Puerto de Tazacorte for dinner and a sunset tipple overlooking the water before resting for the night.

Day 3

Today is all about exploring La Palma's industrious past. Drive from Puerto de Tazacorte to the nearby Museo del Plátano (Calle Miguel de Unamuno 13) to learn about the island's banana trade before driving to its southernmost point, Fuencaliente (p200). See the organic salt pans here before enjoying lunch with a view at the on-site restaurant. Sated, make your way to the Bodegas Carballo vineyard (Ctra a Las Indias 74), best known for its dessert wine – there are soft drinks for the designated drivers – and winery tours. Head back to Puerto de Tazacorte to see off the day on a sunset boat tour.

Day 4

From Puerto de Tazacorte, drive a little further east to join a guided hiking tour of the island's newest volcano: Tajogaite, which last erupted in 2021. It's a fairly easy trek of about 5 km (3 miles) from the Centro de Visitantes de La Caldera de Taburiente, taking around three hours. Refuel after the morning of hiking at the nearby Restaurante Chipi-Chipi (www.chipichipi.es) for a Canarian lunch. When you're ready, drive northwards to San Andrés (p201), one of the oldest towns on the island, to enjoy an evening wander and rest.

Day 5

After a quick breakfast, drive west from San Andrés until you reach the Parque Cultural La Zarza (p198). Enjoy the one-hour walk around this archaeological site, where symbols were carved into the rocks by the Guanche people. Head to Barlovento (p199) for lunch, stopping at the viewpoints along the way. After lunch, drive to the popular Charco Azul, a beautiful natural pool protected from the ocean waves, and stay to watch the sunset. Grab a light bite before finishing your trip with stargazing further south from Mirador San Bartolo.

SANTA CRUZ DE LA PALMA

 13 km (8 miles) S   Plaza de la Constitución s/n; 922 412 106

Situated on a bay known to the Guanches as Timibucar, Santa Cruz de La Palma was the third most important port in the Spanish empire, after Antwerp and Seville. The town's wealth attracted pirates, who plundered it on several occasions. Since recovered, the island's capital is today full of popular sights.

GREAT VIEW
Plaza de España

Climb the stairs in Plaza de España for a gorgeous view over the plaza. You'll take in its lovely Renaissance architecture, marble fountain and the eye-catching Mudéjar-style church, El Salvador.

① Ermita de San Sebastián

📍 Pl de San Sebastián

This small whitewashed chapel, which is usually closed, is one of several in Santa Cruz. The others include the 16th-century Ermita de Nuestra Señora de la Luz, which stands in the picturesque Plaza de San Sebastián, and the Iglesia de El Salvador, which stands in Plaza de España.

Ermita de San Sebastián's simple façade features a bell gable and a small balcony. Inside is a beautiful statue of St Catherine, which was brought here from Antwerp.

② Plaza de España

At the very heart of Santa Cruz lies the Plaza de España. This irregularly shaped public square was known as Plaza de la Constitución in the 19th century, as a tribute to the signing of Spain's first constitution in 1812. It is surrounded by some historic buildings, including the City Hall complex, Iglesia de El Salvador and the fine Monteverde, Lorenzo, Massieu and Pereyra *casas* – all of which are excellent examples of Renaissance architecture.

At the centre of the square is a statue of Manuel Díaz Hernández (1774–1863), a priest of the Salvador church who preached political liberalism in his sermons. There's also a 16th-century artificial fountain in the middle of the plaza.

③ Calle O'Daly

The charming main street, now turned into a pedestrian precinct, bears testimony to

←

Plaza de España with the statue of Manuel Díaz Hernández in the centre

the town's former wealth and prestige. It was named after an Irish banana merchant who settled here. The street is lined on both sides with vibrant, historic houses and residences, as well as boutiques. The most outstanding of these is the Casa Principal de Salazar (No. 22), dating from the early 17th century and featuring distinctive wooden balconies and a handcrafted wooden ceiling. The iconic building is now used as a venue for cultural events and exhibitions. The Casa Pinto (No. 2) is another splendid example of 19th-century Canarian architecture.

> **At the very heart of Santa Cruz lies the Plaza de España. This irregularly shaped public square was known as Plaza de la Constitución in the 19th century.**

④

Iglesia de El Salvador

📍 Plaza de España 3
📞 922 413 250 🕐 10:30am–8:30pm daily

Built at the end of the 15th century, this church acquired its present shape in the second half of the 16th century. This is the most monumental example of the Canary Islands' Renaissance architecture. Its façade has a portal in the form of a triumphal arch dating back to the 16th century, depicting an allegory of Christ and his Church. The tower that adjoins the church was built of volcanic stone blocks. Meanwhile, the interior features a stunning Mudéjar (Spanish-Moorish) coffered wood ceiling and sculptures by the Tenerife artist Fernando

Estévez. The altarpiece of the high chapel has a 19th-century painting of the *Transfiguration* by Sevillian Romantic painter Antonio Maria Esquivel.

↑ The nave and intricate Mudéjar ceiling, Iglesia de El Salvador

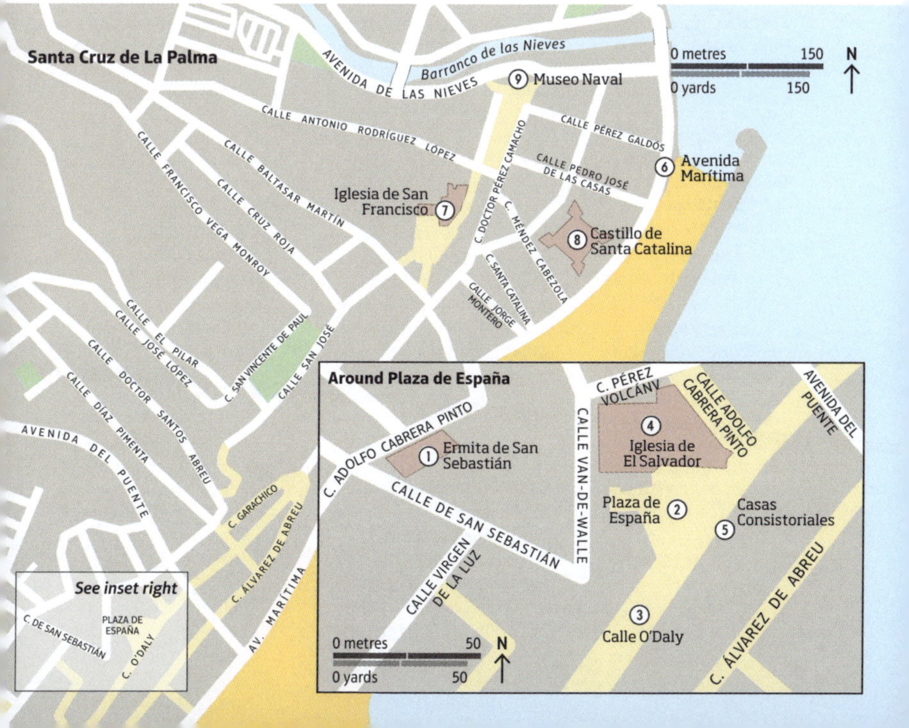

Santa Cruz de La Palma

SHOP

La Margarita Artesanía

This shop has many delicious local culinary products on offer, including *mojos* and traditional Spanish *almendrados* (almond cookies). The store also sells wines, cigars, souvenirs and a range of accessories.

Calle O'Daly 10

La Molina Artesanía

Head to La Molina Artesanía for an incredible selection of locally designed jewellery and accessories, as well as regional wines and delicacies. Don't miss the excellent variety of coffees sourced from Agaete on the island.

Calle O'Daly 17
lamolinartesania.com

Tienda Oficial de la Bajada de la Virgen

A small shop specializing in souvenirs, including stationery, t-shirts and other accessories, which commemorate the island's patron saint festivities.

Calle Anselmo Pérez de Brito 2

La Recova

This municipal market is the place to go for the freshest selection of local produce and regional foods. It's set in a picturesque 16th-century building that was once a hospital.

Avenida el Puente 16

 ⑤

Casas Consistoriales

Plaza de España

The Renaissance-style Casas Consistoriales formerly housed the bishop's palace and now is used as the town hall. It was built in 1559–63 and has several noteworthy architectural features. Its magnificent façade, resting on columned arcades, is decorated with the bust of Philip II, carved in low relief, and bears the crests of La Palma and the Habsburgs. The inside walls and stairwell are decorated with stunning paintings and enormous murals by the artist Mariano de Cassio, depicting island life.

 ⑥

Avenida Marítima

This is regarded as one of the Canary Islands' most beautiful and best-preserved shorelines. At its southern end stands a dragon tree (*p24*), with curiously twisted branches. At the northern end of the shore stands the Casas de los Balcones – a row of picturesque old houses that have been wonderfully restored, with colourful elevations featuring beautiful wooden double balconies. The tall and narrow houses make for a striking sight on the street. The distinctive balconies are enclosed with mullioned windows, a style which is believed to be of Arabic origin. While the balconies face the sea, they are actually found at the back of the houses they adorn; the main façades of these buildings face Calle Real.

 PICTURE PERFECT
Avenida Marítima

Stroll along Avenida Marítima for great photo opportunities. The colourful houses adorned with wooden balconies draped in plants make for a stunning snap.

Walking by the vibrant Casas de los Balcones on Avenida Marítima

local relics, along with Guanche skulls, stuffed animals and several fine Spanish school paintings.

⑧ Castillo de Santa Catalina

🅰 Avda Marítima

This magnificent 16th-century castle is also known as Castillo Real. It was built as part of a series of defences against pirates who plundered ships as they left the port for the Americas with exports of goods such as sugar cane. In 1585, gunfire from the castle prevented Sir Francis Drake from taking over the island. The castle can be viewed only from the outside. The entrance features the coat of arms of the Catholic Kings.

⑨ Museo Naval

🅰 Plaza de la Alameda
🕐 10am–6pm daily (Jul–Sep: to 7pm) 🌐 museo navaldelbarco.es

Near Plaza de la Alameda stands a fine 1940 replica of the Santa María – the tiny ship in which Christopher Columbus set off in 1492 to travel to the Americas.

The inhabitants of Santa Cruz have named the ship El Barco de la Virgen – the Ship of the Holy Virgin. Inside is a modest maritime museum, which

Iglesia de San Francisco

🅰 Plaza de San Francisco 5
📞 928 364 663 🕐 10am–6pm daily

In 1508, Franciscan monks accompanying Alonso Fernándo de Lugo in his conquest of the island began to build their abbey in Santa Cruz. The church, built in the 16th to 17th centuries, is one of the earliest examples of Renaissance architecture on La Palma. Outstanding features include the main altar and the dome-shaped coffered ceiling, as well as the richly painted decor.

Inside, there are numerous art treasures to be enjoyed, such as the superb Flemish sculpture group depicting Saint Anne, the 16th-century *Virgin and Child*, and the *Lord of the Fall*, a carved Sevillian figure dating from the 18th century. Once part of the Royal Convent of La Inmaculada Concepción, today the abbey houses the Museo Insular exhibiting

BAJADA DE LA VIRGEN DE LAS NIEVES

Every five years, Santa Cruz de la Palma marks the Bajada de la Virgen de Las Nieves series of celebrations. In late June, locals in traditional costumes carry a statue of the Virgen de Las Nieves to El Salvador church. This signals the start of the Semana Chica, beginning with the Pandorga lantern procession led by children. This is then followed by Semana Grande in July, featuring parades and the lovely Minué dance. After some symbolic ceremonies, the statue of the Virgen de Las Nieves returns to her sanctuary, ending 40 days of festivities.

traces the history of the island from the 15th century to the present day. The core of its collection consists of old charts, navigational instruments and a variety of ships' flags.

A statue modelled on Napoleon, which stands in front of the Museo Naval

PARQUE NACIONAL DE LA CALDERA DE TABURIENTE

⌂ Carretera General de Padrón 47, El Paso 🕐 9am–6pm daily 🌐 miteco.gob.es

Awarded national park status in 1954, La Caldera de Taburiente is a massive crater formed in the course of several powerful volcanic eruptions. Most people come here seeking out the incredible trails in a wild setting.

The land now known as the Parque Nacional de la Caldera de Taburiente once served as a refuge for the last Benahoares when the Spanish invaded in the 15th century. Today, the national park is a refuge for nature lovers, who come to enjoy hikes among some of the most epic landscapes in the whole archipelago.

💬 INSIDER TIP
Refugio Punta de Los Roques

At the top of the gorge next to La Cumbrecita is the Refugio Punta de Los Roques, a mountain refuge and camp ground. Make sure to come prepared, as there are no facilities on site.

ASTRONOMICAL OBSERVATORY

The International Astrophysical Observatory *(iac.es)* near Roque de los Muchachos was opened in 1985, in the presence of King Juan Carlos and many other European heads of state. Gran Telescopio Canarias (GTC) is the world's largest reflecting telescope, with an effective mirror opening of 10 m (34 ft), and was inaugurated in 2009. Plans for a visitor centre are underway but guided tours are run in the summer months *(Jun–Oct)*. These are booked out well in advance so organize as soon as possible.

→

Admiring the view from Roque de los Muchachos, and *(inset)* the park's observatory

There are plenty of great views to take in, not least from Pico de la Cruz, one of the park's highest peaks. A challenging four- to five-hour walking trail, connecting Pico de las Nieves with Roque de los Muchachos, leads over the peak through some breathtaking scenery. A trail to the Roque de los Muchachos, running along the highest peaks of Caldera de Taburiente, is another highlight of the park; it provides a view over the steep walls of the crater, shrouded with dense fog. For sunset and sunrise views, head to Lomo de las Chozas.

Visitors can also stop at one of the six telescopes that have been placed along the steep, mountain road around Roque de los Muchachos. Nearby, the Mirador de los Andenes holds a natural wonder: bare rocks, eroded by wind and moisture over thousands of years, that have been shaped into natural and artful shapes.

No roads run through the park (although the observatory and viewpoints at Los Brecitos and La Cumbrecita can be reached by car). The best way to enjoy its trails is to come prepared – ensure you have enough provisions for your trip and plan ahead before setting out.

↑ Walking across the volcanic landscape along one of the park's scenic trails

EXPERIENCE MORE

3
Las Nieves

This village, lying among green hills above Santa Cruz de La Palma, is the main pilgrimage centre and the most important religious shrine on the island.

Standing in a picturesque spot is the Santuario de la Virgen de las Nieves. Its small church was built in 1657 on the site of the original chapel. It forms a historic complex together with the neighbouring buildings: the 17th-century Pilgrim's House, the early 18th-century Parish House and several houses that belonged to members of the local aristocracy.

The church is a typical example of colonial Canary architecture, with wooden balcony façades, whitewashed walls and a lovely Mudéjar (Spanish-Moorish) ceiling of Canary pine. The flickering candles, lit by the faithful, and the rich decor give the place its unique atmosphere.

The gilded Baroque main altar is occupied by a 14th-century 82-cm- (32-in-) high terracotta statue of the Madonna of the Snow, the island's patron saint, which was made in Flanders. Her image refers to her miraculous appearance during a freak August snowstorm in Rome. The side walls of the church are decorated with a row of ex-voto canvases. These votive pictures are donated in thanks for miracles performed by the patron saint, including saving a ship caught in a storm and answering the prayers of childless couples.

4
La Zarza

⚑ 10 km (6 miles) W of Barlovento

The archaeological site of La Zarza provides visible evidence of the Benahoares – the former inhabitants of La Palma – who left strange signs carved into the rock in several sites throughout the north of the island, including Roque Faro, Don Pedro and Juan Adalid. These carvings consist mostly of spirals, circles and linear figures, and have survived in their natural environment, though their meaning remains unknown.

The information centre has a small museum illustrating the everyday life of the Benahoares. The exhibition includes a 20-minute video and shows how the ancient inhabitants of the island lived, revealing their diet, medical practices and burial rites. The illuminated screens display images of erupting volcanoes, island scenery, its flora, fauna, and a map pointing out where the rock carvings were found.

When the carvings were discovered here in 1941, they

Did You Know?

La Zarza is home to two species of endemic pigeon: Bolle's pigeon and the laurel pigeon.

became an archaeological sensation. Apart from the puzzling pictures, the ancient inhabitants of the island also left two Aztec-style carved images: one of a man, and an abstract figure of a woman with the head of an insect.

5
Los Tilos

⚑ 3 km (2 miles) W of San Andrés 🛈 Centro de Investigaciones e Interpretación de la Reserva de Biosfera "Los Tilos": 922 451 246; 9am–noon & 1–6:25pm daily

The rocky, almost vertical sides of the Barranco del Agua ravine are overgrown with an evergreen rainforest, which

→ Barlovento's pristine salt-water swimming pools by the ocean

Walking past colourful modern buildings in Tazacorte

includes moss-covered laurel trees – the island's largest concentration of the ancient *laurisilva* – plus lime, myrtle and ferns.

In 1983, Los Tilos was declared a biosphere reserve by UNESCO. A 3-km (2-mile) winding asphalt road, running along the bottom of the ravine, leads to the tourist centre, with its information point and restaurant.

The reserve area, spanning some 5 sq km (2 sq miles), has a number of marked walking trails. One leads to a lovely viewpoint, the Mirador de las Barandas. A longer, more difficult 6-km (4-mile) trail with steep ascents leads in a southwesterly direction to Caldera de Marcos y Cordero, where determined tourists can admire the picturesque waterfalls.

Barlovento

Besides the Iglesia de Nuestra Señora, Barlovento's main claim to fame is its fiesta held every two years in August, when the villagers recreate bloody scenes from the Battle of Lepanto (1571).

Close to the town is the Piscinas de Fajana, located around 6 km (4 miles) to the northeast. It offers a rock pool topped up with cool water from the Atlantic. The lighthouse at Punta Cumplida, also nearby, is the oldest on the island, dating from 1861.

Tazacorte

In 1492, Alonso Fernández de Lugo commenced the conquest of the island from Tazacorte. Today, the skyline of this small town, surrounded by banana plantations, is dominated by the striking Iglesia de San Miguel Arcángel. The church, built in the 16th century, was extended in 1992 and given

a striking, abstract stained-glass window.

The **Museo del Plátano** explores the export of bananas, the economic mainstay in La Palma. Next door, at the **Museo del Mojo**, there is even more about this industry.

Just 12 km (7 miles) north is Mirador del Time, which offers a fine view over Los Llanos de Aridane and Tazacorte.

Museo del Plátano
🏠 Camino de San Antonio
📞 922 480 151 🕐 10am–1:30pm & 4–6pm Mon–Fri, 10am–1pm Sat

Museo del Mojo
🏠 Camino de San Antonio
📞 922 480 803 🕐 For renovation

← Salt flats in Punta Fuencaliente, near Fuencaliente de La Palma

 8

Fuencaliente de La Palma

📠 ℹ️ Pl Minerva, s/n; 922 444 003

The name of this place derives from *fuente caliente*, meaning "hot spring," although the spring has long since been swallowed up by a series of volcanic eruptions. Set amid vineyards, the small town is best known for its sweet, heavy wine and is the home of the oldest and largest winery on the island, established in 1948. Evidence of the town's past can be seen in the small parish church of San Antonio Abad (1730).

Located a little over 10 km (6 miles) to the south is Punta Fuencaliente, La Palma's southernmost point. Here there are two lighthouses and the salt extraction plant of Salinas Teneguía with its numerous brine pools.

 9

Los Llanos de Aridane

📠 ℹ️ 922 402 583

La Palma's second town is a modern affair, with the exception of the Plaza de España. The charming square of Los Llanos de Aridane, with laurel trees casting a pleasant shade over café tables, mainly serves as a venue for concerts.

One side of the square is occupied by the town hall. Opposite it stands the Iglesia de Nuestra Señora de los Remedios. This white 16th-century church is built in the Canarian colonial style. Its Baroque altar features a 16th-century Dutch statue of its patron saint. In the Museo Arqueológico Benahoarita, you can learn more about the Indigenous people of La Palma.

About 3 km (2 miles) to the east is El Paso, a small town famous for its hand-made cigars. Its main feature is the old quarter, with traditional Canary-style buildings surrounding the chapel of Nuestra Señora de Bonanza. Next to the chapel stands a modern church with Neo-Gothic furnishings, dedicated to the same saint.

A short way south of El Paso is the Parque Paraíso de las Aves – a combination of botanical garden and miniature zoo, housing rare and endangered birds from many corners of the world.

 10

Puerto Naos

 📠

A small, quiet resort, Puerto Naos was once a fishing village, but is now being transformed by an ever-increasing number of low-built apartment complexes. Its main attraction is the guaranteed good weather, with some 3,300 annual hours of sunshine.

DIVE AT LAS CRUCES DE MALPIQUE

Near La Palma's southern tip, off the coast of Fuencaliente de La Palma, lies Las Cruces de Malpique. This underwater site features 40 stone crosses honouring 16th-century Jesuit monks who were viciously killed by pirates. With excellent visibility and a maximum depth of 25 m (82 ft), this spot attracts photographers and divers of all levels. It's part of a UNESCO Biosphere Reserve, offering easy shore access and abundant marine life.

INSIDER TIP
See Lava

View the Tojogaite crater and recent lava flow from the Mirador de Tacande. Tour operators in the area offer excursions on buggy and on foot, and bring you within 200 m (655 ft) of the crater.

Set in a beautifully restored mansion in Las Manchas, the Wine Museum provides information on the production of different varieties of wine, and visitors can even taste some of them. Also worth seeing is the mosaic-decorated Plaza de la Glorieta by Luis Morera.

Charco Verde, about 2 km (1 mile) to the south, is a scenic beach, which is sheltered from the waves, and ideal for families.

Mazo

Mazo is famous for its *puros* (handmade cigars). Tourists also shop here for handicrafts including woven baskets and lacework; the Escuela Insular de Artesanía sells these lace products and holds demonstrations of how they are made. Other sights include the Cerámica el Molino, known for its production of replica Guanche vessels, and the Museo de Corpus, which exhibits decorations for the feast of Corpus Christi.

The Iglesia de San Blás (1512) looks out towards Tenerife and was extended in the 19th century. It features a beautiful Baroque altar.

Just 4 km (2 miles) to the south is the historic Parque Arqueológico de Belmaco, a series of caves with original Guanche inscriptions.

San Andrés

This pretty seaside village, with cobbled streets and squares planted with flowers and palms, is filled with typical local houses. At its centre stands the Iglesia de San Andrés Apostól. Built as a fortified church in the 16th century and extended in the 17th century, this is one of the oldest churches in the Canary Islands. The interior features a Baroque main altar and Mudéjar-style coffered ceiling. Look out for the paintings of assorted human limbs on the wall, hung in thanks for the supposed healing powers of the church's patron saint.

San Andrés remains under joint administration with the larger town of Los Sauces, hence the combined name of San Andrés y Los Sauces. The environs of both towns are famous for the cultivation of bananas and sugar cane.

The most noteworthy building in Los Sauces is the Iglesia Nuestra Señora de Montserrat, the largest church on the island, which dates back to 1515. Its present Neo-Romanesque appearance is the result of refurbishment in 1960. Inside is a picture of the Madonna, which has been attributed to the Dutch artist Pieter Poubrus.

A short way to the south is Charco Azul, a tiny village set among banana plantations. High cliffs provide effective shelter for a natural tidal pool of a startling blue shade.

About 7 km (4 miles) to the south is Puntallana, home to the Iglesia San Juan Bautista. However, Puntallana owes most of its popularity to Playa de Nogales, a long black-sand beach backed by steep cliffs.

← The square surrounding Iglesia Nuestra Señora de Montserrat, San Andrés

↑ Approaching a steep volcanic trail along the Ruta de los Volcanes

A LONG WALK
RUTA DE LOS VOLCANES

Distance 19 km (12 miles) **Stopping-off points** Fuencaliente is a good place to stop for a meal **Terrain** Steep slopes, with a combinaiton of paths, forest tracks and roads

A somewhat arduous trail leads along the Cumbre Vieja mountain ridge, from Refugio del Pilar (alt. 1,450 m/4,757 ft) towards Fuencaliente. This section of the Ruta de los Volcanoes hike, which should take some 6 to 7 hours, is unforgettable. Winding round steep volcanic rims, the path leads past striking geological formations and provides magnificent views of the eastern and western coasts of the island.

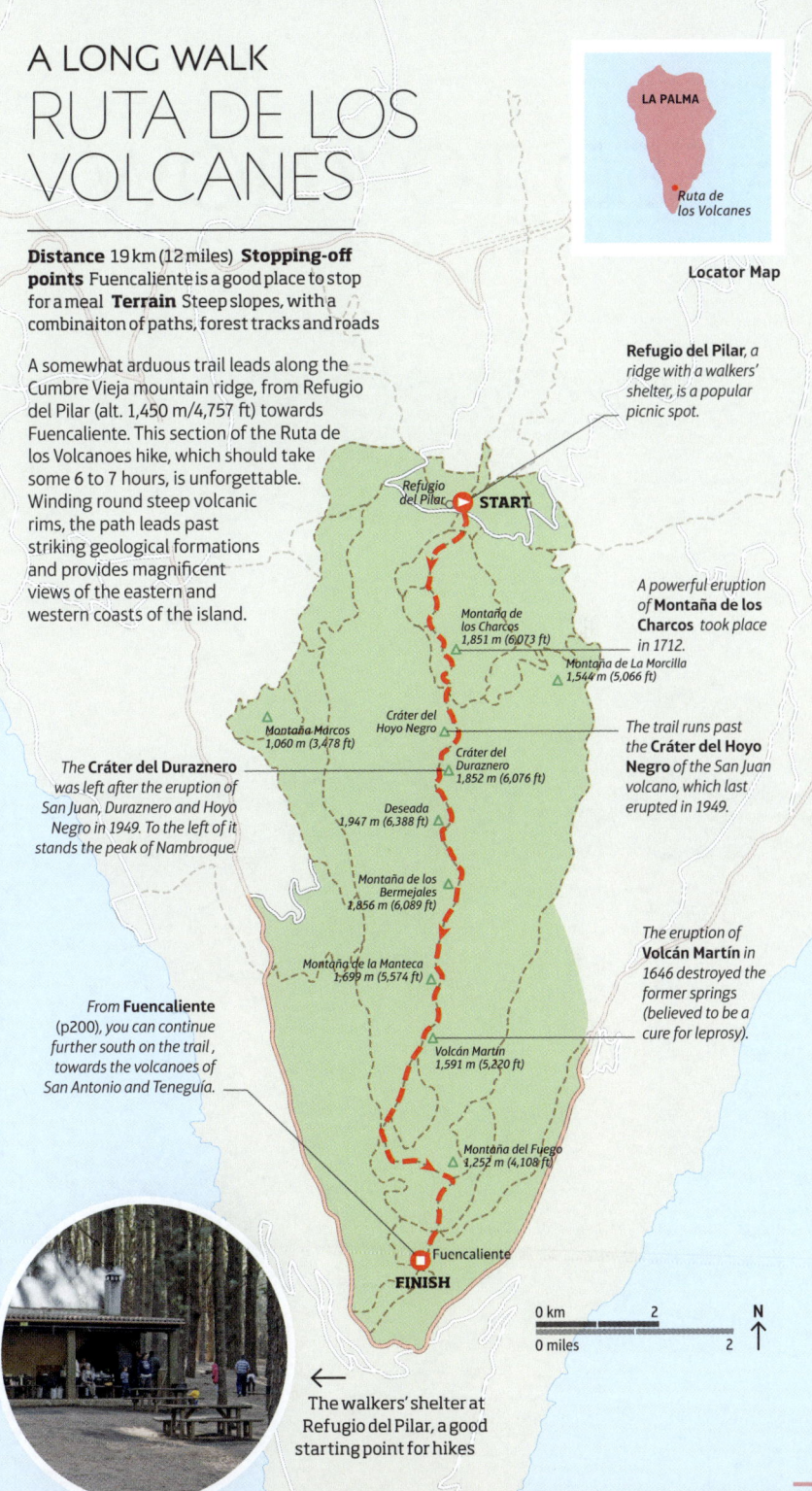

Locator Map

LA PALMA

Ruta de los Volcanes

Refugio del Pilar, *a ridge with a walkers' shelter, is a popular picnic spot.*

Refugio del Pilar   **START**

A powerful eruption of **Montaña de los Charcos** *took place in 1712.*

Montaña de los Charcos 1,851 m (6,073 ft)

Montaña de La Morcilla 1,544 m (5,066 ft)

Montaña Marcos 1,060 m (3,478 ft)

Cráter del Hoyo Negro

Cráter del Duraznero 1,852 m (6,076 ft)

The **Cráter del Duraznero** *was left after the eruption of San Juan, Duraznero and Hoyo Negro in 1949. To the left of it stands the peak of Nambroque.*

The trail runs past the **Cráter del Hoyo Negro** *of the San Juan volcano, which last erupted in 1949.*

Deseada 1,947 m (6,388 ft)

Montaña de los Bermejales 1,856 m (6,089 ft)

Montaña de la Manteca 1,699 m (5,574 ft)

The eruption of **Volcán Martín** *in 1646 destroyed the former springs (believed to be a cure for leprosy).*

From **Fuencaliente** *(p200), you can continue further south on the trail, towards the volcanoes of San Antonio and Teneguía.*

Volcán Martín 1,591 m (5,220 ft)

Montaña del Fuego 1,252 m (4,108 ft)

Fuencaliente   **FINISH**

0 km   2
0 miles   2

N ↑

← The walkers' shelter at Refugio del Pilar, a good starting point for hikes

NEED TO KNOW

A mountain road in Fuerteventura

BEFORE
YOU GO

Things change, so plan ahead to make the most of your trip. Be prepared for all eventualities by considering the following points before you travel.

AT A GLANCE

CURRENCY
Euro

AVERAGE DAILY SPEND

SAVE	SPEND	SPLURGE
€35	€80	€150+

BOTTLED WATER	COFFEE	BEER	DINNER FOR TWO
€2	€2	€3	€40

ESSENTIAL PHRASES

Hello	Hola
Goodbye	Adiós
Please	Por favor
Thank you	Gracias
Do you speak English?	¿Habla inglés?
I don't understand	No comprendo

ELECTRICITY SUPPLY
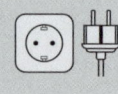
Power sockets are type C and F, fitting a two-prong, round-pin plug. Standard voltage is 220–240v.

Passports and Visas

For entry requirements, including visas, consult your nearest Spanish embassy or check the **Exteriores** website. Citizens of the UK, US, Canada, Australia and New Zealand do not need a visa for stays of up to three months but in future must apply in advance for the European Travel Information and Authorization System (**ETIAS**); roll-out has continually been postponed so check the website for details. Visitors from other countries may also require an ETIAS, so check before travelling.
ETIAS
W travel-europe.europa.eu/etias_en
Exteriores
W exteriores.gob.es

Government Advice

Now more than ever, it is important to consult both your and the Spanish government's advice before travelling. The **UK Foreign, Commonwealth and Development Office (FCDO)**, the **US State Department**, the **Australian Department of Foreign Affairs and Trade**, and the Spanish Exteriores website offer the latest information on security, health and local regulations.
Australian Department of Foreign Affairs and Trade
W smartraveller.gov.au
UK Foreign, Commonwealth and Development Office (FCDO)
W gov.uk/foreign-travel-advice
US Department of State
W travel.state.gov

Customs information

Information on laws on goods and currency taken in or out of Spain is on the **Turespaña** website.
Turespaña
W spain.info

Insurance

We recommend taking out a comprehensive insurance policy covering theft, loss of

belongings, medical care, cancellations and delays, and read the small print carefully. UK citizens are eligible for free emergency medical care in Spain provided they have a valid European Health Insurance Card (EHIC) or UK Global Health Insurance Card (**GHIC**).

GHIC
W ghic.org.uk

Vaccinations

No inoculations are required to visit Spain and the Canary Islands.

Booking Accommodation

Spain offers a wide range of accommodation, from five-star hotels to campsites, including a system of government-run hotels called *paradores*. A useful list of accommodation can be found on the Turespaña website.

As a winter-sun destination, the Canary Islands are busiest from December to March; book your accommodation well in advance during this period. Most hotels quote their prices without including tax (IGIC), which is 6.5 per cent on the Canary Islands.

Money

Major credit and debit cards are accepted by most businesses, while pre-paid currency cards and American Express are accepted in some. Contactless payments are increasingly more common but not universal, so it's wise to carry some cash for small items. ATMs can be found in all cities and most towns, although many charge for cash withdrawals.

Spain does not have a big tipping culture, but rounding up the bill is appreciated and common.

Travellers with Specific Requirements

The Confederación Española de Personas con Discapacidad Física y Orgánica (**COCEMFE**) and Accessible Spain provide information and tailored itineraries for those with reduced mobility, sight and hearing.

Most accommodation and sights generally cater for all visitors, including beaches and nature reserves. Public transport on the islands

includes adapted taxis and buses and the airports provide a free service for passengers with specific requirements.

Accessible Spain
W accessiblespaintravel.com
COCEMFE
W cocemfe.es

Language

The official language of Spain is Spanish. English is widely spoken in cities and other tourist spots, but not always in rural areas.

Opening Hours

Situations can change quickly and unexpectedly. Always check before visiting attractions and hospitality venues for up-to-date opening hours and booking requirements.

Lunchtime Many smaller shops may close for the siesta between 2pm and 5pm; large shopping centres and supermarkets will stay open all day.

Monday Some museums, public buildings and monuments are closed all day; it's worth checking ahead of visiting.

Sunday Churches and cathedrals are closed to the public during Mass.

Public holidays Most museums and many shops either close early or do not open at all.

PUBLIC HOLIDAYS	
1 Jan	New Year's Day
Mar/ Apr	Good Friday
1 May	Labour Day
30 May	Canary Island Day
15 Aug	Assumption Day
12 Oct	Spain's National Day
1 Nov	All Saints' Day
6 Dec	Spanish Constitution Day
8 Dec	Feast of the Immaculate Conception
25 Dec	Christmas Day

GETTING
AROUND

Whether you're visiting one island for a short break or ferry hopping between the islands, discover how best to reach your destination and travel like a pro.

AT A GLANCE

PUBLIC TRANSPORT COSTS

GRAN CANARIA TO FUERTEVENTURA

€55

Ferry
Single journey

TENERIFE TO LA GOMERA

€40

Ferry
Single journey

LANZAROTE TO GRAN CANARIA

€99

Ferry
Single journey

TOP TIP
Avoid on-the-spot fines – be sure to stamp your ticket to validate your journey.

SPEED LIMIT

URBAN ROADS

50 km/h
(31 mph)

DUAL CARRIAGEWAY

100 km/h
(60 mph)

SECONDARY ROAD

90 km/h
(55 mph)

MOTORWAYS

120 km/h
(74 mph)

Arriving by Air

Located south of mainland Spain, the Canary Islands are best reached by airplane. The archipelago is home to a total of eight airports, in addition to seaports. While each island has its own airport, Gran Canaria's **Aeropuerto de Gran Canaria**, Lanzarote's **Aeropuerto César Manrique-Lanzarote** and the two airports of Tenerife are the primary entry points into the Canary Islands. Most international flights and those from mainland Spain arrive at one of these three islands.

Of Tenerife's two airports – **Los Rodeos (Tenerife Norte TFN)** and **Reina Sofia (Tenerife Sur TFS)** – Los Rodeos is closer to the capital city, but it's more commonly used for domestic flights within the Canary Islands. Reina Sofia is the hub for international and charter flights.

Other smaller airports across the islands include **El Matorral** in Fuerteventura and **La Gomera**, **El Hierro**, and **La Palma** on their respective islands. These all provide useful daily connections between the islands of the archipelago.

Aeropuerto de Gran Canaria
W aena.es/en/gran-canaria
Aeropuerto César Manrique-Lanzarote
W aena.es/en/cesar-manrique-lanzarote
Aeropuerto de El Hierro
W aena.es/en/el-hierro
Aeropuerto El Matorral (Fuerteventura)
W aena.es/en/fuerteventura
Aeropuerto de La Gomera
W aena.es/en/la-gomera
Aeropuerto de La Palma
W aena.es/en/la-palma
Los Rodeos (Tenerife Norte TFN)
W aena.es/en/tenerife-norte-ciudad-de-la-laguna
Reina Sofia (Tenerife Sur TFS)
W aena.es/en/tenerife-sur

Domestic Air Travel

The airports on the smaller islands are principally for travelling between islands. Although these are mainly served by a

number of private charter flights, there are also flights with commercial inter-island airlines, like **Binter Canarias Airlines** and **Canaryfly**. Both of these domestic companies offer daily flights and provide a quick way to get between most of the islands. Flight times are usually less than 90 minutes, and flights connect all the islands throughout the day. The tiny island of La Graciosa, meanwhile, has no airport.

Binter Canarias Airlines
W bintercanarias.com/en
Canaryfly
W canaryfly.es/eng

GETTING TO AND FROM THE AIRPORT

Airport	Distance to main city	Journey time
Aeropuerto de Gran Canaria	25 km (16 miles)	30 mins
César Manrique-Lanzarote Airport	7 km (4 miles)	10 mins
El Hierro Airport	10 km (6 miles)	15 mins
El Matorral Airport (Fuerteventura)	6 km (3.5 miles)	10 mins
La Gomera Airport	35 km (22 miles)	50 mins
La Palma Airport	6 km (3.5 miles)	10 mins
Los Rodeos (Tenerife Norte TFN)	14 km (9 miles)	20 mins
Reina Sofía (Tenerife Sur TFS)	63 km (39 miles)	40 mins

JOURNEY PLANNER

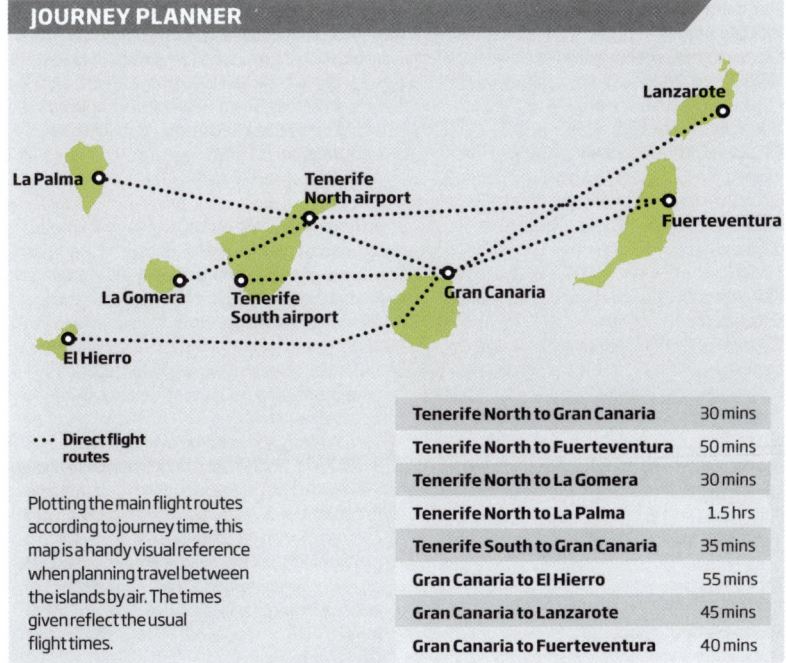

••• Direct flight routes

Plotting the main flight routes according to journey time, this map is a handy visual reference when planning travel between the islands by air. The times given reflect the usual flight times.

Tenerife North to Gran Canaria	30 mins
Tenerife North to Fuerteventura	50 mins
Tenerife North to La Gomera	30 mins
Tenerife North to La Palma	1.5 hrs
Tenerife South to Gran Canaria	35 mins
Gran Canaria to El Hierro	55 mins
Gran Canaria to Lanzarote	45 mins
Gran Canaria to Fuerteventura	40 mins

Public Transport

The main seven islands of the Canaries are all serviced by bus services and different taxi companies. Tenerife has the most comprehnsive public transport network available, making it easy to see most parts of it. Smaller islands, like La Graciosa, don't have public transport options. There's no central public transport authority, so check with local providers for timetables, ticket information and transport maps.

Bus

Buses (also called *guaguas*) are the most common mode of public transport available on the Canary Islands. On the larger of the main seven islands, services run smoothly, but some buses will only run once or twice a day. Buses on the smaller islands will be more infrequent. If you're hoping to get away without hiring a car, you may need to consider using taxis to explore.

Different bus companies operate on each island. **Global** runs services on Gran Canaria; **TITSA** on Tenerife; **Arrecife Bus** offers both city services and intercity routes across Lanzarote; **TIADHE** runs services on Fuerteventura; **GuaguaGomera** on La Gomera; **TILP** on La Palma; and **TransHierro** on El Hierro. Further information on timetables for each company can be found on their websites.

On all the islands you can pay with cash or buy a prepaid transport card to use on the bus system. On the bigger islands, you can also use your contactless card to pay.

Arrecife Bus
W arrecifebus.com/
Global
W guaguasglobal.com/en/
GuaguaGomera
W guaguagomera.com
TIADHE
W tiadhe.com/en/home/
TILP
W tilp.es/en/home/
TITSA
W titsa.com/
TransHierro
W transhierro.com/servicios/transporte-regular/

Taxi

There are many taxi companies available on all the islands; when the bus services are scarce, a taxi may sometimes be the best option. Taxi journeys to and from an airport will often include an additional airport fee and a luggage charge.

Driving

The roads throughout the Canary Islands are generally in a very good condition, and all major towns and villages can be reached by road easily. The larger islands have *auto-carreteras* (motorways), which connect the airports and major tourist hubs.

The island interiors, and the smaller islands in general, have smaller and often winding roads. Driving conditions on mountainous roads can be difficult when it's raining or the clouds descend. The roads can also become wet and slippery, and visibility is often low. Some of the scenic spots of the Canary Islands can only be accessed via rough tracks, which make a 4WD necessary. If renting a 4WD isn't possible, seek out an organized tour.

Driving can be challenging in some of the bigger cities of the islands. Parking is often scarse, meaning cars tend to be parked along the roads as a result.

Rules of the Road

When using a car in Spain, drive on the right and use the left lane only for passing other vehicles. Speed limits on urban roads range between 50 km/h (31 mph) and 20 km/h (12 mph), depending on the number of lanes the road has; always check the speed limit signs to be sure.

Most traffic regulations and warnings to motorists are represented on signs by easily recognized symbols. If you have taken the wrong road, and it has a solid white line, turn round as indicated by a *cambio de sentido* (U-turn) sign. At crossings, give way to the right, unless a sign indicates otherwise.

The blood-alcohol concentration (BAC) limit is 0.5 g/l (or 0.3 g/l for drivers who had their licence for less than two years) and is very strictly enforced. Seatbelts are obligatory, as are car seats or booster seats for children under 135 cm (53 in).

Car Hire

To rent a car, you must be over 21 years of age. Car rental agencies are located on all the islands. The most popular companies in Spain are **Europcar**, **Avis** and **Hertz**, but look out too for local agencies like **Cicar**. All have offices at airports and major train stations, as well as in the larger cities. Price is largely dictated by time of year and car type; advance booking is recommended.

The terms and conditions of hire vary according to individual companies. There are no established rules regarding insurance, mileage or petrol; check carefully before signing any contract. For an ordinary car, the terms will probably include a provision ensuring that you do not drive on unmade roads or take the car by ferry to another island.

Avis
W avis.com

Cicar
🅦 cicar.com
Europcar
🅦 europcar.com
Hertz
🅦 hertz-europe.com

Petrol

The smaller islands have very few petrol stations so if you plan to take a car from a larger island to a smaller one, fill up the tank before you head off on your adventures. When planning your journey, keep in mind that cars will often use more fuel on mountainous roads.

Boats and Ferries

When planning an island-hopping trip around the archipelago, remember that travelling by ferry is cheaper than flying and can be a very pleasant option. Ferries are a great way to get between the islands, although not all of the islands are directly connected with one another. Tenerife is the only one that has a direct ferry connection with every other island. The ferries can also take longer than a plane; the longest service from Gran Canaria takes two days to reach the furthest islands.

From popular cities and resorts, it's possible to find several, daily direct connections by ferry or catamaran between the islands. These usually carry cars, buses and lorries as well as foot passengers. They also often have restaurants and cabins. It's possible to use ferries such as these for day trips to the smaller islands of El Hierro, La Palma or La Gomera.

There are a number of ferry companies operating inter-island routes, including **Trasmediterránea** and **Fred. Olsen Express**. Special deals are sometimes available for routes on Trasmediterránea's Naviera Armas line.

Fred. Olsen Express
🅦 fredolsen.es/en
Trasmediterránea
🅦 armastrasmediterranea.com/en

Main Ferry Ports

Las Palmas de Gran Canaria is the most important ferry port in the Canaries, with ferry connections available to most of the other islands. The only exception are ferries from Gran Canaria to Tenerife, which depart from Agaete.

The rest of the islands also have popular ports. The busiest are usually found in the capital cities of the islands, although there are often some in smaller towns too. In Fuerteventura, the main port can be found in Puerto del Rosario; Lanzarote's main starting point for ferry journeys is the port of Los Mármoles in Arrecife; and

Tenerife's main port can be found in the island's capital city, Santa Cruz de Tenerife.

Cycling

When it comes to cycling in the Canaries, there's really something for everyone. Serious cyclists will enjoy the mountainous regions, while those looking for a gentle and scenic bike ride can enjoy the routes through the coastal flatlands. There aren't many dedicated cycle paths across the islands, meaning cyclists often need to share the road with other vehicles.

There are a number of popular cycling events that take place across the islands annually. **Vuelta al Teide** is a road bike tour held every May on Tenerife. The full circuit is 175 km (109 miles) across the Teide National Park and the Teno Rural Park, and takes cyclists around El Teide, Spain's highest peak. The **Gran Canaria Bike Week** is also held in early December, offering up a variety of routes to cater for cyclists of all abilities.

Bike rental shops can be found on all the main islands offering road bikes, mountain bikes and even e-bikes. In Las Palmas de Gran Canaria, there are also apps like **Moxsi** for easy short-term rentals.

Always wear a helmet when cycling and remember to bring a repair kit with you if heading out of town; there are repair shops available across the islands, but these are mainly found in the cities and towns.

Gran Canaria Bike Week
🅦 grancanariabikeweek.es
Moxsi
🅦 moxsi.es/sitycleta/en/
Vuelta al Teide
🅦 vteide.com

Walking

The Canary Islands are a fantastic destination for people who enjoy walking and hiking. Each island brings its own distinctive terrain and trails, which take walkers through national parks, past rugged peaks and along stunning coastal paths. Thanks to the year-round mild weather, it's also pleasant to walk around the cities and tourist resorts. A firm favourite for scenic walks is green El Hierro; the island may be one of the archipelago's smallest, but it has more hiking trails than it does roads.

All of the official walking routes across the Canary Islands have been approved by professionals and are well marked. **HelloCanaryIslands** has useful links to these official route and is a great resource when planning your hikes across the islands.

HelloCanaryIslands
🅦 hellocanaryislands.com/paths/

PRACTICAL
INFORMATION

A little local know-how goes a long way in the Canary Islands. Here you can find all the essential advice and information you will need during your stay.

AT A GLANCE

EMERGENCY NUMBERS

EMERGENCY
SERVICES

112

TIME ZONE
The Canary Islands are always one hour behind mainland Spain. Western European Time (WET) runs from October to March and Western European Summer Time (WEST) from April to September.

TAP WATER
Tap water in the Canary Islands is safe to drink unless stated otherwise, although it may be heavily treated. Bottled water is widely available if preferred.

USEFUL WEBSITES

España
Spain's official tourism website (www.spain.info/en/).
HelloCanaryIslands
The official tourism website of the Canary Islands (www.hellocanaryislands.com).

Personal Security

The Canary Islands are generally a safe destination, but petty crime does exist. Pickpockets are known to work in tourist areas and busy streets. Use your common sense and be alert to your surroundings. If you do have anything stolen, report the crime within 24 hours to the nearest police station and take ID with you. Get a copy of the crime report (denuncia) to make an insurance claim. Contact your embassy if your passport is stolen or in the event of a serious crime.

As a rule, Spaniards are very accepting of all people, regardless of their race, gender or sexuality. Homosexuality was legalized in Spain in 1979, and in 2007, the government recognized same-sex marriage and adoption rights for same-sex couples. The archipelago is generally a welcoming destination for all races, religions and orientations. The Canary Islands are a particularly great destination for the LGBTQ+ community, with popular Pride events taking place each year. That being said, the Catholic church still holds a lot of sway here and some conservative attitudes prevail, especially outside of urban areas. If you do feel unsafe, head for the nearest police station.

Health

Spain has a worldclass healthcare system. Emergency medical care in Spain is free for all UK and EU citizens. If you have an EHIC or GHIC (p207), be sure to present this as soon as possible. You may have to pay after treatment and reclaim the money later.

For visitors coming from outside the UK or EU, payment of medical expenses is the patient's responsibility, so it is important to arrange comprehensive travel insurance before travelling.

In case of illness or injury, head for the emergency department of the nearest hospital. Most hospitals have English-speaking staff who can help with translations. In case of an accident, call for an ambulance on 112 for a multilingual,

24-hour emergency helpline. If your medical problem is non-urgent, head to a pharmacy (*farmacia*) for help and advice. Many pharmacists in the Canary Islands speak English. Each pharmacy displays a card in the window showing the address of the nearest all-night pharmacy.

Smoking, Alcohol and Drugs

Smoking is banned in public spaces and is a fineable offence. Many bars and restaurants have designated outdoor areas where smoking is permitted.

Spain has a relaxed attitude towards alcohol consumption, but being openly drunk is frowned upon. The legal drinking age is 18, and alcohol can only be purchased between the hours of 10am and 10pm (unless it's bought in a regulated venue). In some popular tourist spots, this time period can end even earlier. The blood-alcohol concentration (BAC) limit is strictly enforced; it's 0.5 g/l of blood or 0.3 g/l for drivers who have had their licence for less than two years. This limit is also applied for cyclists and motorized scooter users.

Recreational drugs are illegal, and possession of even a very small quantity can lead to a hefty fine. Amounts that suggest an intent to supply drugs to others can lead to custodial sentences.

ID

By law you must carry identification with you at all times in Spain. A photocopy of your passport should suffice, but you may be asked to report to a police station with the original document. Passports may be required when travelling between islands.

Visiting Places of Worship

Most churches and cathedrals will not permit visitors during Sunday Mass. Generally, entrance to churches is free; however, a fee may apply to enter special areas, like cloisters. When visiting religious buildings, ensure that you are dressed modestly and keep noise to a minumum.

Responsible Travel

The climate crisis is having a big impact across Spain, including in the Canary Islands, with heatwaves and droughts becoming more frequent. There may be water restrictions in place during certain months of the year. You can help water conservation efforts by taking quick showers and reusing towels if staying in hotel accommodation.

In the Canary Islands, forest fires are also becoming increasingly frequent. Make sure to carefully dispose of any cigarette butts, glass bottles and other flammable litter. Starting a forest fire, even if accidental, is deemed a criminal offence.

It pays, too, to follow basic leave no trace principles, especially when visiting nature spots: take rubbish with you, stick to designated paths and steer well clear of wildlife.

Mobile Phones and Wi-Fi

Free Wi-Fi hotspots are widely available in city centres. Cafés and restaurants will usually give you their Wi-Fi password on the condition that you make a purchase. Do not rely on mobile phones or other devices for navigation or emergency communications in remote areas where mobile reception can be intermittent. Check with your network provider if you will be liable for data roaming charges. Pay-as-you-go SIM cards are available at newsagents and supermarkets.

Post

Post offices are usually prominently located in city centres and town squares. Stamps can be bought from post offices. Allow up to 10 days when sending post to the UK, and up to 15 days for the US or Australia.

Taxes and Refunds

The Canary Islands have a different tax system from mainland Spain and Europe in general. The equivalent to VAT in the Canary Islands is the Canary Island General Indirect Tax, or IGIC, generally charged at just 7 per cent.

Under certain conditions, non-EU residents are entitled to claim a rebate of these taxes, providing they request a tax receipt and regular retail receipt when purchasing goods. Present a form and your receipts to a customs officer at your point of departure.

INDEX

PHRASE BOOK

IN AN EMERGENCY

Help!	Socorro	soh-**koh**-roh
Stop!	¡Pare!	**pah**-reh
Call a doctor!	¡Llame a un médico!	**yah**-meh ah oon **meh**-dee-koh
Call an ambulance!	¡Llame a una ambulancia!	**yah**-meh ah **oonah** ahm-boo-**lahn**-thee-ah
Call the police!	¡Llame a la policía!	**yah**-meh ah lah poh-lee-**thee**-ah
Call the fire brigade!	¡Llame a los bomberos!	**yah**-meh ah lohs bohm-**beh**-rohs
Where is the nearest telephone?	¿Dónde está el teléfono más próximo?	**dohn**-deh ehs-**tah** ehl teh-**leh**-foh-noh mahs prohx-ee-moh
Where is the nearest hospital?	¿Dónde está el hospital más próximo?	**dohn**-deh ehs-**tah** ehl ohs-pee-**tahl** mahs prohx-ee-moh

COMMUNICATION ESSENTIALS

Yes	Sí	see
No	No	noh
Please	Por favor	pohr fah-**vohr**
Thank you	Gracias	**grah**-thee-ahs
Excuse me	Perdone	pehr-**doh**-neh
Hello	Hola	**oh**-lah
Goodbye	Adiós	ah-dee-**ohs**
Goodnight	Buenas noches	bweh-nahs noh chehs
Morning	La mañana	lah mah-**nyah**-nah
Afternoon	La tarde	lah **tahr**-deh
Evening	La tarde	lah **tahr**-deh
Yesterday	Ayer	ah-**yehr**
Today	Hoy	oy
Tomorrow	Mañana	mah-**nyah**-nah
Here	Aquí	ah-**kee**
There	Allí	ah-**yee**
What?	¿Qué?	keh
When?	¿Cuándo?	**kwahn**-doh
Why?	¿Por qué?	pohr-**keh**
Where?	¿Dónde?	**dohn**-deh

USEFUL PHRASES

How are you?	¿Cómo está usted?	**koh**-moh ehs-**tah** oos-**tehd**
Very well, *thank you.*	Muy bien, gracias.	mwee bee-**ehn grah**-thee-ahs
Pleased to meet you.	Encantado de conocerle.	ehn-kahn-**tah**-doh deh koh-noh-**thehr**-leh
See you soon.	Hasta pronto.	ahs-tah **prohn**-toh
That's fine.	Está bien.	ehs-**tah** bee-**ehn**
Where is/are ...?	¿Dónde está/están ...?	**dohn**-deh ehs-**tah**/ehs-**tahn**
How far is it to ...?	¿Cuántos metros/ kilómetros hay de aquí a ...?	**kwahn**-tohs meh-trohs/kee-**loh**-meh-trohs eye deh ah-**kee** ah
Which *way to...?*	¿Por dónde se va a ...?	pohr **dohn**-deh seh bah ah
Do you speak English?	¿Habla inglés?	**ah**-blah een-**glehs**
I don't understand	No comprendo	noh kohm-**prehn**-doh
Could you speak more slowly, please?	¿Puede hablar más despacio, por favor?	pweh-deh ah-**blahr** mahs dehs-pah-thee-oh pohr fah-**vohr**
I'm sorry.	Lo siento.	loh see-**ehn**-toh

USEFUL WORDS

big	grande	**grahn**-deh
small	pequeño	peh-**keh**-nyoh
hot	caliente	kah-lee-**ehn**-teh
cold	frío	**free**-oh
good	bueno	**bweh**-noh
bad	malo	**mah**-loh
enough	bastante	bahs-**tahn**-the
well	bien	bee-**ehn**
open	abierto	ah-bee-**ehr**-toh
closed	cerrado	thehr-**rah**-doh
left	izquierda	eeth-key-**ehr**-dah
right	derecha	deh-**reh**-chah
straight on	todo recto	toh-doh **rehk**-toh
near	cerca	**thehr**-kah
far	lejos	**leh**-hohs
up	arriba	ah-**ree**-bah
down	abajo	ah-**bah**-hoh
early	temprano	tehm-**prah**-noh
late	tarde	**tahr**-deh

entrance	entrada	ehn-**trah**-dah
exit	salida	sah-**lee**-dah
toilet	lavabos, servicios	lah-**vah**-bohs sehr-bee-**thee**-ohs
more	más	mahs
less	menos	**meh**-nohs

SHOPPING

How much does this cost?	¿Cuánto cuesta esto?	**kwahn**-toh kwehs-tah ehs-toh
I would like ...	Me gustaría ...	meh goos-ta-**ree**-ah
Do you have ...?	¿Tienen...?	tee-**yeh**-nehn
I'm just looking, thank you.	Sólo estoy mirando, gracias.	soh-loh ehs-**toy** mee-**rahn**-doh **grah**-thee-ahs
Do you take credit cards?	¿Aceptan tarjetas de crédito?	ah-**thehp**-tahn tahr-**heh**-tahs deh **kreh**-dee-toh
What time do you open?	¿A qué hora abren?	ah **keh** oh-rah **ah**-brehn
What time do you close?	¿A qué hora cierran?	ah keh oh-rah thee-**ehr**-rahn
This one.	Éste.	**ehs**-the
That one.	Ése.	**eh**-she
expensive	caro	**kahr**-oh
cheap	barato	bah-**rah**-toh
size, clothes	talla	**tah**-yah
size, shoes	número	**noø**-mehr-oh
white	blanco	**blahn**-koh
black	negro	**neh**-groh
red	rojo	**roh**-hoh
yellow	amarillo	ah-mah-**ree**-yoh
green	verde	**behr**-deh
blue	azul	ah-**thool**
antiques shop	la tienda de antigüedades	lah tee-ehn-dah deh ahn-tee-gweh-**dah**-dehs
bakery	la panadería	lah pah-nah-deh-**ree**-ah
bank	el banco	ehl**bahn**-koh
book shop	la librería	lah lee-breh-**ree**-ah
butcher's	la carnicería	lah kahr-nee-theh-**ree**-ah
cake shop	la pastelería	lah pahs-teh-leh-**ree**-ah
chemist's	la farmacia	lah fahr-**mah**-thee-ah
fishmonger's	la pescadería	lah pehs-kah-deh-**ree**-ah
greengrocer's	la frutería	lah froo-teh-**ree**-ah
grocer's	la tienda de comestibles	lah tee-**yehn**-dah deh koh-mehs-**tee**-blehs
hairdresser's	la peluquería	lah peh-loo-keh-**ree**-ah
market	el mercado	ehl mehr-**kah**-doh
newsagent's	el kiosko de prensa	ehl kee-**ohs**-koh deh prehn-sah
post office *nah*	la oficina de correos	lah oh-fee-**thee**-deh kohr-**reh**-ohs
shoe shop	la zapatería	lah thah-pah-teh-**ree**-ah
supermarket	el supermercado	ehl soo-pehr-mehr-**kah**-doh
tobacconist	el estanco	ehl ehs-**tahn**-koh
travel agency	la agencia de viajes	lah ah-**hehn**-thee-ah deh bee-**ah**-hehs

SIGHTSEEING

art gallery	el museo de arte	ehl moo-**seh**-oh deh **ahr**-the
cathedral	la catedral	lah kah-teh-**drahl**
church	la iglesia la basílica	lah ee-**gleh**-see-ah lah bah-**see**-lee-kah
garden	el jardín	ehl hahr-**deen**
library	la biblioteca	lah bee-blee-oh-**teh**-kah
museum	el museo	ehl moo-**seh**-oh
tourist information office	la oficina de turismo	lah oh-fee-**thee**-nah deh too-**rees**-moh
town hall	el ayuntamiento	ehl ah-yoon-tah-mee-**ehn**-toh
closed for holiday	cerrado por vacaciones	thehr-**rah**-doh pohr bah-kah-cee-**oh**-nehs
bus station	la estación de autobuses	lah ehs-tah-thee-**ohn** deh owtoh-**boo**-sehs
railway station	la estación de trenes	lah ehs-tah-thee-**ohn** deh treh-nehs

STAYING IN A HOTEL

Do you have a vacant room?	¿Tienen una habitación libre?	tee-**eh**-nehn oo-nah ah-bee-tah-thee-**ohn** lee-breh
double room	habitación doble	ah-bee-tah-thee-**ohn** doh-bleh

with double bed	con cama de matrimonio	kohn **kah**-mah deh mah-tree-**moh**-nee-oh
twin room	habitación con dos camas	ah-bee-tah-thee-**ohn** kohn dohs **kah**-mahs
single room	habitación individual	ah-bee-tah-thee-**ohn** een-dee-doo-**ahl**
vee- room with a bath	habitación con baño	ah-bee-tah-thee-**ohn** kohn **bah**-nyoh
shower	ducha	**doo**-chah
porter	el botones	ehl boh-**toh**-nehs
key	la llave	lah **yah**-veh
I have a reservation.	Tengo una habitación reservada.	tehn-goh **oo**-na ah-bee-tah-thee-**ohn** reh-sehr-**bah**-dah

EATING OUT

Have you got a table for ...?	¿Tienen mesa para ...?	tee-**eh**-nehn **meh**-sah pah-**rah**
I want to reserve a table.	Quiero reservar una mesa.	kee-eh-roh reh-sehr-**bahr** **oo**-nah **meh**-sah
The bill, please.	La cuenta, por favor.	lah **kwehn**-tah pohr fah-**vohr**
I am a vegetarian	Soy vegetariano/a	soy beh-heh-tah-ree-**ah**-no/na
waitress/ waiter	camarera/ camarero	kah-mah-**reh**-rah/ kah-mah-**reh**-roh
menu	la carta	lah **kahr**-tah
fixed-price menu	menú del día	meh-**noo** dehl **dee**-ah
wine list	la carta de vinos	lah **kahr**-tah deh **bee**-nohs
glass	un vaso	oon **bah**-soh
bottle	una botella	oo-nah boh-**teh**-yah
knife	un cuchillo	oon koo-**chee**-yoh
fork	un tenedor	oon teh-neh-**dohr**
spoon	una cuchara	oo-nah koo-**chah**-rah
breakfast	el desayuno	ehl deh-sah-**yoo**-noh
lunch	la comida/ el almuerzo	lah koh-**mee**-dah/ ehl ahl-**mwehr**-thoh
dinner	la cena	lah **theh**-nah
main course	el segundo plato	ehl pree-**mehr** **plah**-toh
starters	los primeros	lohs ehn-treh **meh**-sehs
dish of the day	el plato del día	ehl **plah**-toh dehl **dee**-ah
coffee	el café	ehl kah-**feh**
rare	poco hecho	poh-koh eh-choh
medium	medio hecho	**meh**-dee-oh **eh**-choh
well done	muy hecho	mwee **eh**-choh

MENU DECODER

asado	ah-**sah**-doh	roast
el aceite	ah-**thee-eh**-teh	oil
las aceitunas	ah-theh-**toon**-ahs	olives
el agua mineral	ah-gwa	mineral water mee-neh-**rahl**
sin gas/con gas	seen gas/kohn gas	still/sparkling
el ajo	**ah**-hoh	garlic
el arroz	ahr-**rohth**	rice
el azúcar	ah-**thoo**-kahr	sugar
la carne	**kahr**-neh	meat
la cebolla	theh-**boh**-yah	onion
la cerveza	thehr-**beh**-thah	beer
el cerdo	**therh**-doh	pork
el chocolate	choh-koh-**lah**-teh	chocolate
el chorizo	choh-**ree**-thoh	red sausage
el cordero	kohr-**deh**-roh	lamb
el fiambre	fee-**ahm**-breh	cold meat
frito	**free**-toh	fried
la fruta	**froo**-tah	fruit
los frutos secos	froo-tohs **seh**-kohs	nuts
las gambas	**gahm**-bahs	prawns
el helado	eh-**lah**-doh	ice cream
al horno	ahl **ohr**-noh	baked
el huevo	oo-**eh**-voh	egg
el jamón serrano	hah-**mohn**	cured ham sehr-**rah**-noh
el jerez	heh-**rehz**	sherry
la langosta	lahn-**gohs**-tah	lobster
la leche	**leh**-cheh	milk
el limón	lee-**mohn**	lemon
la limonada	lee-moh-**nah**-dah	lemonade
la mantequilla	mahn-teh-**kee**-yah	butter
la manzana	mahn-**thah**-nah	apple
los mariscos	mah-**rees**-kohs	seafood
la menestra	meh-**nehs**-trah	vegetable stew

la naranja	nah-**rahn**-hah	orange
el pan	pahn	bread
el pastel	pahs-**tehl**	cake
las patatas	pah-**tah**-tahs	potatoes
el pescado	pehs-**kah**-doh	fish
la pimienta	pee-mee-**yehn**-tah	pepper
el plátano	**plah**-tah-noh	banana
el pollo	**poh**-yoh	chicken
el postre	**pohs**-treh	dessert
el queso	**keh**-soh	cheese
la sal	sahl	salt
las salchichas	sahl-**chee**-chahs	sausages
la salsa	**sahl**-sah	sauce
seco	**seh**-koh	dry
el solomillo	soh-loh-**mee**-yoh	sirloin
la sopa	**soh**-pah	soup
la tarta	**tahr**-tah	pie/cake
el té	teh	tea
la ternera	tehr-**neh**-rah	beef
las tostadas	tohs-**tah**-dahs	toast
el vinagre	bee-**nah**-greh	vinegar
el vino blanco	**bee**-noh **blahn**-koh	white wine
el vino rosado	**bee**-noh roh-**sah**-doh	rosé wine
el vino tinto	**bee**-noh **teen**-toh	red wine

NUMBERS

0	cero	**theh**-roh
1	uno	**oo**-noh
2	dos	dohs
3	tres	trehs
4	cuatro	**kwa**-troh
5	cinco	**theen**-koh
6	seis	says
7	siete	see-**eh**-the
8	ocho	**oh**-choh
9	nueve	**nweh**-veh
10	diez	dee-**ehth**
11	once	**ohn**-theh
12	doce	**doh**-theh
13	trece	**treh**-theh
14	catorce	kah-**tohr**-theh
15	quince	**keen**-theh
16	dieciséis	dee-eh-thee-**seh-ees**
17	diecisiete	dee-eh-thee-see-**eh**-the
18	dieciocho	dee-eh-thee-**oh**-choh
19	diecinueve	dee-eh-thee-**nweh**-veh
20	veinte	**beh**-een-the
21	veintiuno	beh-een-tee-**oo**-noh
22	veintidós	beh-een-tee-**dohs**
30	treinta	**treh**-een-tah
31	treinta y uno	treh-een-tah ee **oo**-noh
40	cuarenta	kwah-**rehn**-tah
50	cincuenta	theen-**kwehn**-tah
60	sesenta	seh-**sehn**-tah
70	setenta	seh-**tehn**-tah
80	ochenta	oh-**chehn**-tah
90	noventa	noh-**vehn**-tah
100	cien	thee-**ehn**
101	ciento uno	thee-**ehn**-toh oo-noh
102	ciento dos	thee-**ehn**-toh dohs
200	doscientos	dohs-thee-**ehn**-tohs
500	quinientos	khee-nee-**ehn**-tohs
700	setecientos	seh-teh-thee-**ehn**-tohs
900	novecientos	noh-veh-thee-**ehn**-tohs
1,000	mil	meel
1,001	mil uno	meel **oo**-noh

TIME

one minute	un minuto	oon mee-**noo**-toh
one hour	una hora	oo-na **oh**-rah
half an hour	media hora	meh-dee-**a oh**-rah
Monday	lunes	**loo**-nehs
Tuesday	martes	**mahr**-tehs
Wednesday	miércoles	mee-**ehr**-koh-lehs
Thursday	jueves	hoo-**weh**-vehs
Friday	viernes	bee-**ehr**-nehs
Saturday	sábado	**sah**-bah-doh
Sunday	domingo	doh-**meen**-goh

ACKNOWLEDGMENTS

DK would like to thank the following for their contribution to the previous edition: Jürgen Bingel, Magdalena Borzęcka, Zbigniew Dybowski, Joanna Egert-Romanowska, Daniel Poch, Javier Lopez Silvosa, Damian Sosa

The publisher would like to thank the following for their kind permission to reproduce their photographs:

Key: a-above; b-below/bottom; c-centre; f-far; l-left; r-right; t-top

123RF.com: charles03 10bl.

4Corners: Reinhard Schmid 104–105ca.

Adobe Stock: Juan Carlos Alonso 20–21bc; Tomasz Czajkowski 110-111t; EyesTravelling 10–11bc; Denis Feldmann 41bc; JaviJfotografo 202; JFL Photography 10ca; K I Photography 89cla; Tamara Kulikova 41cb; Frank Lambert 37tr; Martin 11br; mehdi33300 199tr; Miroslaw 157tl; olenatur 25bc; Alexandre ROSA 98-99b; stu.dio 147tr; Szymek 162cr; unai 162bl; underworld 123br; vasanty 176crb.

Alamy Stock Photo: Phil Crean A 99tr, 141br; AJD images 75crb; Alan Dawson Photography 42cb; ALANDAWSONPHOTOGRAPHY 39crb; Album 41cla; Album / Archivo ABC / Valdivielso 44crb; ALLTRAVEL / Peter Mross 144ca; Jonathan Alonso 117b; Steve Taylor ARPS 29crb; Artefact 43cra; B.O'Kane 23tr; Nia Bell 24bc, 29tr; Frank Bienewald 11crb; Cavan Images 28t; Cavan Images / David Santiago Garcia 38cr; Charles Stirling (Travel) 77tr; Chronicle 44t; Classic Image 44bl; Helmut Corneli 36–37bc; Stephen Coyne 67cb; Craig Jack Photographic 129tr, 136–137t, 138tl, 148tl; CW Images / Chris Warren 82crb; DanitaDelimont.com 19t, 172, 61tc, 63br, 143cra, 157br, 197tr; Dave 86–87t, Alan Dawson 33br, 45cla, 72bc; en.photo 45bl; Greg Balfour Evans 107cr, 194–195t; F1online digitale Bildagentur GmbH / Dumrath 112ca; Andrew Fare 40t, 41tr; Jose Luis Mendez Fernandez 29cla; Florapix 25bl; Olga Gillmeister 21c; GL Archive 43tl; Hemis.fr / BIBIKOW Walter 133tr; Hemis.fr / Fabien Olart 150–151b; hemis.fr / Franck Guiziou 88–89b; hemis.fr / Pierre Jacques 61br; hemis.fr / Richard Soberka 42bc; Hemis.fr / Walter Bibikow 72–73t; Shawn Hempel 27bl; Shawn Hempel 111clb; Image Professionals GmbH - LOOK-foto 185bl; Image Professionals GmbH / Juergen Richter 35cla, 38clb; Image Professionals GmbH / LOOK-foto 18cb, 158; Image Professionals GmbH / LOOK-foto 63cl; Image Professionals GmbH / LOOK-foto 176t; Image Professionals GmbH / Sabine Lubenow 56t; imageBROKER.com GmbH & Co. KG / . / . 24br; imageBROKER.com GmbH & Co. KG / Christian Handl 155t; imageBROKER.com GmbH & Co. KG / Daniel Schoenen 39tl; imageBROKER.com GmbH & Co. KG / K. Kreder 192t; imageBROKER.com GmbH & Co. KG / Markus Lange 181tl; imageBROKER.com GmbH & Co. KG / Martin Siepmann 93b, 97br, 165crb; imageBROKER.com GmbH & Co. KG / Michael Nitzschke 109, 112bl; imageBROKER.com GmbH & Co. KG / Oliver Gerhard 48–49; imageBROKER.com GmbH & Co. KG / Sonja Jordan 30tr; Islandstock 33clb, 37br, 38cl, 43crb, 57cra, 62cla, 68tr, 147cra; iWebbstock 45tl; Jon Arnold Images Ltd / Michele Falzone 162t; Jon Arnold Images Ltd / Walter Bibikow 4, 152tl; Andrea Katrinecz 64b, 69tr; lophius_sub 22bl; mauritius images GmbH / Catharina Lux 128tl, 150crb; mauritius images GmbH / Gerhard Wild 135br; mauritius images GmbH / Marco Simoni 70bl; mauritius images GmbH / Maria Breuer 119cl, 119b; mauritius images GmbH / Martin Siepmann 43bc; mauritius images GmbH / Peter Schickert 164, 169crb; mauritius images GmbH / Udo Bernhart 8cl; mauritius images GmbH / Urs Flüeler 39tr; mauritius images GmbH / Walter Bibikow 67crb, 76bl, 176bl; Samuel Mederos Medina 39cr; Mehdi33300 27crb; Wilhelm Menze 31bl; Juan Carlos Muñoz 54cr; Niday Picture Library 45cr; Klaus Ohlenschlaeger 25bc; Pictorial Press Ltd 40cb; Prisma by Dukas Presseagentur GmbH / Gerth Roland 123tr; M Ramírez 190t, 201b; Nando Rivero 21tr; robertharding / Christian Kober 190cr; robertharding / Markus Lange 71crb; robertharding / Sergio Pitamitz 11t; Felipe Rodriguez 21br, 84cb; Peter Schickert 162crb; Sipa US 45crb; Jacek Sopotnicki 31cr; Stephen Taylor 139br; E.D. Torial 195br; travelbild.com 65tr; travelstock44.de / Juergen Held 190crb; Jorge Tutor 104tl; VWPics 120bl; Westend61 GmbH 151tr; Westend61 GmbH / Maria Breuer 58tr, 59tc; Wild Places Photography / Chris Howes 31cla; Jan Wlodarczyk 145bl.

AWL Images: Walter Bibikow 6–7, 82t; Marco Bottigelli 18tl, 124; Davide Camesasca 19bl, 186, 96–97t; ClickAlps 8–9b,16c, 50; Alan Copson 54bl; Neil Farrin 26–27tc, 35br, 154–155b; Roland Gerth 184; Gavin Hellier 106–107b, 204–205; Katja Kreder 190bl; Markus Lange 17t, 78, 54t, 94b; Sabine Lubenow 105tr.

Bridgeman Images: © Florilegius 40bc.

Dreamstime.com: Aiacob9 156bl; Cristian M

Main Contributors Lynnette McCurdy Bastida, Ross Clarke, Ben Ffrancon Dowds

Senior Editors Dipika Dasgupta, Zoë Rutland

Senior Designers Laura O'Brien, Stuti Tiwari Bhatia

Project Editor Tijana Todorinović

Editor Anjasi Nongkynrih Nyshadham

Assistant Art Editor Divyanshi Shreyaskar

Proofreader Stephanie Smith

Indexer Helen Peters

Picture Research Team Nishwan Rasool, Virien Chopra, Manpreet Kaur

Publishing Assistant Simona Velikova

Jacket Designers Laura O'Brien, Divyanshi Shreyaskar

Jacket Picture Researcher Harriet Mills

Illustrator Mohd Zishan

Senior Cartographer Subhashree Bharati

Senior Executive Cartographic Editor James Macdonald

Cartography Manager Suresh Kumar

Senior DTP Designer Tanveer Zaidi

DTP Designers Rohit Rojal, Mohd Rizwan, Jagtar Singh

Pre-Production Manager Balwant Singh

Senior Production Controller Samantha Cross

Managing Editor Beverly Smart

Managing Art Editor Gemma Doyle

Senior Managing Art Editor Priyanka Thakur

Editorial Director Hollie Teague

Art Director Maxine Pedliham

Publishing Director Georgina Dee

First edition 2003

Published in Great Britain by
Dorling Kindersley Limited,
20 Vauxhall Bridge Road, London SW1V 2SA

The authorised representative in the EEA is
Dorling Kindersley Verlag GmbH. Arnulfstr.
124, 80636 Munich, Germany

Published in the United States by DK Publishing,
1745 Broadway, 20th Floor, New York, NY 10019, USA

Copyright © 2003, 2025 Dorling Kindersley Limited
A Penguin Random House Company

24 25 26 27 10 9 8 7 6 5 4 3 2 1

A CIP catalog record for this book
is available from the British Library.

A catalog record for this book is available
from the Library of Congress.

ISSN: 1542 1554
ISBN: 978 0 2417 1901 5

Printed and bound in China

www.dk.com

MIX
Paper | Supporting
responsible forestry
FSC™ C018179
www.fsc.org

This book was made with Forest
Stewardship Council™ certified
paper – one small step in DK's
commitment to a sustainable future.
Learn more at **www.dk.com/uk/
information/sustainability**

A NOTE FROM DK

The rate at which the world is changing is constantly
keeping the DK travel team on our toes. While we've
worked hard to ensure that this edition of Canary
Islands is accurate and up-to-date, we know that
opening hours alter, standards shift, prices fluctuate,
places close and new ones pop up in their stead. So,
if you notice we've got something wrong or left
something out, we want to hear about it.
Please get in touch at travelguides@dk.com